Jean Anouilh

Also published by Hill and Wang

Jean Anouilh

(SEVEN PLAYS)

Volume III

A Mermaid Dramabook

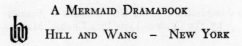

Hill and Wang – New York

842
ANOUILH

Manufactured in the United States of America
by The Colonial Press Inc., Clinton, Mass.

CHRONOLOGY OF PLAYS BY JEAN ANOUILH

Taken from *Jean Anouilh* by Edward Owen Marsh. The dates following the titles indicate the year written.

  *Published in DRAMABOOKS MD 10, *Jean Anouilh* Volume 1.
 **Published in DRAMABOOKS MD 13, *Jean Anouilh* Volume 2.
***Published in DRAMABOOKS MD 39, *Jean Anouilh* Volume 3

CHRONOLOGY OF PLAYS BY JEAN ANOUILH

CONTENTS

CONTENTS

THIEVES' CARNIVAL

(Le Bal des Voleurs)

A play in four acts

Translated by
LUCIENNE HILL

CHARACTERS

PETERBONO ⎫
HECTOR ⎬ *thieves*
GUSTAVE ⎭
LORD EDGARD
LADY HURF
EVA ⎫
JULIETTE ⎬ *her nieces*
DUPONT-DUFORT SENIOR
DUPONT-DUFORT JUNIOR
THE TOWN CRIER
THE POLICEMEN
THE NURSEMAID
THE LITTLE GIRL
THE MUSICIAN
A SERVANT

THIEVES' CARNIVAL

ACT ONE

The public gardens of a watering place which saw its heyday in the 1880's. In the middle, a bandstand. The orchestra is represented by a single MUSICIAN, *who at the rise of the curtain is executing a solo of superlative virtuosity on the clarinet. A woman deck-chair attendant goes to and fro. The summer visitors stroll up and down to the rhythm of the music. In the foreground* EVA *and* HECTOR *are locked in a dramatic screen embrace. The music stops. So does the kiss, from which* HECTOR *emerges, reeling a little. Applause for the* MUSICIAN.

HECTOR [*covered in confusion*]. I say, steady. They're applauding us!

EVA [*bursts out laughing*]. Of course not, it's the orchestra. I must say you appeal to me enormously.

HECTOR [*instinctively fingering his hair and mustache*]. What do you like about me specially?

EVA. Everything. [*She blows him a kiss.*] We mustn't stay here, it's too risky. I'll see you tonight at eight in the Phoenix Bar. And if you should meet me with my aunt, whatever you do, pretend you don't know me.

HECTOR [*yearningly*]. Your little hand, once more.

EVA. Careful. My aunt's old friend Lord Edgard is over there by the bandstand reading his paper. He'll see us. [*She holds out her hand, but turns away to watch* LORD EDGARD.]

HECTOR [*passionately*]. I want to inhale the perfume of your hand!

He bends over her hand, and surreptitiously draws a jeweler's eyeglass from his pocket to take a closer look at EVA's *rings.* EVA *withdraws her hand, unaware of the maneuver.*

EVA. Till tonight. [*She goes.*

HECTOR [*weak at the knees*]. My beloved . . . [*He follows her out of sight, then comes downstage again, putting*

away his eyeglass, and mutters with icy self-possession.]
A good two hundred thousand. And not a flaw in the lot.

At this point the TOWN CRIER *enters with his drum and
the crowd gathers around to listen.*

TOWN CRIER. Townsmen of Vichy! The Municipality,
anxious to preserve the well-being and security of the in-
valids and bathers, issues a warning for their information
and protection! Numerous complaints from visitors have
been lodged at the Town Hall and at the main police station, Market Street. A dangerous pack of picklepockets—
[*He has a little trouble with this word, at which the clarinet plays a little accompaniment. The* TOWN CRIER
swings around on him, furious.]—a dangerous pack of
pockpickets—[*Again the clarinet renders the word in
music.*]—is at this very hour within our gates. The local
police are on the watch. Members of the force, in plain
clothes and in uniform, are ready to protect our visitors.
. . . [*Indeed, even as he speaks* POLICEMEN *are thread-
ing their several ways gracefully through the crowd.*] Visitors are nevertheless requested to exercise the greatest
possible caution, particularly on the public highway, in
public parks, and in all other places of public amusement.
A reward is offered by the Tourist Association to anyone
supplying information leading to the apprehension of the
felons! Tell your friends!

A roll of drums. During the proclamation HECTOR *has re-
lieved the* TOWN CRIER *of his enormous copper watch and
bulging purse. The crowd scatters, and the drum and the
harangue are heard again farther off.* HECTOR *takes a seat,
and the chair woman approaches.*

CHAIR WOMAN. Will you take a ticket, sir, please?
HECTOR [*largely*]. Since it's customary . . .
CHAIR WOMAN. That'll be five francs, please.

While HECTOR *feels for the money, the woman steals his
wallet, then the huge watch and the purse he has just taken
from the* TOWN CRIER.

HECTOR [*seizing the hand on its next trip into his pocket*].
Hey! What do you think you're up to? [*The woman
struggles to free herself and loses her wig.*] Have you
gone crazy? [*He lifts his own wig and mustache a trifle.*]
It's me!

The chair attendant readjusts her wig. It is PETERBONO.

PETERBONO. Sorry, old chap. It's me, too. Had a good day?

HECTOR. The purse and a watch, and a cigarette lighter.

PETERBONO [*examining them*]. I know that watch. It's the town crier's and it's made of copper. I put it back into his pocket, the poor devil, that and the purse, which you'll find if you check up contains just fifteen cents and the receipt for a registered parcel. As for the lighter, we've already got nine hundred and three, out of which only a couple work. I've known you to do better, my lad!

HECTOR. I've a date tonight with a girl who'll be mine before you can say mischief, and who wears over two hundred thousand francs' worth of diamonds on her middle finger.

PETERBONO. We'll look into it. Have you noticed that little thing over there? The necklace?

HECTOR [*examining the girl through the field glasses he wears around his neck*]. Phew! The stones are enormous!

PETERBONO. No wishful thinking. They're smaller to the naked eye. Still, off we go. Small-change Maneuver. I get offensive and you interfere. [*They cross to the girl with a terrible affectation of indifference.*] Ticket? Ticket? [*The girl gives him a coin;* PETERBONO *begins to yell.*] I've got no change! I tell you I've got no change! No change, do you hear? No change at all, I keep on telling you!

HECTOR. What's this? No change, eh? Excuse me, mademoiselle, allow me to put this insolent baggage in her place!

There follows a tussle under cover of which HECTOR *investigates the clasp of the girl's necklace.*

THE GIRL [*violently freeing herself*]. No, you don't!

HECTOR [*taken aback*]. What do you mean, no, you don't!

PETERBONO. No, you don't what?

THE GIRL [*lifting her wig; it is* GUSTAVE]. It's me.

HECTOR [*falling into a chair*]. Charming!

PETERBONO [*exploding*]. That's what comes of not working to plan! I can't rely on anybody! Running errands, that's all you're fit for! Errand boys! If it weren't for your poor old mothers, who put you in my charge to learn the business, you'd be out on your ear, the pair of you. Do you hear me? Out on your ear! And without your week's pay in lieu of notice, make no mistake! And complain to the

union if you dare! I'll tell them a thing or two, the dance
you've led me, both of you! [To GUSTAVE.] You! You
haven't done a stroke today, naturally!

GUSTAVE. Yes, I have. I've done two. First, there's this
magnificent wallet.

PETERBONO. Let's have a look. [He examines it, then
searches himself anxiously.] Where did you get this? Who
from?

GUSTAVE. I got it in the Boulevard Ravachol off an old
gentleman with a long white beard. . . .

PETERBONO [terrible in his anger]. Check trousers, olive-
green jacket, and deerstalker cap; am I right, pigeon-
brain?

GUSTAVE [quaking]. Yes, sir. Did you see me?

PETERBONO [sinks into a chair, flattened by this latest blow].
That was me, idiot, that was me! At this rate we'll be
lucky if we cover our expenses!

GUSTAVE. But I've got something else, Mr. Peterbono, sir.

PETERBONO [profoundly discouraged]. If it's something else
you stole from me, you can imagine my curiosity.

GUSTAVE. It isn't a thing, it's a girl. And she looks rich.

HECTOR [jumping up]. Good God! Don't say it's the same
girl. A redhead? About twenty-five? Name of Eva?

GUSTAVE. No. Dark hair, about twenty. Name of Juliette.

HECTOR. Oh, that's all right.

PETERBONO. What did you get?

GUSTAVE. Nothing yet. But I helped her fish a kid out of
the Thermes Fountain. We sat in the sun to dry and we
got talking. She told me she liked me.

PETERBONO. Any jewels?

GUSTAVE. One very fine pearl.

PETERBONO. Good. We must look into that. Hector, can
you spare a moment this afternoon, other engagements
permitting?

GUSTAVE. No! I'd like to handle this myself.

PETERBONO. What's this? What's this? Handle it yourself,
would you? Well, whatever next?

GUSTAVE. It was me she took a fancy to.

PETERBONO. All the more reason. Hector will swallow her
in one.

GUSTAVE. No, I tell you! Not this one!

PETERBONO [severely]. Gustave, listen to me. Your mother
put you in my care, and I took you into the firm as assist-

ant decoy. You're young and you're ambitious. That's fine. I was ambitious myself when I was your age. But just a minute! In our profession, as in all professions, you have to work your way up from the bottom. Hector here is the finest professional seducer I know this side of Monte Carlo. There's a chap who hits the bull's-eye three times out of four, and take it from me, that's a pretty handsome average. You don't mean to tell me that you, a mere apprentice, expect to turn out better work than that?

GUSTAVE. To hell with it! I'll get her for myself.

PETERBONO [tight-lipped]. If you wish to do a job on the side in your spare time, there's nothing to stop you. You'll owe me just the sixty-five percent on what you make, that's all.

HECTOR [who has been watching a NURSEMAID during this altercation]. Peter?

PETERBONO. Hector?

HECTOR. That nursemaid over there. See the gold chain?

PETERBONO [contemptuously]. Pooh! It's probably wire.

HECTOR. Listen, it's ten to seven. We've ten minutes to go before supper.

PETERBONO. Very well, if you're set on it. We'll give her the Three Musketeers Maneuver.

HECTOR. Three Musketeers Maneuver?

PETERBONO. It's the classic routine for nursemaids. Number one gets off with her, number two plays ten little pigs with the baby, and number three starts whistling bugle calls without a break to make her senses reel.

They go. Enter LADY HURF *and* JULIETTE.

JULIETTE. The little boy was barely five years old. He was only in up to his waist, but he was frightened and he kept falling over. He would have drowned, I'm sure.

LADY HURF. How dreadful! Have you noticed all these little chimney-pot hats everywhere? How absurd they look!

JULIETTE. Fortunately this young man came to the rescue. He was wonderful, and very sweet.

LADY HURF. All children are sweet at five. But at twelve they begin to get silly. That's why I never wanted any.

JULIETTE. I was talking about the young man, Aunt.

LADY HURF. Oh yes, of course. There's another of those grotesque little hats. The young man was very sweet—yes, go on.

JULIETTE. That's all.

LADY HURF. We must invite him to dinner.

JULIETTE. He's gone. I'd never seen him before.

LADY HURF. Good. One always knows far too many people. Besides, I can't stand stories about drowning. Your poor uncle swam like a lump of lead. He drowned himself seven times; I could have hit him. Ah, there's Edgard. Edgard, have you seen Eva?

LORD EDGARD [appearing from behind his paper]. How are you, my dear?

LADY HURF. I asked if you'd seen Eva.

LORD EDGARD. Eva? No, I haven't. That's very odd. Now what can I have done with her? Perhaps she's at the Baths.

LADY HURF. At seven o'clock at night? Don't be silly.

JULIETTE. Shall we try the Phoenix Bar? She often goes there.

LADY HURF. Edgard, don't stir from this spot for any reason whatsoever.

LORD EDGARD. Very good, my dear.

LADY HURF [going]. But of course if you see her, run after her.

LORD EDGARD. Very good, my dear.

LADY HURF. Or better still, don't; you'd only lose her—just come and tell us which way she went.

LORD EDGARD. Very good, my dear.

LADY HURF. On second thought, no. You'd never manage to find us. Send one attendant after her, another attendant to let us know, and put a third in your place to tell us where you've gone so we can pick you up on the way home if we should happen to be passing.

LORD EDGARD. Very good, my dear.

He retires, stunned, behind his paper. Exit LADY HURF with JULIETTE. Enter the DUPONT-DUFORTS, father and son, accompanied by the little jig on the clarinet, which is their signature tune.

D.D. SENIOR. Let's follow. We'll meet them casually on the promenade, and try to tempt them to a cocktail. Didier, I don't know what's come over you. You, a hard-working, conscientious lad, brimful of initiative, and look at you. You're not paying an atom of attention to young Juliette.

D.D. JUNIOR. She snubs me.

D.D. SENIOR. What does that matter? To begin with, you aren't just anybody. You are Dupont-Dufort Junior. Her aunt thinks a great deal of you. She's prepared to make any investment on your recommendation.

D.D. JUNIOR. That ought to be enough for us.

D.D. SENIOR. Son, in matters of money there's no such thing as enough. I'd far and away prefer you to pull off this marriage. Nothing short of that will put our bank fairly and squarely on its feet again. So let me see a bit of charm, a little fascination.

D.D. JUNIOR. Yes, Dad.

D.D. SENIOR. We couldn't wish for more propitious circumstances. They're bored to tears, and there's nobody here in the least presentable. So let's make ourselves agreeable, superlatively agreeable.

D.D. JUNIOR. Yes, Dad.

Exeunt the DUPONT-DUFORTS. LORD EDGARD, *who has heard every word, looks over his* Times *to watch them go.* PETERBONO, HECTOR, *and* GUSTAVE *come in dressed as soldiers as the* MUSICIAN *begins his second number. The* POLICEMEN *enter at the same time from the other side. They all perform a flirtatious little ballet around the* NURSEMAID, *the maneuvers of the* POLICEMEN *seriously impeding those of the three thieves. The* NURSEMAID *finally goes; the* POLICEMEN, *twirling their white batons behind their backs, make gallant attempts to hinder her departure. During the ballet* LADY HURF *returns alone and goes to sit beside* LORD EDGARD. *The music stops at the exit of the* POLICEMEN *and the* NURSEMAID.

PETERBONO [*thwarted*]. Lads, that's the first time I've ever known the Three Musketeers Maneuver to miscarry.

LADY HURF [*to* LORD EDGARD]. Well, Edgard, my dear, and what have you done with yourself today?

LORD EDGARD [*surprised and embarrassed as always at* LADY HURF's *customary abruptness*]. I—er—I read *The Times*.

LADY HURF [*sternly*]. The same as yesterday?

LORD EDGARD [*ingenuously*]. Not the same copy as yesterday.

HECTOR [*who has been watching the scene, gives a whistle of admiration*]. See those pearls?

PETERBONO. Four million!

HECTOR. How about it? What's it to be? Russian princes?

PETERBONO. No. She knows her onions by the look of her. Ruined Spanish noblemen.

GUSTAVE. That's bright of you. Whenever you masquerade as Spaniards you're rigged out like a couple of rats.

PETERBONO. Quiet, shaver! You're speaking of a trade you know nothing about.

GUSTAVE. Well, anyway, if you think I'm dressing up as your ecclesiastical secretary like the last time, it's no go. I'm not wearing a cassock in this heat.

PETERBONO. Gustave, you're trying my patience! Come along, home! Hector and I will be Spanish grandees, and you'll put on that cassock, heat or no heat.

The unwilling GUSTAVE *is borne away, to the accompaniment of a little jig on the clarinet.*

LADY HURF [*who has been deep in thought*]. Edgard, the situation is grave. . . .

LORD EDGARD. I know. According to *The Times*, the Empire . . .

LADY HURF. No, no. Here.

LORD EDGARD [*looking around him anxiously*]. Here?

LADY HURF. Listen to me. We have two tender creatures in our care. Intrigues are fermenting—marriages are brewing. Personally, I can't keep track of them—it gives me the vertigo. Who is to uncover them, Edgard; who is to supervise them?

LORD EDGARD. Who?

LADY HURF. Juliette is a scatterbrain. Eva is a scatterbrain. As for me, I haven't a notion what's going on and the mere idea of it bores me to extinction. Besides, I've no more common sense than those two senseless girls. That leaves you in the midst of these three scatterbrains.

LORD EDGARD. That leaves me.

LADY HURF. Which is another way of saying nobody. I am perplexed, excessively perplexed. Anything may happen in this watering place. Intrigues spring up under one's very feet like so much jungle vegetation. Should we do better to leave Vichy, I wonder? Ought we perhaps to bury ourselves in some rustic backwater? Edgard, for heaven's sake, say something! You are the guardian of these two young things, aren't you?

LORD EDGARD. We might ask Dupont-Dufort his advice.
He seems to be a man of character.

LADY HURF. A deal too much character. What a ninny you
are. He's the last man from whom we want advice. The
Dupont-Duforts are after our money.

LORD EDGARD. But they're rich.

LADY HURF. Exactly. That's what worries me. They're after
a lot of money. An investment or a marriage settlement.
Our two little ones with their millions are exceptionally
tempting morsels.

LORD EDGARD. Could we not telegraph to England?

LADY HURF. What for?

LORD EDGARD. Scotland Yard might send us a detective.

LADY HURF. That would be a great help, I must say! They're
crooked as corkscrews, the lot of them!

LORD EDGARD. The problem, then, is in effect insoluble.

LADY HURF. Edgard, you simply must bestir yourself. Our
fate, the girls' and mine, is in your hands.

LORD EDGARD [looks at his hands, very worried]. I don't
know that I am very well equipped.

LADY HURF [sternly]. Edgard, do you call yourself a man?
And a gentleman?

LORD EDGARD. Yes.

LADY HURF. Then make a decision!

LORD EDGARD [firmly]. Very well! I shall nevertheless sum-
mon a detective from Scotland Yard, with a special pro-
viso that I want him honest.

LADY HURF. Over my dead body! If he's honest, he'll phi-
lander with the kitchenmaids and he won't wash. It will
be insufferable. And yet I don't know why I should be
telling you all this. What do I want with absolute security? I'm as bored as a piece of old carpet!

LORD EDGARD. Oh, my dear . . . !

LADY HURF. That's all I am, a piece of old carpet.

LORD EDGARD. You, who were once so beautiful.

LADY HURF. Yes, in the nineteen hundreds. Oh, I could
scream with rage! I want to enjoy my last few years—I
want to laugh a little. Sixty years I've spent deluded into
thinking life a serious business. That's sixty years too
long. I am in the mood, Edgard, for a gigantic piece of
folly.

LORD EDGARD. Nothing dangerous, I hope?

LADY HURF. I don't know. I'll see what occurs to me. [*She leans toward him.*] I think I should like to massacre the Dupont-Duforts.

In they come, accompanied by their particular little tune, with EVA *and* JULIETTE.

D.D. SENIOR. How are you today, milady?

D.D. JUNIOR. Milady.

D.D. SENIOR. Ah, dear Lord Edgard.

LORD EDGARD [*drawing him aside*]. Take the greatest possible care.

D.D. SENIOR. But why, milord?

LORD EDGARD. Hush! I can't tell you. But take care. Leave Vichy.

D.D. JUNIOR. We ran into these ladies on the promenade.

EVA. Vichy's an impossible place. Nothing to do, nowhere to go, and all the men are hideous.

D.D. JUNIOR. Oh, how true! Quite, quite hideous, all of them!

D.D. SENIOR. All of them! [*Aside to his son.*] Excellent thing for us.

EVA. I have an engagement tonight, Aunt. I shall be late for dinner—if I'm back at all.

D.D. SENIOR [*aside to his son*]. With you?

D.D. JUNIOR. No.

JULIETTE. Eva, I haven't told you. I rescued a little boy who fell into the Thermes Fountain, and I met an enchanting young man, who helped me to save him.

LADY HURF. Juliette talks of nothing else.

The DUPONT-DUFORTS *look at each other anxiously.*

D.D. SENIOR. Wasn't that you?

D.D. JUNIOR. No.

JULIETTE. We sat in the sun till we were dry, and chatted. You've no idea how pleasant he was! He's slight, with dark hair, and—he's not the same as yours by any chance?

EVA. No. Mine's tall, with red hair.

JULIETTE. Thank goodness!

D.D. SENIOR [*whispers*]. Son, you have absolutely *got* to sparkle. [*Raising his voice.*] Didier, dear boy, have you been to the swimming pool with these ladies yet? You must give them a demonstration of your impeccable crawl. You could have rescued the toddler with the greatest of ease.

JULIETTE. Oh, the crawl would have been quite useless. The Thermes Fountain is only eighteen inches deep.

Toward the end of this scene, PETERBONO, *as a very noble —all too noble—old Spanish gentleman,* HECTOR *as a grandee, an equally spectacular achievement, and* GUSTAVE, *their ecclesiastical secretary, come in and slowly approach the others.*

PETERBONO. Careful. This is big game. Stay close, and take no risks.

HECTOR. Your monocle.

PETERBONO. The big act: Noblesse Oblige. Wait for the word "go." Gustave, two paces behind.

The clarinet strikes up a march, heroic and ultra-Spanish. Suddenly LADY HURF, *who has been watching this curious trio, runs to them and throws her arms around* PETERBONO's *neck.*

LADY HURF. Why, if it isn't that dear, dear Duke of Miraflores!

Music stops.

PETERBONO [*surprised and uneasy*]. Huh?

LADY HURF. Don't say you've forgotten! Biarritz, 1902. The luncheon parties at Pampeluna! The bullfights! Lady Hurf.

PETERBONO. Ah . . . ! Lady Hurf. Bullfights. Lunch. Dear friend. [*To the other two.*] I must have made up like one of her acquaintances.

LADY HURF. I am so, so happy! I was disintegrating with boredom. But where is the Duchess?

PETERBONO. Dead.

Tremolo from the orchestra.

LADY HURF. Oh, heavens! And your cousin, the Count?

PETERBONO. Dead.

Tremolo from the orchestra.

LADY HURF. Oh, heavens! And your friend, the Admiral?

PETERBONO. Also dead. [*The orchestra begins a funeral march.* PETERBONO *turns to his friends.*] Saved!

LADY HURF. My poor friend. So many funerals.

PETERBONO. Alas! However, may I present my son, Don Hector? And my ecclesiastical secretary, Dom Petrus?

LADY HURF. Lord Edgard, whom you knew years ago. It

was he whom you beat each morning at golf, and who
was always losing his golf balls.

PETERBONO. Ha, golf—yes. Dear friend.

LORD EDGARD [*panic-stricken, to* LADY HURF]. But, my
dear——

LADY HURF [*sternly*]. What's the matter? Do you mean to
say you don't remember the Duke?

LORD EDGARD. This is insane. Come now, think back——

LADY HURF. Your memory is abominable. Don't say another word or I shall lose my temper. My nieces, Eva
and Juliette, who worry me so dreadfully because they're
both very marriageable and their dowries are exceptionally tempting to fortune hunters.

The DUPONT-DUFORTS *look at each other.*

D.D. SENIOR. Dignity, lad, dignity.

D.D. JUNIOR. She can't mean us.

PETERBONO *and* HECTOR *indulge in violent nudging.*

LADY HURF. I am so delighted to have met you again.
Vichy is such a dull hole. Tell me, do you remember
the Ridottos on the Riviera?

PETERBONO. I should think I do!

D.D. JUNIOR [*to his father*]. We're forgotten.

D.D. SENIOR. Let's introduce ourselves. Dupont-Dufort
Senior.

D.D. JUNIOR. Junior.

During the introductions EVA *stares hard at* HECTOR, *who
simulates an enormous interest in the conversation.* GUS-
TAVE *has all but disappeared into his brief case and rummages feverishly among his papers to avoid* JULIETTE's
gaze, which is fixed on him in puzzled interest.

LADY HURF. You must be as bored as I am. It's an un-
dreamed-of stroke of fortune, our meeting, don't you
think?

PETERBONO [*nudging* HECTOR]. Undreamed of.

HECTOR [*nudging* PETERBONO]. Yes. Undreamed of—absolutely undreamed of.

*In their glee, they go much too far, but no one seems to
notice.*

LADY HURF. Your son is most charming. Don't you think
so, Eva?

EVA. Yes.

PETERBONO. He was the most dashing officer in the entire
    Spanish army—before the revolution.

LADY HURF. Alas! You suffered a great deal?

PETERBONO. A great deal.

LADY HURF. Where are you staying? Not at a hotel?

PETERBONO [vaguely]. Yes.

LADY HURF. It's out of the question, Edgard! The Duke
    is staying at a hotel!

LORD EDGARD. But, my dearest, I assure you——

LADY HURF. Be quiet! Dear Duke, you cannot, you simply
    cannot stay at a hotel. Will you do us the honor of ac-
    cepting our humble hospitality? Our villa is enormous,
    and we shall put the west wing entirely at your disposal.

PETERBONO. Certainly, certainly, certainly, certainly——

Stupendous nudging between PETERBONO *and* HECTOR. *The*
    DUPONT-DUFORTS *exchange crestfallen glances.*

LADY HURF. You may, needless to say, bring your entou-
    rage. [She looks inquiringly at GUSTAVE.] Is he looking
    for something?

PETERBONO. A document, yes. Dom Petrus!

GUSTAVE [emerging from the brief case]. Your Grace? [He
    has put on some dark glasses.]

LADY HURF. Has he got bad eyes?

PETERBONO. Oh, very bad. His condition requires a cer-
    tain amount of care. I couldn't burden you with his pres-
    ence. Dom Petrus, we shall accept Lady Hurf's generous
    offer of hospitality. Call at the hotel, will you, and have
    our luggage sent on. And stay there until further notice.
    You will collect the mail and come to us each morning
    for instructions.

GUSTAVE [furious]. But, your Grace . . .

PETERBONO. Enough!

GUSTAVE. Your Grace——

PETERBONO. Off with you!

HECTOR *gives* GUSTAVE *a push, and he wanders reluctantly*
    away.

LADY HURF [moved]. Just as he used to be! That same
    commanding tone—the vocal magic of the Miraflores!
    Your cousin had it too.

PETERBONO. Alas!

LADY HURF. How did he die?

PETERBONO. Er, how he died?

LADY HURF. Yes—I was so fond of him.

PETERBONO. You want me to relate the circumstances of his passing?

LADY HURF. Yes.

PETERBONO [*turns to* HECTOR *in his panic*]. Well, he died . . .

HECTOR *mimes a motor accident, but this* PETERBONO *cannot grasp.*

PETERBONO. He died insane.

LADY HURF. Ah, poor fellow! He always was eccentric. But your wife, the dear Duchess?

PETERBONO. Dead.

LADY HURF. Yes, I know. But how?

HECTOR *touches his heart several times.* PETERBONO *is slow to take the suggestion, but since he has no imagination whatever himself, he gives way.*

PETERBONO. Of love.

LADY HURF [*in confusion*]. Oh, I beg your pardon! And your friend, the Admiral?

PETERBONO. Ah, now, the Admiral . . . [*He looks at* HECTOR, *who indicates that he has run out of ideas. He again misinterprets the pantomime.*] Drowned. But please excuse me, you are reopening wounds which time has not yet healed.

LADY HURF. Oh, forgive me, dear friend, forgive me! [*To the others.*] What breeding! What grandeur in adversity! Don't you think so, Edgard?

LORD EDGARD. My dear, I still insist that——

LADY HURF. Do stop insisting. Can't you see the Duke is suffering?

D.D. SENIOR [*to his son*]. Let us join in the conversation.

D.D. JUNIOR. What an appalling avalanche of misfortunes!

D.D. SENIOR. Falling on such venerable heads!

No one listens.

LADY HURF [*in a peal of laughter*]. How beautiful Biarritz was in those days. Do you remember the balls?

PETERBONO. Ah, the balls . . .

LADY HURF. And Lina Veri?

PETERBONO. Lina Veri. I can't quite recall . . .

LADY HURF. Come, come. Why, you were intimate! [*To the others.*] He's aged so much.

PETERBONO. Oh, Lina Veri. Of course. The darling of Italian society.

LADY HURF. No, no, no. She was a dancer.

PETERBONO. Oh yes, but her mother was the darling of Italian society.

LADY HURF [to the others]. He's wandering a little. He's very tired. My dear Duke, I would like to show you your apartments right away. The villa is close by, at the end of the avenue.

PETERBONO. With pleasure.

GUSTAVE comes running in, this time as his own charming self, but magnificently dressed.

GUSTAVE. Good morning, Father!

PETERBONO [off balance]. Stinker! Allow me to present my second son, Don Pedro, whom I'd forgotten to mention.

LADY HURF. Gracious, you have another son? By whom?

PETERBONO [panicking again]. Ah, that's a long story——
[He looks at HECTOR, who signs to him to go carefully.]
But that one also opens wounds as yet unhealed by time.

LADY HURF. Come along, Edgard.

LORD EDGARD. But, my dear——

LADY HURF. And keep quiet!

They go, HECTOR paying elaborate attentions to EVA, who has continued to stare at him.

JULIETTE [to GUSTAVE]. Now, will you kindly tell me what is going on?

GUSTAVE. Ssh! I'll explain later.

They go too. The DUPONT-DUFORTS are left alone.

D.D. JUNIOR. Father, they've forgotten us——!

D.D. SENIOR. All the same, we'll follow. And, Didier, twice the affability. Let's hope these young men are already attached or better still that they aren't interested in women!

They go.

ACT TWO

A drawing room in LADY HURF's *house. It is evening, after dinner, and* JULIETTE *and* GUSTAVE *are sitting side by side; a little romantic air is heard in the distance.*

JULIETTE. It's nice here. No one is disturbing us tonight.

GUSTAVE. Yes, it is nice.

JULIETTE. For three days now you've been sad. Are you homesick for Spain?

GUSTAVE. Oh no.

JULIETTE. I'm sorry now I wouldn't work at my Spanish at school. We might have spoken it together. It would have been fun.

GUSTAVE. I only speak a few words myself.

JULIETTE. Do you? That's funny.

GUSTAVE. Yes, it is rather.

A silence.

JULIETTE. It must be amusing to be a prince.

GUSTAVE. Oh, one gets used to it, you know.

A silence.

JULIETTE. Don Pedro, what's the matter? We were much friendlier three days ago.

GUSTAVE. Nothing's the matter.

A pause. LORD EDGARD *crosses the room, laden with papers.*

LORD EDGARD [*muttering*]. Though I should die in the endeavor, I'll set my mind at rest. [*He drops his papers. They jump up to help him, but he bars their path.*] Don't touch them! Don't touch them! [*He picks up the papers himself and goes out muttering.*] This momentous discovery, if discovery there be, must be surrounded with the greatest possible precautions.

GUSTAVE. What is he looking for? He's done nothing but ferret about among those old papers since we came here.

JULIETTE. I don't know. He's a little mad. Only he's painstaking as well, you see, so sometimes the results are quite prodigious.

18

A Little Girl *comes in.*

Juliette. Oh, here's my little friend.

Little Girl. Mademoiselle Juliette, I've picked some daisies for you.

Juliette. Thank you, darling.

Little Girl. They haven't very many petals. Daddy says they aren't the ones that lovers use.

Juliette. Never mind.

Little Girl. Shall I get some others?

Juliette. No. Yes. You're very sweet. [*She kisses her.*] Run away now.

The Little Girl *goes.* Juliette *turns to* Gustave, *shame-faced.*

Juliette. Do you think it's silly of me?

Gustave. No.

Juliette. You said you loved me, Don Pedro, yet for three days now you haven't even looked at me.

Gustave. I do love you, Juliette.

Juliette. Then why——?

Gustave. I can't tell you.

Juliette. My father wasn't titled, I know, but my aunt is a Lady, and my grandfather was an Honorable.

Gustave. How funny you are. It isn't that.

Juliette. Do you think the Duke of Miraflores would consent to my marrying you?

Gustave [*smiling*]. I'm sure he would.

Juliette. Why do you look so sad then, if you love me and everyone approves?

Gustave. I can't tell you.

Juliette. But you do feel, don't you, that our lives might meet and join one day?

Gustave. I would be lying if I told you I felt that.

Juliette [*turning away*]. That's unkind of you.

Gustave. Careful. Here's your cousin.

Juliette. Come into the garden. It's getting dark. I want you to tell me everything.

The music fades as they go. Eva *comes in, followed by* Hector, *in a totally different make-up from the one he wore in Act One.*

Hector. There, you see, they've left us the place to ourselves.

Eva. But I don't in the least need a place to myself—that's

the pity of it—I could adapt myself quite easily to a great crowd around us.

HECTOR. How cruel you are!

EVA. I don't like you. I'm cruel to those I dislike. It's in my nature. But, on the other hand, when someone appeals to me, there's hardly anything I wouldn't do for him.

HECTOR [*in despair*]. Why, why can I not manage to appeal to you a second time?

EVA. You know perfectly well why. You're not the same now.

HECTOR. What abominable absent-mindedness! This disguise, I tell you, is the fancy of an aristocrat wearied to death of his own personality, a pastime which affords him an escape from his oppressive self. And for this accursed fancy, must I lose my love?

EVA. I remember with delight a young man who spoke to me in the park. Find him for me. I might still think him lovable.

HECTOR. This is ridiculous! Won't you even tell me if I'm getting warm? At least tell me, did I have a beard when I first appealed to you?

EVA. But it wouldn't amuse me if I were to tell you.

HECTOR [*who has turned away to change his make-up, turns back again wearing a completely new face*]. It wasn't like this, I suppose?

EVA [*in a burst of laughter*]. No, oh no!

HECTOR. Yet you remember my voice, my eyes?

EVA. Yes, but it isn't enough.

HECTOR. I'm the same height as I was. I'm tall, well built —I assure you I am, very well built.

EVA. I only judge by faces.

HECTOR. This is horrible! Horrible! I'll never find the face that pleased you, ever! It wasn't as a woman, by any chance?

EVA. What do you take me for?

HECTOR. Or as a Chinaman?

EVA. You're evidently out of your mind. I'll wait till you're in it again. [*She goes to sit farther off; he starts to follow her and she turns on him.*] No, no, no! For heaven's sake, will you stop following me around and changing your beard every five minutes! You're making my head spin.

HECTOR [*stricken*]. And to think that idiot Peterbono
keeps on swearing it was as a test pilot!

LORD EDGARD *crosses the room laden with papers.*

LORD EDGARD. This is unthinkable! I must find this letter,
from which the truth will spring in such a curious fashion.
[*He sees* HECTOR *in his latest make-up, drops his papers,
and leaps on him.*] At last! The detective from Scotland
Yard.

HECTOR. No, sir. [*He makes to go.*]

LORD EDGARD. Excellent! The perfect answer. I specially
stipulated secrecy. But don't be afraid. I am Lord
Edgard in person. You may disclose your identity.

HECTOR. I tell you I'm not the man you're expecting.
[*He goes.*

LORD EDGARD [*following him*]. I see! I see! Perfect! You're
keeping word for word to my instructions! I stressed the
need for caution!

LADY HURF *enters, holding a magazine.*

LADY HURF. My little Eva is bored, isn't she?

EVA *smiles and says nothing. Unseen by* LADY HURF,
HECTOR *comes back in another make-up, which he silently
shows* EVA. *She shakes her head and he retires, heavy-
hearted.* LADY HURF *puts down her magazine with a sigh.*

LADY HURF. My little Eva is as bored as she can be.

EVA [*with a smile*]. Yes, Aunt.

LADY HURF. So am I, darling, very bored.

EVA. Only I'm twenty-five, so you see, it's rather sad.

LADY HURF. You'll see how much sadder it can be when
you are sixty. For you there's always love. As you may
guess, it's several years now since I officially renounced it.

EVA. Oh, love!

LADY HURF. *What* a deep sigh! Since you've been a widow,
surely you've had lovers?

EVA. I never had a single one who loved me.

LADY HURF. You want the moon. If your lovers bore you,
marry one of them. That will give the others an added
fascination.

EVA. Marry? Whom?

LADY HURF. Needless to say these Dupont-Duforts exasperate us both. What about the Spaniards?

EVA. Prince Hector chases after me changing his mustache

in the hope of rediscovering the one that first appealed to me.

LADY HURF. Truly appealed to you?

EVA [*smiling*]. I don't remember.

LADY HURF. They're curious individuals.

EVA. Why?

LADY HURF. Oh, I don't know. I tell you, I'm an old carcass who doesn't know what to do with herself. I've had everything a woman could reasonably, or even unreasonably, wish for. Money, power, lovers. Now that I'm old, I feel as alone inside my skin as I did as a little girl and they made me face the wall when I'd been naughty. And here's the rub; I know that between that little girl and this old woman, there has been, under the charivari and the noise, nothing but an even greater loneliness.

EVA. I've always thought of you as happy.

LADY HURF. You don't see much, do you? I am playing a part. Only, like everything else I do, I play it well, that's all. Yours now, you play badly, little girl. [*She strokes her hair.*] Child, child, you will always find yourself pursued by desires with changing beards and never have the courage to tell one of them: stay as you are—I love you. Don't think yourself a martyr now. All women are the same. My little Juliette, though, will come through because she is romantic. Her simplicity will save her. It's a favor only granted to few.

EVA. There are some who can love.

LADY HURF. Yes. There are some who love a man. Who kill him with loving, who kill themselves for him, but they are seldom heiresses to millions. [*She strokes her hair again, with a rueful smile.*] Ah, you'll finish up like me, an old woman covered in diamonds who plays at intrigues in an effort to forget that she has never lived. And yet, I'd like to laugh a little. Here am I, playing with fire, and the fire won't even burn my fingers.

EVA. What do you mean, Aunt?

LADY HURF. Shush—here come our marionettes.

PETERBONO *and* HECTOR *appear in the doorway, preceded by the* MUSICIAN *and followed almost at once by the* DUPONT-DUFORTS. *They all rush toward the ladies, but it is the thieves who get there first to kiss their hands.*

LADY HURF [*jumps to her feet and utters a sudden cry*]. Ah! I have an idea!

PETERBONO [*frightened, to* HECTOR]. She scares the life out of me. Every time she screams like that, I think my beard's loose.

LADY HURF. Where is Juliette?

EVA. In the garden, with Prince Pedro. They're inseparable.

PETERBONO. Ah, the dear children!

LADY HURF [*calling*]. Juliette!

JULIETTE [*coming in with* GUSTAVE]. Did you want me, Aunt Emily?

LADY HURF [*drawing her aside*]. Your eyes are red, child. Now mind, you mustn't be unhappy, or I cut the strings and the puppets will fall down.

JULIETTE. What do you mean, Aunt?

LADY HURF. If I appear to be talking through my hat, it's precisely so you won't understand me. Come along, both of you. [*She takes them by the waist and leads them into the garden.*] I have an idea to brighten up this evening; I want you to tell me what you think of it.

They go. The DUPONT-DUFORTS *look at each other.*

D.D. SENIOR. After them, my boy. And a hundred times more charm. Remember, it's our future that's at stake.

D.D. JUNIOR. Yes, Dad.

Left alone, the three thieves can unbend.

HECTOR [*offering* PETERBONO *a box of cigars*]. Would you care for a cigar?

PETERBONO [*helping himself*]. I'm savoring them. They're remarkably good.

HECTOR [*pouring out*]. A little brandy?

PETERBONO. Thank you.

They drink.

HECTOR. Another cigar, perhaps?

PETERBONO [*grabbing a fistful without more ado*]. You're too kind. No, no, really, you embarrass me. [*He feels a slight remorse and takes the box.*] But may I in return press you to a cigar?

HECTOR [*pulling them out of his pockets in handfuls*]. Thank you so much. I'm all right just now.

There is a moment of beatitude and exquisite refinement.

They spread themselves blissfully on the sofa. Suddenly
HECTOR *indicates* GUSTAVE, *sitting sad and somber in his*
corner.

PETERBONO [*rises and goes to him*]. What's wrong, laddie?
  Why so sad? Here you are with a wonderful room, lovely
  food, and a pretty little thing to flirt with, you're playing
  at princes, and for all that you can manage to be gloomy?
GUSTAVE. I don't want to stay here.

The other two give a start.

PETERBONO. Huh? You want to leave?
GUSTAVE. Yes.
PETERBONO. Leave here?
GUSTAVE. Yes—leave here.
PETERBONO. Hector, the boy's lost his reason.
HECTOR. What do you want to leave for?
GUSTAVE. I'm in love with Juliette.
HECTOR. Well then?
GUSTAVE. Really in love.
HECTOR. Well then?
PETERBONO. Why not? You've never been better off. She
  takes you for a prince, and rich at that. Go in and win,
  lad, she's as good as yours.
GUSTAVE. I don't want to take her for a day and then be
  forced to leave her.
PETERBONO. You'll have to leave her one day.
GUSTAVE. And—I'm ashamed of this game I have to play
  with her. I'd rather go away, now, and never see her
  again.
HECTOR. He's out of his mind.
PETERBONO. Completely.
GUSTAVE. Look, what are we here for?
PETERBONO. What are we here for? We're working, lad.
  It's the height of our season.
GUSTAVE. We're here to do a job. Let's do it, then, and go.
PETERBONO. And the preliminaries? Have you spared a
  single thought for the preliminaries?
GUSTAVE. They've gone on long enough, your damn pre-
  liminaries!
PETERBONO. I ask you, Hector, isn't it painful? Having to
  listen to an apprentice teaching us our trade!
HECTOR. Of course we'll do a job—that's what we came

for—but have you even the first idea what that job's going to be?

GUSTAVE. Strip the drawing room?

PETERBONO. With carpetbags, eh? Like raggle-taggle gypsies! The lowness, Hector, the abysmal lowness of this youngster's mind! Understand, boy, that we haven't yet decided on the job we're going to do. And if our behavior strikes you, a novice, as peculiar, tell yourself it's because we're in the process of investigating the possibilities of this—establishment.

GUSTAVE. You're lingering on here for the brandy and cigars, and because Hector still hopes he'll get Eva to remember him. But in actual fact you haven't the smallest inkling what you want to do. I may be an apprentice, but I'll tell you something—that's no way to work.

PETERBONO [*running to* HECTOR]. Hector, hold me back!

HECTOR [*still blissfully smoking*]. Gustave, don't be difficult. Try to understand.

PETERBONO. Hector, hold me back!

HECTOR. You see, we're wavering . . .

PETERBONO. Hold me back, Hector! Hold me back!

HECTOR [*takes his arm to please him*]. All right, I've got you.

PETERBONO [*deflated*]. Just as well.

HECTOR [*to* GUSTAVE]. We're wavering between several possible courses of action. . . .

GUSTAVE. Which?

HECTOR. Shall we confide in him, Pete? Is it safe to risk the indiscretion of a youth?

PETERBONO [*shrugs*]. Oh, confide in him, do. Since we're answerable to him now.

HECTOR. Right. Tell him your idea first, Pete.

PETERBONO. After you, Hector, after you.

HECTOR [*embarrassed*]. Aaaaaaah . . . well . . .

GUSTAVE. You haven't thought of a thing!

HECTOR [*in righteous rage*]. We haven't thought of a thing?!!! We're wavering between the trick of the bad check given in exchange for real jewels on a Saturday, which gives us the weekend to make our getaway, or the trick of the good check received in exchange for fake jewels under the same conditions. We've also considered giving Lady Hurf some orchids sprayed with ether (tak-

ing good care not to smell them ourselves) so as to relieve
her of the pearls as soon as she nods off.

PETERBONO [equally incensed]. Or we might provoke the
Dupont-Duforts to a duel! We wound them and then in
the commotion we make off with the silver!

GUSTAVE. What if you're the ones to get wounded?

PETERBONO. Impossible!

GUSTAVE. Why?

PETERBONO [yelling]. I don't know. But it's impossible!

HECTOR. Or, again, we could make out we'd been robbed
and demand a colossal sum for hush money!

PETERBONO. Pretend we found a pearl in the oysters at
dinner, for instance, and swap it for a pearl of Lady
Hurf's, or something.

GUSTAVE. There's no "r" in the month.

PETERBONO. I said, for instance!

GUSTAVE. In other words, you just don't know. Well, I'm going to do the job tonight, and then I'm off.

PETERBONO. Tonight? And why not right away?

GUSTAVE. Yes, why not right away? I want to go away.
I want to leave here as soon as possible.

PETERBONO. He'll be the ruin of us! Gustave, think of
your poor old mother, who put you in my care!

GUSTAVE. No!

PETERBONO. I'll put my curse on you! Naturally you don't
care a rap if I put my curse on you?

GUSTAVE. No.

PETERBONO [bellowing]. Hector! Hold me back! [He seizes
GUSTAVE.] Just another two weeks. We'll do the job all
right, but it's nice here, and it isn't so often we're in a
nice place. . . .

GUSTAVE. No. I'm too unhappy.   [He goes.

HECTOR [leaps after him]. After him! We've got to stop
him before he starts a scandal.

PETERBONO [calling after him]. I've got an idea! Suppose
we pretended not to know him?

HECTOR shrugs his shoulders and goes out, refusing even
to consider such a solution. Enter LORD EDGARD, preceded
by the MUSICIAN playing a succession of tremolos as if he
had intimations of a sudden blow of destiny. LORD EDGARD
is rummaging in his ever-present pile of papers. All of a
sudden he utters a loud cry and falls in a dead faint among

his scattered letters. The MUSICIAN *runs for help, emitting isolated notes from his instrument.* JULIETTE *comes in.*

JULIETTE. Uncle, Uncle, what's the matter? [*She props him up against a sofa and feels his hands.*] Ice cold! What's this? [*She picks up a letter, reads it, and hurriedly thrusts it into her pocket! Running out.*] Aunt Emily! Aunt Emily! Come quickly!

The clarinet in great confusion multiplies the tragic tremolos. Everyone comes rushing in shouting at once.

ALL. Stroke!
    At his age!
    No, he's only fainted.
    Stand back—give him air.
    Get a doctor!
    He's coming around.
    He's all right now.
    A sudden shock.
    Perhaps he found what he was looking for.
        The music stops. An enormous silence.

PETERBONO [*breathes to* HECTOR *in the silence*]. The chance of a lifetime.

HECTOR. Yes. But what do we do about it?

PETERBONO. Well, nothing, obviously, but it's still the chance of a lifetime.

LORD EDGARD [*sitting up slowly, says in a toneless voice*]. My friends, I have a ghastly piece of news for you. The Duke of Miraflores died in Biarritz in 1904.

Everyone looks at PETERBONO, *who is very ill at ease. An impish little jig on the clarinet.*

PETERBONO. Nonsense!

HECTOR [*aside*]. Talk about the chance of a lifetime!

PETERBONO. This is a fine time to be funny! Ease over to the window.

LADY HURF. Edgard, are you out of your mind?

LORD EDGARD. No, I tell you. I've found the notification. I knew I'd find it eventually. Ever since the day . . . [*He searches himself.*] Where is it? This is too much! Where is it? I had it a moment ago! Oh, my goodness! It's gone again.

D.D. SENIOR. Everything is coming to light!

D.D. JUNIOR. We are saved! [*To* PETERBONO, *who is im-*

perceptibly edging toward the window.] Aren't you staying to make sure your host is all right?

PETERBONO. Yes, oh yes!

LADY HURF. Edgard, that's a ridiculous joke to play on the dear Duke.

LORD EDGARD. But, my dear, I guarantee——

LADY HURF. Come along, dear Duke, and show him you aren't dead.

PETERBONO [*uneasy*]. No, no. I'm not dead.

LORD EDGARD. Yet I found the notification. . . .

LADY HURF [*pinching him*]. Edgard, you're making a mistake, I'm sure. You must apologize.

LORD EDGARD [*rubbing his arm*]. Ouch! Why yes, now that you mention it, I think I must have been confusing him with the Duke of Orléans.

LADY HURF. Of course. Shall we call the incident closed?

PETERBONO [*in great relief*]. Completely closed.

LADY HURF. Let's go outside, shall we? I've ordered coffee on the terrace. I want to tell you about my idea.

D.D. SENIOR [*in step with her*]. I think it's a wonderful idea.

LADY HURF [*exasperated*]. Wait a minute, my dear man, I haven't told you yet. Listen. They're holding a Thieves' Carnival tonight at the Casino. We're all going to dress up as thieves and go to it.

D.D. SENIOR *and* JUNIOR [*immediately burst out laughing*]. He! He! He! How terribly, terribly amusing!

D.D. SENIOR [*to his son as they go out*]. Play up to her, son.

PETERBONO [*furious, as he goes out with* HECTOR]. I call that in very poor taste, don't you?

JULIETTE *is alone. She stands motionless a moment. The music is heard some way away, playing a romantic theme.*
JULIETTE *takes out the fatal letter and reads it.*

JULIETTE. "We regret to announce the sad death of His Serene Highness the Duke of Miraflores y Grandes, Marquis of Priola, Count of Zeste and Galba. The funeral will take place . . ." [*She stands in thought a moment.*] If his father isn't the Duke of Miraflores—then who can he be? Why has he taken the car out of the garage? Why is he hiding from me?

LITTLE GIRL [*entering*]. Mademoiselle Juliette, I found some. Look, daisies with lots of petals.

JULIETTE. Haven't you gone to bed yet?

LITTLE GIRL. I was picking daisies for you.

JULIETTE. Thank you, you're an angel. [*She kisses her.*] His father may be an adventurer, but, you see, he loves me. He does love me, doesn't he?

LITTLE GIRL. Yes, of course he does.

JULIETTE. We don't care, do we, if he's an adventurer, or worse? If you were me, you'd love him, wouldn't you, just the same? Only why does that hard look come into his eyes whenever I ask him about himself? If he has designs on me, and he'd be wise to have because I'm very rich, he should be very pleasant to me all the time —whereas—do you think he prefers Eva? That would be terrible——

LITTLE GIRL. I don't know.

JULIETTE. No, of course you don't. Come along, I'll take you home. Are you afraid of the dark?

LITTLE GIRL. No.

JULIETTE. That's a good girl. Nor am I. There's nothing to be afraid of, you know. Thieves won't hurt you.

They go.

ACT THREE

The same set. The room is dark; a figure is seen moving about with a flashlight. It is GUSTAVE, *dressed in dark clothes and wearing a cap. He is silently examining the objects in the drawing room. Suddenly he hears a noise and switches off the flashlight; a low whistle; two dark figures spring up, two flashlights light up and focus on* GUSTAVE.

GUSTAVE. Who's that?

FIRST FIGURE. Tonight's the night.

GUSTAVE. Peterbono?

FIRST FIGURE. No. We're the new ones.

SECOND FIGURE. The new bandits.

GUSTAVE. For God's sake, what's going on? [*He draws a revolver.*] Hands up!

D.D. SENIOR [*it is no other*]. Ha-ha-ha! That's good! Where did you get the gun? It's magnificent!

GUSTAVE. Stay where you are or I fire!

D.D. SENIOR. Come quietly! The game's up.

GUSTAVE. Stay where you are, damn you! [*He fires.*]

D.D. SENIOR [*blissfully unaware of his danger*]. Oh, well done! Bravo!

GUSTAVE. What do you mean, bravo? [*He fires again.*]

D.D. JUNIOR. It's a wonderful imitation! Where on earth did you buy those caps?

GUSTAVE. For the last time, stay where you are! [*He fires again and shatters a vase, which falls with a terrible clatter.*]

D.D. SENIOR. Didier, why do you have to be so clumsy!

D.D. JUNIOR [*protesting in the dark*]. But, Dad, I didn't do it!

D.D. SENIOR. Well, it can't have been I, can it? I'm in the middle of the room.

D.D. JUNIOR. But, Dad, so am I!

D.D. SENIOR [*suddenly anxious*]. Well then, who broke the vase?

LORD EDGARD [*enters and switches on the light; he is dressed up as a policeman*]. Now, now, what is all this noise? How do you like my helmet?

30

D.D. SENIOR [*who has got himself up, along with his son,
in a terrifying apache disguise*]. Superb, my lord, superb!
[*Exit* LORD EDGARD. D.D. SENIOR *goes to* GUSTAVE.] My
word, I don't think much of your costume. It doesn't
come off—it's much too simple. It's the little touches
that mean so much. For instance, look, this little scar
here.

D.D. JUNIOR. And the black eye patch.

GUSTAVE. What are you doing dressed up like that?

D.D. SENIOR. We're going to the Casino.

D.D. JUNIOR. To the Thieves' Carnival. And so are you.

GUSTAVE. Oh? Oh yes, of course. So am I.

D.D. SENIOR. Only if I were you, I'd touch up your make-
up, my boy. It's a shade too simple. You don't look a bit
like a thief.

GUSTAVE. You're quite right. I'll see to it at once. [*He turns
at the door.*] Tell me, is everybody going to the Thieves'
Carnival?

D.D. SENIOR. Of course—everybody.

GUSTAVE. That's fine. See you later.   [*He goes.*

D.D. SENIOR. Not an ounce of imagination in him, that
boy.

D.D. JUNIOR. If the other two have rigged themselves up
as absurdly as that, which they probably have, we're well
on the way. The girls will have eyes for nobody but us!

D.D. SENIOR. Have you seen the latest batch of telegrams?

D.D. JUNIOR. Yes.

D.D. SENIOR. If we don't leave this house with a fat settlement, it's the colonies for us, I can tell you. Make yourself
irresistible, there's a good boy.

D.D. JUNIOR. I'm doing my best, Dad.

D.D. SENIOR. I know you are. You're an honest, conscientious lad, but you mustn't slacken for one moment. The
success of this evening's entertainment means a great
deal to us. What's more, there's something shady about
our rivals which is bound to give rise to a scandal one of
these days. It was quite obviously Lady Hurf who made
the old duffer keep quiet this afternoon when he insisted
the Duke of Miraflores died in 1904. Keep your eyes open,
and be ready for any emergency.

D.D. JUNIOR. We have got to get rid of these adventurers.
It's a matter of life and death.

D.D. SENIOR. We'll let them dig their own graves, while

we'll be more and more agreeable. Ssh! Here comes Lady Hurf.

Enter LADY HURF *and* EVA *as thieves in petticoats. The* DUPONT-DUFORTS *cough desperately to attract attention.*

LADY HURF [*seeing them*]. Oh, breath-taking! Aren't they, Eva? Breath-taking! Who would have thought they had it in them! What do you think of our guests, Eva?

EVA. What a spectacular effect! How in the world did you manage it?

D.D. SENIOR [*simpering*]. We're delighted . . .

D.D. JUNIOR. . . . that we delight you.

LADY HURF. They always look as though they're waiting for a tip.

EVA. Which, in a way, they are.

LADY HURF. The Duke and his sons are being very slow.

EVA. I called out to them as I went by. They can't manage to dress up as thieves, they said.

LADY HURF [*as she goes*]. Go up and fetch them, gentlemen, if you would be so good, and give them a few wrinkles.

D.D. SENIOR. Certainly! Certainly! [*Aside to his son.*] Let us be pleasant.

D.D. JUNIOR. Very, very pleasant. [*They bow themselves out.*]

JULIETTE *crosses furtively.*

EVA. Why, you're not dressed!

JULIETTE. I'm going up now.

EVA. You'll make us late.

JULIETTE. Go on ahead. I'll take the two-seater.

EVA [*unexpectedly*]. Are you in love with this boy?

JULIETTE. Why do you ask me?

EVA. Yes indeed, why does one ask people if they're in love, when one can tell at a glance, always?

JULIETTE. Can you tell?

EVA. Yes.

JULIETTE. Well, you're wrong. I'm not in love with any-one.

She turns to go when EVA *calls her back.*

EVA. Juliette! Why do you look upon me as your enemy?

JULIETTE. You are my enemy.

EVA. No, I love you very much. Sit down.

JULIETTE [*turning on her*]. You're in love with him, too—
that's it, isn't it? You're going to take him away from
me, and you want to warn me first so that I won't be
hurt too much? Why, you've even agreed on that between you, probably. You have, haven't you? Haven't
you? For heaven's sake, say something! Why do you
smile like that?

EVA. How lucky you are to be in love as much as that.

JULIETTE. You're prettier than I am; you can get any man
you want.

EVA. Oh, if I could only bring myself to want one.

JULIETTE. Don't you want him, then?

EVA. No, little silly.

JULIETTE. Have you never spoken to him when I wasn't
looking?

EVA. Had I ever wanted to, I should have found it very
difficult. He only has to come near me by accident and
you can't take your eyes off us.

JULIETTE. I'm wary. I love him, you see.

EVA. Lucky you.

JULIETTE. You swear you've never set out to attract him?

EVA. I swear.

JULIETTE. Even the day you danced with him twice running?

EVA. The orchestra had struck up a second tango.

JULIETTE. Even the day you went out on the river while
the Dupont-Duforts tried to teach me roulette?

EVA. Even then. He looked so sad that I suggested he
should row straight back, but we couldn't find you anywhere.

JULIETTE. That day I'm not so sure. He had a strange look
in his eyes that evening.

EVA. Because he'd asked me if I thought you cared for
him, and I said you were an unpredictable little girl and
there was no knowing what went on inside your heart.

JULIETTE. Was that truly why? [*A little pause.*] All the
same, I do think you might have told him something
else.

EVA. Are you satisfied now?

JULIETTE. Did you never try to attract him, not even at
the beginning, not even the very first day?

EVA. Not even the first day.

JULIETTE. Yes, then, I'm satisfied.

Eva. Why will you never trust me? I feel like an old woman beside you sometimes.

Juliette. You're so much better-looking than I am, so much more poised, more feminine.

Eva. Do you think so?

Juliette. It surprises me, you know, in spite of what you say. You must admit that he's a good deal more attractive than Hector, and you don't mind *his* attentions.

Eva. Do you think I couldn't have denied myself a mere flirtation when I could see you were so much in love?

Juliette. That's grand of you.

Eva. Oh no. I wish I could have wanted him so much that I'd have sacrificed you without giving you a moment's thought.

Juliette. When you chew your pearls, I know there's something wrong.

Eva. Yes, there's something wrong.

Juliette. Yet you look so lovely tonight. You'll have all the men around you at the ball.

Eva. All of them.

Juliette. I'm not joking.

Eva. Nor am I. I'll have them all. And yet it's very sad.

Juliette. Aren't you happy?

Eva. No.

Juliette. Yet it's so easy. You only need to let yourself go. Why, hardly a moment goes by that one isn't unhappy, yet I think that must be what it means, to be happy.

Eva. You've always thought me cleverer, stronger, more beautiful than you because the men flocked around me. And yet you see, there's only you who is alive, in this house—you're the only one perhaps in Vichy, perhaps in the whole world.

Juliette [*smiling, lost in her dream*]. Yes, I am alive.

Eva. And untouched, and eager to believe. . . .

Juliette. To believe everything.

Eva. You've never had, as I have, a man without love in your bed. You haven't even a jewel at your throat, not a ring on your finger. You're wearing nothing but this simple linen dress, and you're twenty years old, and you are in love. [Juliette *sits motionless, yielding to the unseen with a faint smile.* Eva *looks sharply at her.*] Juliette, why aren't you in thieves' dress like the rest of us?

JULIETTE [*bursting with sudden joy*]. Oh, I'm too happy!
I haven't the courage to stay beside you who are sad.
When I'm a little less happy, I'll think of you, I swear
I will! [*She kisses her and runs off.*] Ssh!

EVA. All this mystery! What are you trying to say?

Enter LADY HURF *with the* DUPONT-DUFORTS.

LADY HURF. We will make a truly magnificent entrance.

D.D. SENIOR. The Spanish gentlemen are ready.

LADY HURF. Do they look all right?

D.D. SENIOR. That's a matter of taste.

D.D. JUNIOR. Anyway, here they come.

Enter PETERBONO *and* HECTOR. *They have contrived to
disguise themselves as absolutely ludicrous comic-opera
bandits. They are greeted with shrieks of laughter.*

HECTOR. What are they laughing at?

PETERBONO. What do they *think* thieves look like? Don't
they ever go to the theatre?

LADY HURF. But, my dear Duke, what are you supposed
to be?

PETERBONO. A thief.

HECTOR [*to* EVA]. It wasn't like this, I suppose?

EVA. Heavens, no!

PETERBONO [*to* LADY HURF]. Don't you like us?

LADY HURF. Enormously!

PETERBONO. Admit there's something wrong.

LADY HURF. My dear friend, one really can't expect a
Spanish grandee to make much of a showing as a common thief.

PETERBONO. Well said, eh, Hector?

Enormous nudgings.

LADY HURF. Come along, all of you. The car's waiting.
Where is Lord Edgard? Still glued to the mirror, I suppose. Edgard!

*He appears, still in his own suit, and wearing his police
helmet, but he has shaved off his mustache.*

LORD EDGARD. Do you think I did well to shave off my mustache?

LADY HURF [*without looking at him*]. I don't know! Come
along! To the carnival!

*The music immediately strikes up a lively quadrille, which
the thieves dance with the ladies, without the* DUPONT-

DUFORTS *getting a sporting chance. Then follows a piece of extremely vulgar jive, and the* DUPONT-DUFORTS, *making the best of a bad job, finish up by dancing together with tremendous spirit. All the characters dance their way out.*

D.D. SENIOR [*bringing up the rear with his son*]. Things are getting better and better and better.

D.D. JUNIOR. Let's be as witty as the very devil!

D.D. SENIOR. And, remember, Didier, twice as nice.

The room remains empty for an instant. A SERVANT *comes in to close the windows and turn out the lights. Another moment of silence, and* GUSTAVE *appears and listens. The car is heard driving off. He goes around the room, examining its contents one by one. All of a sudden he flattens himself against the wall.* JULIETTE *enters, dressed for a journey.*

JULIETTE. Here I am.

GUSTAVE. What are you doing here? Why didn't you go with the others?

JULIETTE. I've come to find you.

GUSTAVE. Get out of here, will you?

JULIETTE. Why are you so harsh with me?

GUSTAVE. Go on, get out!

JULIETTE. I'll go, of course, if you don't want me, only I thought you would want me. What's the matter?

GUSTAVE. I've got a headache. I want to stay here.

JULIETTE. Why this yarn, to me?

GUSTAVE. It isn't a yarn. Get out, will you. Go on, quick march!

JULIETTE. But—you've never spoken to me like this!

GUSTAVE. There's a first time for everything.

JULIETTE. What have I done?

GUSTAVE. Nothing in particular. It's too difficult to explain, and anyway you wouldn't understand.

JULIETTE. But, Señor Pedro . . .

GUSTAVE. There isn't any Señor Pedro, for a start. My name is Gustave. And, secondly, will you please go away?

JULIETTE. And there was I thinking that you loved me——

GUSTAVE. We all make mistakes, don't we?

JULIETTE. But you used to tell me so.

GUSTAVE. I was lying.

JULIETTE. Oh no! I don't believe it!

GUSTAVE [*going to her purposefully*]. Listen, my little pet,
I'm telling you to get out of here, double quick.

JULIETTE. Why?

GUSTAVE. You'll see why later on. In the meantime go up
to your room and weep over your lost illusions. [*He takes
her arm to lead her to the door.*] What are you dressed
up in this coat for? What kind of a costume is that
meant to be?

JULIETTE. Traveling costume.

GUSTAVE. Traveling costume? You're mad.

JULIETTE. Please don't be angry. I came to find you so we
could go away. You told me once we'd go away together.

GUSTAVE. I was joking. Anyway, how do you know I mean
to go away?

JULIETTE. I know.

GUSTAVE. You look as though you know a lot of things.
Come along with me.

JULIETTE. We might meet one of the servants in the passage. [*He looks at her.*] We'd better not move from here.
We'll be quite safe in this room.

GUSTAVE. The Dupont-Duforts must be waiting for you.
Go and dress up as a pickpocket like the rest of them.

JULIETTE. Don't pickpockets ever wear traveling clothes?

GUSTAVE. You're not going to travel. You're going to a
carnival.

JULIETTE. Once they've stolen, thieves go away as a rule.
Why won't you let me come with you, since you're going away?

GUSTAVE [*seizes her*]. You know too much, my girl!

JULIETTE. Oh, please, don't hurt me!

GUSTAVE. Don't be afraid. Just a precaution.

He ties her to a chair and searches in her handbag.

JULIETTE. Oh, don't rob my bag. There's nothing in it.
Anyway, I give it to you.

GUSTAVE. Thank you. All I want is a handkerchief.

JULIETTE. What for?

GUSTAVE. To gag you with. [*He finds her handkerchief,
which is microscopic.*] I ask you, what's the point of a
handkerchief that size? Never mind, mine's clean.

JULIETTE. I'm not going to scream—I swear I won't scream
—Señor Pedro! Gustave—Gusta——

He gags her.

GUSTAVE. There. If you think this a Thieves' Carnival, my
lass, you'll have to think again. I'm a real thief, I am.
So is Hector, and so is the Duke of Miraflores. Except
that those two, they're imbeciles as well. You've built
yourself a castle in the air, that's all, and your aunt, who's
got bats in her belfry, has built herself a dozen. But let
me tell you *I* came to do a job, and I intend to do it.
[*She struggles.*] All right. All right. It's no good trying to
soften me. I'm used to girls. [*He begins to fill his sacks
with the most unlikely objects in the room. After a while
he looks at her with misgiving.*] It's not too tight, is it?
[*She shakes her head.*] That's a good girl. You see, old
girl, I did a bit of billing and cooing, I know, but to be
frank I didn't mean a word of it. I had to do it for the
job. [*She struggles again.*] Does that upset you? Yes, I
know, it isn't very pretty. But then in every trade there's
always a little bit like that which isn't very pretty. Apart
from that, I'm an honest sort of chap in my own way.
I follow my trade, simply, without frills and fancies. Not
like Hector and Peterbono. Peterbono has to be the
Duke of Miraflores. One must be honest in one's own
particular line. Life's not worth living otherwise. [*He
takes a furtive look at her.*] You sure it's not too tight?
[*He gives her a smile.*] It worries me a bit, playing a trick
like that on you, because you know, I lied just now. I am
fond of you really. [*He goes back to his work.*] After all,
when God invented thieves he had to deprive them of
a thing or two, so he took away from them the esteem of
honest folk. When you come to think of it, it's not so
terrible. It could have been much worse. [*He shrugs and
laughs, without daring to meet her eyes.*] In a little
while, you'll see, we'll have forgotten all about it. [*He
goes on collecting objects. She struggles again, and he
looks at her.*] If there's anything you care for specially,
you must tell me. I'll leave it for you as a souvenir. I
mean, I'd *like* to give you a little present. [*She looks at
him and he stops in embarrassment.*] Please, don't look
at me like that! You're breaking my heart! Can't you see
I've got to do this? So just let me get quietly on with my
job. [*She moves.*] Are you uncomfortable? You're not
choking, are you? Look, Juliette, if you swear not to call
out, I'll take the gag off. Do you swear? [*She nods.*]
All right, then, I trust you. [*He removes the handker-

chief.] What are you going to say to me, now that you know I'm a real thief? [*He sits down, resigned.*]

JULIETTE [*the moment she is ungagged*]. This is absurd! Absolutely absurd. Untie me at once!

GUSTAVE. *Oh,* no! I'm a good sort, but business is business.

JULIETTE. At least listen to me!

GUSTAVE. What do you want to say?

JULIETTE. You don't imagine I came to find you, wearing my traveling coat, merely in order to sit here like a nincompoop bound and gagged in a chair? Of course I know you're a thief. If you weren't a real thief, I wouldn't have thought you were planning to leave in the middle of the night, would I, seeing you're a guest of my aunt's?

GUSTAVE. What are you talking about?

JULIETTE. I've been telling you over and over again for the last hour. I love you. I saw you take a car out of the garage, I guessed you really were a thief, and that tonight was the night. Since I supposed you'd go the minute the job was done, I dressed and got ready to go with you. You don't intend to stay, do you?

GUSTAVE. That's no question to ask a thief.

JULIETTE. Well then, take me with you.

GUSTAVE. But I'm a thief.

JULIETTE [*crying out in exasperation*]. I tell you I know you're a thief! There's no need to go on and on about it. I wonder you don't draw attention to yourself. Come along, untie my hands.

GUSTAVE. But, Juliette——

JULIETTE. Untie my hands. They're terribly painful.

GUSTAVE. Do you swear not to run away and raise the alarm?

JULIETTE. Yes, yes, I swear. Oh, how stupid you are!

GUSTAVE. I trust you of course, but I just don't understand.

He unties her. She immediately powders her face and then gets up with determination.

JULIETTE. We've wasted at least a quarter of an hour. Make haste. It wouldn't do to get caught now. Have you enough? [*She indicates the sacks with her foot.*]

GUSTAVE. What are you doing?

JULIETTE. Really, I shall begin to wonder if you're all there soon. Yes, or no, do I appeal to you?

GUSTAVE. Oh yes, but——

JULIETTE. Good. That's the main thing. Now, listen to me. Gustave, if you like me, I love you and I want to be your wife—oh, don't worry, if you're afraid of awkward questions at the License Bureau, we won't get properly married. There. Now then——[*She picks up one of the sacks.*] Is this all we're taking with us?

GUSTAVE [*snatching the sack from her*]. Juliette, no! You don't know what you're doing! You mustn't come with me. What would become of you?

JULIETTE. I'd help you. I'd keep a lookout, and I'd whistle when I saw someone coming. I can whistle beautifully. Listen—— [*She gives an earsplitting whistle.*]

GUSTAVE [*terrified*]. Ssssh! For heaven's sake!

They listen for a moment.

JULIETTE [*humbly*]. I'm sorry. What a fool I am. Take me away. I'll whistle very quietly, I promise you, and then only when it's absolutely necessary.

GUSTAVE. Juliette, this is only a whim. You're playing with me. It's unkind of you.

JULIETTE. Oh no, you mustn't think that! Never think that! I love you.

GUSTAVE. But do you know the dangers of this kind of life?

JULIETTE. Yes. Kiss me.

GUSTAVE. Juliette, it's good-by to your tranquillity.

JULIETTE. It was on the way to killing me, my tranquillity. Kiss me.

GUSTAVE. But you're happy here, Juliette. You don't know what it means to be on the run, to be afraid. You're used to luxury.

JULIETTE. Why, we're rich! Look at this! If it worries you, we won't steal as long as the police are out looking for me.

GUSTAVE. Thieves aren't wealthy folk. You get precious little for what you sell.

JULIETTE. Well, we'll be poor then. Kiss me.

They join in a long kiss.

JULIETTE [*radiantly*]. I am so happy. Now, hurry. [*She stops.*] Why, you haven't taken the little Fragonards. You're mad, my darling; they're the most valuable things in the house. [*She runs to take them down.*] And the little enamels. [*She rummages in the sack.*] Leave the candlesticks. They're imitation bronze. You see how useful I am to you. I shall be such a help, you'll see. Kiss me.

GUSTAVE [*taking her in his arms again*]. My little robber.
They go.

ACT FOUR

In the conservatory an hour later. The clarinet, which has begun by playing the carnival theme, takes it up again in a nostalgic manner. The characters wander in in single file, heads hanging, and sit down, vexed and dejected.

LADY HURF. It's positively absurd.

HECTOR. I do think they might have let us in.

LADY HURF. Too absurd. Fancy writing the title of the carnival in microscopic lettering. Economy is an absolute obsession with the French.

LORD EDGARD. We were turned away in the most humiliating fashion.

EVA. What do you expect, Uncle? I can quite see that our attire alarmed them.

LADY HURF. A Carnival of Leaves! The idiocy of it! A Carnival of Leaves!

D.D. SENIOR. What puzzles me is how you could confuse a Carnival of Leaves with a Carnival of Thieves.

LADY HURF. You should have consulted the notices yourself then, my good friend, if your eyesight is so sharp.

D.D. SENIOR. But, damn it . . .

D.D. JUNIOR. Don't be rash, Dad.

LADY HURF. To begin with, it's thanks to your disguises that our party was shown the door.

PETERBONO. I should definitely have got in, for one. It's a funny thing. They really thought I was going as a palm tree.

LADY HURF. Of course, but for them we should all have been admitted. What abominable taste! Look at them, will you? They might be a couple of pantomime buccaneers.

D.D. SENIOR. I should have thought for a Carnival of Thieves . . .

LADY HURF. Leaves! Leaves! Leaves! Are you going to spend the rest of the evening calling it a Carnival of Thieves?

D.D. JUNIOR. Keep calm, Father. [*To* LADY HURF.] We are dreadfully sorry.

D.D. SENIOR [*abjectly*]. We'll never do it again.

42

LADY HURF. A fine time to say so!

LORD EDGARD. Couldn't we perhaps spend the evening as we are, among ourselves, so as not to waste our efforts altogether?

LADY HURF. Edgard, what an insane idea. Let us go up and change. We'll play yet one more stupefying game of bridge.

She sighs and the guests sigh with her.

LORD EDGARD. If I'd known we were going to play bridge, I would have preferred to keep my mustache.

LADY HURF [*distractedly*]. So would I! [*To* PETERBONO, *on her way out.*] My dear Duke, can you forgive me for this wasted evening?

PETERBONO [*nudging* HECTOR]. No evening is ever really wasted.

LADY HURF. Another time I'll be more careful when I read the posters, and more discriminating in my choice of company.

She goes out with EVA *and* LORD EDGARD.

PETERBONO. Ring. Pearls.

HECTOR. Pocketbook.

PETERBONO. Perfect.

The DUPONT-DUFORTS *find themselves alone.*

D.D. SENIOR. Things are going badly.

D.D. JUNIOR. Very badly.

D.D. SENIOR. These gay dogs are here on the same errand we are, that's quite obvious, but everything is going their way and nothing is coming ours.

D.D. JUNIOR [*looking in a mirror*]. Yet we achieved a really lovely make-up.

D.D. SENIOR. Not for a Carnival of Leaves.

D.D. JUNIOR. Fancy organizing a Carnival of Leaves!

D.D. SENIOR. Fancy, what's more, reading "Carnival of Thieves" when it's down in black and white on all the posters "Carnival of Leaves." The old goose!

D.D. JUNIOR [*catching sight of the drawing room through the open window*]. Dad!

D.D. SENIOR. What is it?

D.D. JUNIOR. Look at the wall!

D.D. SENIOR. What about the wall?

D.D. JUNIOR. The Fragonards!

D.D. SENIOR. If you think at a time like this I feel like going into ecstasies over a lot of paintings . . . !

D.D. JUNIOR. Dad, the Fragonards aren't on the wall. [*He rushes into the room.*]

D.D. SENIOR. Well?

D.D. JUNIOR [*from the room*]. Nor are the enamels! The bronze candlesticks are missing! And the snuffboxes! All the drawers are open! [*Rushing out again.*] Dad, there's been a burglary!

D.D. SENIOR. Let's go. They'll think we did it.

D.D. JUNIOR. Don't be ridiculous! We were at the carnival with everybody else! Dad! There's been a robbery here!

D.D. SENIOR [*who has looked to make sure*]. You're absolutely right. There's been a robbery. But what are you so pleased about? That won't set our affairs to rights.

D.D. JUNIOR. Don't you understand? There's been a robbery while we were at the Casino. Don't you see suspicion can only fall on the one person who made himself conspicuous by his absence? Now then, who, I ask you, made himself conspicuous by his absence?

D.D. SENIOR. Young Pedro?

D.D. JUNIOR. Of course! Young Pedro.

D.D. SENIOR. In that case, surely the others would be his accomplices.

D.D. JUNIOR. They are his accomplices. They came with us to allay suspicion, that's quite clear. But now you may be sure they're gone, or will have before very long.

D.D. SENIOR. Didier, you're magnificent! You do my old heart good. Kiss me, Son! At last they are unmasked. They're done for, laddie, and our affairs have never looked so promising.

D.D. JUNIOR. We must clinch matters. There's to be no escape and no denial. We must telephone the police at once. [*He picks up the receiver.*] Give me the police please. And hurry!

D.D. SENIOR [*trundling around the drawing room and bellowing*]. The Fragonards! The enamels! The candlesticks! The snuffboxes! Two drawers burst open! Magnificent!

D.D. JUNIOR. Hello? Is that the police station? This is the Villa des Boyards. A serious robbery has just taken place. Yes, the thieves are still on the premises. You'll catch them red-handed if you hurry. Hurry!

D.D. Senior [*coming back radiant*]. Come to your father, laddie!

They embrace.

D.D. Junior. Let's call the company and confront the rascals! Hey there! Come quickly, everybody!

D.D. Senior. Hey there! Hey!

Lord Edgard [*entering; he, and likewise the others when they come down, have all changed back into their usual clothes*]. What's the matter?

D.D. Junior. There's been a burglary!

Lord Edgard. That's no surprise to anybody in these troubled times. Where?

D.D. Junior. Here!

Lord Edgard. Here!

D.D. Senior [*breathless with excitement*]. Here! Here in this very room!

Lord Edgard. In the drawing room? What did they take?

D.D. Senior [*like a street hawker*]. Fragonards! Enamels! Snuffboxes! Candlesticks! Drawers! Come in and see! Come and see!

Lord Edgard *goes into the room, comes back, and staggers into an armchair.*

Lord Edgard. Terrible! Terrible! I had an idea this would happen.

D.D. Senior *and* Junior. So did we!

Lord Edgard. Do you know who did it?

D.D. Senior. We have an idea!

Lord Edgard. So have I!

Enter Eva.

Lord Edgard. My child, we've just been burgled!

Eva. What?

D.D. Senior [*off again*]. The Fragonards! The enamels! The candlesticks! The snuffboxes!

Eva. I'm glad about the candlesticks; they were appalling. But it's a shame about the Fragonards.

Hector *enters triumphantly in new make-up.*

Hector. Eva, this time I've got it!

Eva. No.

Lord Edgard [*leaping on him*]. At last! The detective! My dear fellow, you're in the nick of time. A serious robbery has just been committed. We suspect some impostors whom we are entertaining at the moment, owing to a curious fancy of my cousin's. Kindly arrest them at once, my dear fellow.

EVA. What's come over you, Uncle? That's Prince Hector. Hector, do take off that beard.

HECTOR [*modestly, as he reveals himself*]. Yes, sir, it's me.

LORD EDGARD [*in a sudden rage*]. How much longer do you intend to make a fool of me, young man?

HECTOR [*backing imperceptibly toward the door*]. But, your Lordship, I'm not making a fool of you, really.

LORD EDGARD. I can take a joke, in doubtful taste though it is with a man of my years, but don't repeat it a dozen times a day!

HECTOR [*nearing the door*]. But I'm not making a fool . . .

He bumps into the DUPONT-DUFORTS, *who have cut off his retreat.*

D.D. JUNIOR. Oh no.

D.D. SENIOR. Of course you're not making a fool of him. Don't go. Everything will be all right.

HECTOR. Look here, what's going on? Am I under suspicion?

EVA. Gentlemen, will you please leave his Highness alone?

HECTOR. I should think so. Why, it's absurd, isn't it, Eva?

LADY HURF [*entering with* PETERBONO]. What is all this shouting? I've never heard such a commotion!

PETERBONO. We simply can't hear ourselves speak!

LORD EDGARD. It's terrible! There's been a dreadful robbery! I had my suspicions all along. I told you he died in 1904! I told you they were all impostors!

D.D. SENIOR [*at the same time*]. The Fragonards! The enamels! The snuffboxes! The candlesticks! The drawers!

LADY HURF. One at a time, please! I don't know what you're talking about. First of all, I must sit down. I'm worn out.

During the ejaculations of the others and the silence which follows, HECTOR *is desperately indicating to* PETERBONO *that they must be off.* PETERBONO *thinks his cuff links are undone, his tie crooked, or that something is hanging down. He brushes himself, looks in the mirror, still fails to understand, and finally shrugs his shoulders and gives up.*

LADY HURF. Now. Tell me all about it.

PETERBONO [*engagingly*]. Splendid idea. Tell us all about it.

LORD EDGARD [*before they stop him*]. Didn't I tell you he died in——

D.D. SENIOR [*at the same time*]. Everything! Everything! The Fragonards! The . . .

They look at each other and stop dead.

EVA. There's been a burglary.

LADY HURF. A burglary?

EVA. Yes. While we were out the enamels were stolen, and the Fragonards, and, believe it or not, the candlesticks.

LADY HURF. Oh, good. They were imitation.

LORD EDGARD. I told you so! I told you so!

LADY HURF. One of the servants, I expect. Are they all here?

EVA. I don't know.

D.D. SENIOR. We must inform the police.

LADY HURF. No.

D.D. SENIOR. What do you mean, no?

LADY HURF. No, I tell you. I will not have policemen in my house.

D.D. JUNIOR. But we've already telephoned, your Ladyship.

LADY HURF. My good sirs, have you completely forgotten your manners? I beg you to remember that this is my house. You appear to have abandoned every vestige of constraint these last few days.

D.D. JUNIOR. But we——

D.D. SENIOR. You see, we——

LADY HURF. Eva, call them back at once and tell them not to come.

D.D. SENIOR. Too late. They're bound to be on the way.

All this time PETERBONO *and* HECTOR *have been quietly edging toward the door. When* LADY HURF *tells* EVA *to call off the police, they stop, still hopeful. At these last words, they make a frenzied dash for it.*

D.D. SENIOR. Look! They're getting away!

D.D. JUNIOR. This is too much! We'll save you, whether you like it or not! Hands up!

D.D. SENIOR. Hands up!

They cover the thieves with their revolvers.

LADY HURF. Gentlemen, I am mistress in this house! I order you to put away those firearms!

D.D. JUNIOR. No!

D.D. SENIOR. No. You'll thank us for it later on.

LADY HURF. Eva, I'm going to have hysterics! Call the servants! Emile! Here, quickly! Joseph! Help!

Enter POLICEMEN *during her cries.*

POLICEMAN. Here we are! Horace, you take the fat one!

They have seen these two horrible bandits pointing their guns at the gentry. Without a moment's indecision, they hurl themselves on the DUPONT-DUFORTS.

POLICEMAN. Aha, me beauties! We've got you!

D.D. SENIOR *and* JUNIOR [*backing away*]. But—but——
We didn't do anything! No, no, not us! Not us! Quite the reverse! We're the ones who telephoned! This is preposterous! It's them!

They collide as they retreat, try to escape the other way and collide again in the course of a droll little ballet which culminates in their capture.

POLICEMEN [*hoisting them onto their shoulders with the showmanship of circus acrobats*]. Upsy-daisy! [*To* HECTOR.] If you'd like to give us a hand, sir, by taking the trouble to open the door, sir, it'd be much appreciated.

HECTOR. No trouble. Absolutely no trouble at all.

The POLICEMEN *carry off the* DUPONT-DUFORTS *despite their agonizing protestations.*

LORD EDGARD [*wildly*]. But, my dear . . .

LADY HURF [*sternly*]. Edgard! Be quiet.

D.D. SENIOR [*yelling in vain as he is borne away*]. For God's sake, say something! Tell them! Tell them!

D.D. JUNIOR [*as he whirls past her*]. Mademoiselle Eva!

They have gone, ushered out by their own little melody.

LADY HURF [*calmly*]. There! That's a relief. Three whole weeks those people have been here, and I hadn't a notion how to get rid of them.

LORD EDGARD [*overcome by so many emotions, falls semi-conscious into an armchair*]. When I think I came here to cure my liver trouble!

LADY HURF. Eva dear, run up and get your uncle his smelling salts.

EVA *goes.* LADY HURF *looks at* PETERBONO, *who ever since the arrest of the* DUPONT-DUFORTS *has been choking in the grip of irrepressible hysteria.*

LADY HURF. My dear man, save your laughter. I know perfectly well you are the real thief. [*He stops dead. She feels in his pocket.*] Give me back my pearls. You haven't been very clever.

PETERBONO. What do you mean?

LADY HURF. Have you a lot of luggage? How long will it take you to pack?

PETERBONO [*piteously*]. Not long.

LADY HURF. Then I advise you to make the greatest possible haste upstairs.

PETERBONO. Yes.

Enter HECTOR.

HECTOR [*superbly*]. There. The rascals are in good hands, your Ladyship. [PETERBONO *coughs*.] Father dear, aren't you feeling well?

LADY HURF. No, he's not feeling at all well. I think you had both better go up to your rooms.

HECTOR. Really, Father? Where's the trouble exactly?

LORD EDGARD [*himself once more*]. I told you the Duke of Miraflores died in 1904!

LADY HURF. I knew it long ago, my dear.

HECTOR [*still not understanding* PETERBONO's *desperate dumb show, says waggishly*]. Ha-ha-ha! Still the same old joke, eh?

LADY HURF. The Duke died in my arms, or near enough. So that I knew quite well whom we were dealing with. Only you see, my poor old Edgard, I was so very, very bored.

HECTOR [*finally going to* PETERBONO]. What's the matter, for heaven's sake?

PETERBONO. Idiot! I've been trying to tell you for the last half hour. The game's up, but she's letting us go free.

HECTOR. Huh? Don't be silly, they've arrested the others.

LADY HURF [*going to them with a smile*]. You don't, I'm sure, want to await the visit of the inspector of police, gentlemen.

HECTOR. This is unthinkable! What are we accused of? We were with you the whole evening!

PETERBONO. Don't be canny. Come on.

HECTOR. My dear Father, I don't know what you're talking about. Madame, we are here as your guests, and this robbery is no reason to treat us, the Miraflores y Grandes, in this cavalier fashion.

PETERBONO [*unable to suppress a giggle, despite the tragic situation*]. Miraflores y Grandes! Oh, my Lord! You're off your head, old chap. Come on.

LADY HURF. Go along, sir, do, as everyone advises you.

HECTOR. I will not tolerate this attitude. [*To* PETERBONO.] Play up, will you?

EVA [*coming back*]. Here are the salts.

HECTOR. I will not tolerate this attitude. Because if you consider our presence undesirable, I laugh to scorn—do you hear, to scorn—your utterly unfounded and insulting allegations. There's someone here, I know, who will think my presence far from undesirable. Eva, Eva, my darling, I've found my face at last! [*He turns away and rapidly re-creates the appearance he had in the first scene.*]

PETERBONO. Hector, stop playing around. The police are on their way.

HECTOR [*making up*]. Let me alone. We're saved, I tell you!

LADY HURF [*sits down, dispirited*]. Edgard, if this head-strong child falls in love with him again, the situation is absolutely hopeless.

LORD EDGARD. I have not the faintest idea what is going on. What is he doing? Is this another joke? He goes very much too far, that boy.

HECTOR [*turning around triumphantly*]. Eva, beloved! It *was* like this, wasn't it?

A silence. EVA *looks at him. The others hold their breath.*

EVA [*calmly breaking the tension*]. Yes, that's how you were. Only I must have looked at you too hastily, I think, because now you don't appeal to me at all.

LADY HURF [*leaping up*]. Heaven be praised! Now, off with you! Quickly, off with you!

HECTOR. But, Eva, listen! Eva, I can't believe . . .

PETERBONO [*in a whisper*]. Hurry, idiot, hurry! She's taken back the necklace, but I've still got the ring.

They go with great dignity. A gay little tune signals their departure.

LADY HURF [*watching them go with a tender little smile*]. Poor old fellow. I let him keep the ring. They stayed here a full two weeks after all, because of me. We haven't any right to make them waste their time. I imagine it's a trade that doesn't bring in all that much.

LORD EDGARD. What I don't fathom is where the boy comes in. [*The two women look at him in sudden anguish.*] The boy, the young one, who was so pleasant, you remember?

EVA. Juliette! Where's Juliette?

LADY HURF. Juliette! She didn't come to the carnival. Isn't she upstairs? Perhaps in the morning room? Or in the garden?

EVA. I'll run and see. Oh, it's inconceivable.

LORD EDGARD. What is inconceivable? I don't understand, quite. [LADY HURF *drops onto the sofa and plays nervously with her pearls.*] Why do you look so tragic? It's all over now, isn't it?

LADY HURF. No, stupid, it is not all over. This boy has carried off Juliette along with the pictures in the drawing room. How many times did I tell you to bestir yourself and take precautions if we didn't want disaster?

EVA [*coming back*]. She's not upstairs. The servants are combing the grounds.

LADY HURF. It's horrible!

LORD EDGARD. Juliette, our little Juliette. Is it possible? Can she have been stolen?

EVA. Yes.

LORD EDGARD. But she's a big girl now. She could have defended herself. Or called for help. The house is overrun with staff.

LADY HURF. Can't you understand? She's in his power! He's bewitched her. He'll make her steal for him, or walk the streets!

LORD EDGARD. The streets. [*It dawns on him.*] The streets!

He staggers under the blow. The clarinet plays an air heavy with tragedy. The three of them lapse into pensive and painful silence. The clarinet resumes its tragic theme with an overtone of mockery, and then leads into the romance which is indeed altogether fitting at this moment, for GUSTAVE *enters on tiptoe, laden with so many things that he cannot see where he is going. He is carrying* JULIETTE, *who is asleep, and his various sacks. He crosses the drawing room, unseen by anybody; suddenly he bumps into an armchair. He drops his sacks with a clatter and startles the others, who see him and cry out.*

LADY HURF. He's killed her!

A *tremolo from the clarinet.* GUSTAVE, *terrified, starts to
put* JULIETTE *down on the sofa, but at the cries she wakens
and clings to him.*

JULIETTE. No, no, no! Why did you bring me back? No,
  he's not to go! If he goes I'm going with him!

LADY HURF. Juliette!

LORD EDGARD. My child.

JULIETTE [*screaming through a flood of tears*]. Yes, you
  despise him, I know, but I love him. Don't try to tell me
  anything—I want to go with him because I love him.
  Don't say a word, I'd only hate you for it. Gustave,
  Gustave, why did you bring me back? [*He struggles and
  tries to run away but she clutches him.*] No. Stay here,
  or let me come with you. Why did you bring me back?
  Was I too stupid for you? Too naïve? Is it because I fell
  asleep beside you in the car that you don't want me? It's
  true one doesn't as a rule doze off on the night of one's
  elopement, but I was tired, my darling. I'm not used to
  staying up so late. [*She hides her head in his arms.*]

LORD EDGARD. What is she saying?

LADY HURF [*moved*]. Do be quiet! It's very lovely what she
  is saying.

JULIETTE [*turning to them like a little fury, without letting
  go of* GUSTAVE]. No, no, I'm not ashamed! I'm not
  ashamed! You can say anything you like, I'll never be
  ashamed! I love him. I want him for my lover, since you
  will never let him be my husband. Look. I'm going to kiss
  him now in front of you.

*She throws her arms around his neck. He holds back for
a second; then as he sees her tousled hair and her radiant
tear-stained face, he too forgets the others.*

GUSTAVE. I love you, Juliette.

JULIETTE. You see, we're kissing here, in front of them.

                    They kiss.

LORD EDGARD [*adjusting his pince-nez*]. Why, they're kissing.

LADY HURF. That's right. They're kissing. What about it?
  Did you never do as much? [*She contemplates them, en-
  tranced.*] How enchanting they are!

LORD EDGARD. Aren't they? Do you remember, Emily?

LADY HURF. They make a delightful couple, don't they?

LORD EDGARD [*lost in his memories*]. Delightful. Do you
  remember? The Crystal Palace?

LADY HURF. She's nearly as tall as he is. He is adorable.
Look at the breeding in that profile. The exquisite shyness
and yet the strength of it. He will make a fairy-tale husband for our terrible, gentle little Juliette. [*She stops.*]
Edgard, what are you talking me into? He's a thief!

LORD EDGARD [*smiling*]. Ah yes, a thief.

LADY HURF. Well then, it's out of the question. He must
go at once.

The clarinet stops from shock.

LORD EDGARD [*crestfallen*]. But—but they love each other.

LADY HURF. I know they love each other. But it's the only
thing to do. Absolutely the only thing. She simply cannot marry a boy who has neither a father nor a mother.

LORD EDGARD. Ah! [*He thinks furiously for a moment, then
cries suddenly.*] Wait a minute! Wait a minute!

GUSTAVE *and* JULIETTE, *startled by his cry, come out of their
embrace.* LORD EDGARD *runs out like one demented.*

LADY HURF. Where do you suppose he's going?

JULIETTE. I'll never leave him, never, never, never.

GUSTAVE [*holding her to him, says by way of explanation*].
We love each other.

The clarinet plays a little supplication.

LADY HURF. I gather so. But there it is. You're nothing but
a nobody, if not worse. I'm afraid you'll have to go.

Another entreaty from the clarinet.

JULIETTE. If he goes I go with him.

LADY HURF. This time we will be here to stop you. [*The
clarinet's plea becomes heart-rending.* LADY HURF *turns
furiously on the* MUSICIAN.] As for you, my good sir,
you're beginning to get on my nerves! Go away! [*The
clarinet attempts a musical protest.*] Get out of here this
instant!

She drives him out. Pathetically the MUSICIAN *goes, ex-
pressing his despair on his instrument.* LORD EDGARD *returns like a meteor, carrying ribbons, medals, and a photograph. He marches threateningly over to* GUSTAVE.

LORD EDGARD. You are twenty years old, are you not?

GUSTAVE. Yes.

LORD EDGARD. Right. [*He looks at the photograph, looks
at it a second time, backs, screwing up his eyes in the
manner of a painter scrutinizing a picture.*] Hold your

head up. Fine. Open your shirt. Fine. Now for the mark behind the ear. [*He turns back his ear.*] Fine. [*He shows him the medal.*] Do you recognize this medal?

GUSTAVE. No.

LORD EDGARD [*throwing it away*]. Never mind. You are my son! My son who was stolen from me at a tender age. [*He falls into his arms.*]

LADY HURF. Edgard, have you taken leave of your senses?

GUSTAVE [*furiously*]. Let me go, sir. I don't know what you're talking about. [*To* JULIETTE.] What's the matter with him?

LORD EDGARD [*to* LADY HURF]. Do you deny that a son was stolen from me at a tender age? [*To* GUSTAVE.] Do you deny that you are uncertain of your paternal origins? Yes, yes, you are my son, my own son, my beloved son! [*He falls on his neck again.*]

JULIETTE. Isn't that lucky! Gustave, isn't that lucky!

GUSTAVE [*freeing himself roughly*]. No, it won't work.

LORD EDGARD. What won't work?

GUSTAVE. I'm quite sure I'm not your son.

LORD EDGARD. So I shall have waited twenty years for Heaven to give me back my child, and now when Heaven at last sees fit to give him back to me, it is this very child who refuses to acknowledge his own father!

GUSTAVE. No. It's all a scheme because you can see your little girl is in love with me, but I'm sorry, I can't accept.

LADY HURF. That's very honorable of him.

LORD EDGARD. This is horrible! Horrible! My son denies me! [*He prances with rage.*]

GUSTAVE. No, I can't accept. It's nice of you to do it, very nice of you. But I can't. I'm not one of your kind.

LADY HURF. It is really unfortunate that this boy should be the only one among us to suffer from class consciousness.

LORD EDGARD. I am abominably humiliated. Such contempt from my own son! I shall crumple up with sorrow. [*He does in fact crumple up with sorrow on the nearest sofa.*] Here I am, crumpled up. How much longer do I have to stay crumpled?

LADY HURF. Couldn't you see your way to accepting? You're making your father very unhappy.

GUSTAVE. How can I! I haven't any reason——

JULIETTE. Oh, but you have! Come into the garden as you did before. I'm going to explain all your reasons to you.

Do come, please. Come, anyway. You haven't anything to lose, after all, by coming into the garden. [*She drags him out.*]

LADY HURF [*as soon as they're gone*]. Edgard, it's not true! You never had a son stolen from you at a tender age!

LORD EDGARD. No, it isn't true. It's a picture I cut out of a magazine.

LADY HURF. So you've acted like an imbecile for over fifty years and yet you had it in you to think of that all by yourself.

EVA. How happy they are going to be.

LADY HURF [*dreamily*]. Yes.

EVA. And I shall continue to play the young and charming widow who is always such a great success.

LADY HURF. My poor Eva, faith is a gift, alas, and there's no learning it. It's over, our fine escapade. Here we are alone again, like bobbing corks. It's only for those who have played it with all the zest of youth that the comedy is a success, and only then because they were playing their youth, a thing which succeeds always. They were not even conscious of the comedy.

Enter a bearded gentleman.

BEARDED GENTLEMAN. I am from Scotland Yard.

LORD EDGARD [*lets out a roar, leaps onto him, and pulls his beard*]. Oh no, it won't work this time!

DETECTIVE. Stop it! You're hurting me!

LORD EDGARD [*greatly astonished*]. What! Do you mean it's your own?

DETECTIVE. Of course it's my own!

LORD EDGARD. Then you really are the detective I sent for?

DETECTIVE. I've just said so, haven't I?

LORD EDGARD. Well, we don't need you any more. The entertainment is over.

DETECTIVE [*blithely*]. In that case . . .

He pulls his clarinet out of his pocket—for it is none other than the MUSICIAN—*and strikes up a quickstep which does duty as a finale. The characters come in through all the doors, dancing and exchanging beards.*

MEDEA

(Médée)

A "black" play in one act

English version by
LUCE *and* **ARTHUR KLEIN**

Medea by Jean Anouilh, English version by Luce and Arthur Klein. Copyright ©, 1957 by Arthur Klein.

CHARACTERS

MEDEA
JASON
CREON
THE NURSE
THE BOY
THE GUARDS
THE CHILDREN

MEDEA

When the curtain rises, MEDEA *and the* NURSE *are seen squatting on the ground before a wagon. Vague music and singing are heard in the distance. They listen.*

MEDEA. Do you hear it?

NURSE. What?

MEDEA. Happiness. Prowling around.

NURSE. They are singing in the village. Today may be a feast day for them.

MEDEA. I hate their feast days. I hate their joy.

NURSE. It does not concern us. [*A silence.*] At home our feast days came earlier. In June. The girls put flowers in their hair and the boys paint their faces red with their blood, and then in the small hours of the morning, after the first sacrifices, they begin to fight. How handsome our Colchis boys look when they fight!

MEDEA. Be still.

NURSE. Afterward they spend all day taming wild animals. And in the evening they set large fires before your father's palace—large yellow bonfires made with herbs that smelled so strongly. Have you forgotten the fragrance of our native plants, child?

MEDEA. Be still. Not another word, good woman.

NURSE. Ah, I am old now and the way is so long. . . . Why, why did we leave, Medea?

MEDEA [*shouts*]. We left because I loved Jason, because I stole from my father for him, because I killed my brother for him! Be still, good woman. Be still. Do you think it is wise to repeat these things over and over again?

NURSE. You had a palace with walls of gold and now we squat here like two beggars before a fire which always dies out.

MEDEA. Go and fetch some wood.

The NURSE *gets up moaning and walks away.*

MEDEA [*suddenly shouts*]. Listen! [*She stands up.*] Someone is coming on the road.

NURSE [*listens, then says*]. No. It is the wind.

59

MEDEA *again crouches. The singing is once more heard in the distance.*

NURSE. Do not wait for him any longer, my dove. You are eating your heart out. If it is true this is a feast day, they have surely invited him there. And your Jason is dancing now, dancing with the daughters of Pelasgus, and here we are, you and I.

MEDEA [*in a hollow tone*]. Be quiet, old hag.

NURSE. I won't say a word.

A pause. She bends down and blows on the fire. Music is heard.

MEDEA [*suddenly*]. Smell!

NURSE. Smell what?

MEDEA. Their happiness. How it stinks even to this very fire. Yet they have confined us far enough from their village! They were afraid we would steal their chickens during the night. [*She stands tall and cries out.*] But why do they sing and dance? Do I sing? Do I dance?

NURSE. They are fortunate. They are in their own homes. Their day's work is done. [*She dreams.*] Do you remember? How white the palace looked at the end of the cypress road when we returned from our long rides? You would give your horse to the slave and you would throw yourself on the divans. Then I would call the maidens to bathe you and dress you. You were the mistress and the King's daughter and nothing was too beautiful for you. They would bring you dresses from the great chests, and you would make your choice, calm and naked, while you were rubbed with oil.

MEDEA. Quiet, you fool. You are too stupid. Do you think I miss a palace, dresses, and slaves?

NURSE. On the run, always on the run, ever since!

MEDEA. I could have gone on running away.

NURSE. Chased, beaten, scorned, without a country, without a home.

MEDEA. Scorned, chased, beaten, without a country, without a home, but not alone.

NURSE. And you drag me with you, old as I am. And if I die, where will you leave me?

MEDEA. In a hole, on the side of the road, anywhere, old hag. And I too, I accepted that. But not alone.

NURSE. He is leaving you, Medea.

MEDEA [*cries out*]. No! [*She stops.*] Listen.

NURSE. It is the wind. It is the feast day. He will not return tonight again.

MEDEA. But what is this feast day? What happiness is it that stinks even here from their sweat, their cheap wine, and their greasy food? People of Corinth, why do you shout so and dance? What makes you so gay this evening while I am so choked and oppressed? Nurse, Nurse . . . tonight I feel as if I were in labor. I suffer and I am scared as when you helped me pull a child from my womb. . . . Help me, Nurse. Something stirs in me as in the old days, and it is something that says no to their joy over there, something that says no to happiness. [*She clings to the old woman, trembling.*] Nurse, if I cry out, you will put your hand over my mouth, and if I struggle, you will hold me tight, won't you? You won't let me suffer all alone. . . . Oh, hold me, Nurse. Hold me with all your strength. Hold me as you did when I was a little girl, as you held me on the night when I almost died in childbirth. I still have something to bring into the world tonight, something bigger and more alive than myself, and I do not know if I will be strong enough. . . .

A BOY *enters suddenly and stops.*

BOY. Are you Medea?

MEDEA [*shouts to him*]. Yes! Speak up! I know!

BOY. Jason sent me.

MEDEA. He won't come back? He is wounded? He is dead?

BOY. He sends word that you are saved.

MEDEA. He won't return?

BOY. He sends word that he will come, and that you are to wait for him.

MEDEA. He won't return? Where is he?

BOY. He is with Creon the King at his palace.

MEDEA. Imprisoned?

BOY. No.

MEDEA [*again shouts*]. Yes! This feast day is for him? Speak! You can see that I know. It is for him?

BOY. Yes. It is for him.

MEDEA. What has he done? Come, tell me quickly. You have run all the way, your face is flushed, and you are anxious to go back. They are dancing, are they not?

BOY. Yes.

MEDEA. And drinking?

BOY. The people are helping themselves to wine from six large barrels in front of the palace.

MEDEA. And they play games, and fireworks and guns light up the sky. Come, tell me, child, and you will have played your part and you can return at once and enjoy yourself. You do not know me. What difference can it make to you what you are going to tell me? Why does my face frighten you? Do you want me to smile? There you are. I am smiling. Besides, it must be good news since they are dancing. So tell me quickly, child, since I know!

BOY. He is marrying Creon's daughter, Creüsa. The wedding is tomorrow morning.

MEDEA. Thank you, child! Go and dance now with the girls of Corinth. Dance all night long, as much as you can. And when you are old remember that you were the one who broke the news to Medea.

BOY [takes a step]. What shall I say to him?

MEDEA. To whom?

BOY. Jason.

MEDEA. Tell him that I thanked you.

The BOY exits.

MEDEA [suddenly shouts]. Thank you, Jason! Thank you, Creon! Thank you, night! Thank you, all of you! How simple it was. Now I am freed . . . !

NURSE [approaches]. My proud eagle, my little vulture . . .

MEDEA. Leave me alone, woman! I no longer have need of your hands. This time my child has come by itself. Oh, my newly born hatred . . . ! How soft you are, how good you smell. Oh, little black girl, now you are the only thing I have left in the world to love.

NURSE. Come, Medea . . .

MEDEA [stands tall with folded arms]. Leave me alone. I am listening.

NURSE. Take no heed of their music, and let us go inside.

MEDEA. I do not hear it any more. I am listening to my hatred. . . . Oh, sweetness! Oh, lost strength! What had he done to me, Nurse, with his large warm hands? He had only to enter my father's palace and touch me with a single caress. Ten years have gone by and Jason's hand no longer grips mine. I have found myself again. Have I been dreaming? Now again I am Medea! I am no longer that woman bound to the smell of a man, that bitch in heat who waits. Oh, shame! Shame! My cheeks are burning, Nurse. All day long I waited for him, my legs open, maimed. . . . Humbly, that part of myself that he could take and give back, that middle of my womb was his. . . . I had to obey him and smile at him and adorn myself to please him, since he took my life with him when he left every morning, only too happy when he returned in the evening and brought my life back to me. How could I help but give him the Golden Fleece when he wanted it, and all of my father's secrets? How could I help but kill my brother for him, and afterward follow him in his flight . . . poor and criminal with him? I did all I had to do, that is all, and I could have done even more. You know all of that, good woman, for you too have loved.

NURSE. Yes, my vulture.

MEDEA [shouts]. Maimed . . . ! Oh, Sun, if it is true that I come from you, why was I born maimed? Why have you made me a girl? Why these breasts, this weakness, this open wound in the middle of myself? Would not the boy Medea have been handsome? Would he not have been strong? His body strong as stone, made to take and then to go . . . firm, intact, and complete. Ah! Then Jason could have come with his large and powerful hands; then he could have tried to touch me with them! Each of us with his knife—yes!—and the stronger kills the other and walks away free; yes, free. Not this struggle where I only yearned to yield, this wound I was craving for. Woman! Woman! Bitch! Flesh made with a little mud and a man's rib! A mere piece of man! Whore!

NURSE [kisses her]. Not you, Medea, not you!

MEDEA. I as well as the others . . . ! More cowardly and more open than the others. Ten years! But tonight it is over, Nurse. I have become Medea again. How good it is.

NURSE. Calm yourself, Medea.

MEDEA. I am calm, Nurse. I am subdued. Do you not hear how softly I speak. I am dying. I am killing everything in me softly. I am strangling.

NURSE. Come now. You frighten me. Let us go in.

MEDEA. I too am frightened.

NURSE. What are they going to do with us now?

MEDEA. Why bother about that? What you should rather

ask is what are we going to do with them. Yes, I am
frightened too, but not of their music, their shouting,
their wretched King, or their orders! I am afraid of myself. Jason, you put her to sleep, but now Medea is awak-
ening again. Hatred. Hatred! You great bountiful wave,
you are washing me and I am reborn.

NURSE. They are going to drive us away, Medea.

MEDEA. Perhaps they will.

NURSE. Where shall we go?

MEDEA. There will always be a country for us, good woman,
where Medea will be Queen. Either this side of life or the
other. Oh, my black kingdom, you are mine once more.

NURSE [moans]. Now we shall have to pack everything
again.

MEDEA. Yes, we shall pack again, old woman. Afterward!

NURSE. After what?

MEDEA. Must you ask?

NURSE. What do you want to do, Medea?

MEDEA. What I did for him when I betrayed my father,
when I had to kill my brother so we could escape. What
I did to old Pelias when I tried to make Jason King of
his island. What I have done for him ten times over. But
this time, at long last, I will do it for myself!

NURSE. You are mad! You cannot.

MEDEA. What can I not, good woman? I am Medea, all
alone in front of this wagon; abandoned on the shore of
this strange sea, expelled, disgraced, hated! But nothing
is too much for me! [The music grows stronger in the
distance. MEDEA's voice overpowers it.] Let them sing,
let them sing their wedding songs! And quickly, too. Let
them be swift in adorning the bride in her palace. There
is a long night before tomorrow's wedding. . . . Ah!
Jason, you know me, though; you know what a virgin you
took in Colchis. What could you imagine? Did you think
I was going to cry? I followed you in blood and crime,
and I need blood and crime to leave you.

NURSE [throws herself against her]. Be still! I beg you, say
no more! Bury your moans in the bottom of your heart;
bury your hatred. Endure it. Tonight they are stronger
than we.

MEDEA. What difference does that make, Nurse?

NURSE. You will take your revenge, my little wolf; you will
revenge yourself, my little vulture. One day you too will

hurt them. We are nothing here. We are only two
strangers in their wagon with their old mare. Two chicken
thieves at whom the children throw stones. Wait one day,
my child; wait a year, and soon you will be the strongest.

MEDEA. Stronger than tonight? Never.

NURSE. But what can you do in this hostile island? Colchis
is far away and even from there you were driven out.
And now Jason is also leaving us. What have you left?

MEDEA. Myself!

NURSE. Poor child! Creon is King and it is only because he
permitted it that we were allowed to stay on their land.
Were he to say a word, were he to give his permission,
they will all be upon us with their knives and their spears.
They will kill us.

MEDEA [softly]. They will kill us. But too late.

NURSE [throwing herself at MEDEA's feet]. Medea, I am an
old woman and I don't want to die! I followed you, I
gave up everything for you. But the earth is still full of
good things—the sun on our faces when we stop, the
warm soup we sip at midday, the feel in our hands of the
little coins we have earned, the nip which warms one's
heart before going to sleep.

MEDEA [pushes her aside with contempt]. Carcass! Yesterday I too wanted to live, but now it is no longer a matter
of living or dying.

NURSE [clinging to her legs]. I want to live, Medea!

MEDEA. I know. You all want to live. It is because Jason
wants to live, too, that he is leaving.

NURSE [suddenly vile]. You no longer love him, Medea. You
have not desired him for a long time now. One cannot
help knowing everything squeezed together in this wagon.
He was the first to tell you that he was too warm one
night, and that he wanted to sleep outside. And you let
him go and I heard you relax and heave a contented sigh
to have the bed all to yourself that night. One kills for a
man who still takes you, not for a man you let out of
your bed at night.

MEDEA [takes her by the collar and lifts her brutally before
her face]. Take care, woman! You know too much. You
say too much. I sucked your milk all right, and I have
put up with your whinings. But it is not from milk that
Medea has grown. I owe no more to you than I would to
the goat I might have suckled in your place. So listen:

you have said too much, you and your carcass, with your little nip and your sun on your rotten flesh. . . . To your dishes, old hag. To your broom and your potato peelings with the others of your kind. The game we are playing is not for the likes of you. And if you happen to die by mischance and without knowing why, then it is your hard luck. And that is all.

She throws her on the ground. At that moment the old woman shouts:

NURSE. Look out, Medea! Someone is coming!

MEDEA *turns around.* CREON *is before her, accompanied by two or three men.*

CREON. Are you Medea?

MEDEA. I am.

CREON. I am Creon, the King of this city.

MEDEA. Greetings.

CREON. I have heard of your story. Your crimes are known here. In the evening—here as well as in all the islands off this shore—women tell them to their children to frighten them. I have put up with you and your wagon on this plain for several days. But now you will have to go.

MEDEA. What have I done to the people of Corinth? Have I looted their farms? Did I make their cattle sick? Have I poisoned their fountains when I went and drew water for my meals?

CREON. No, not yet. But all that you might do one day. Go away.

MEDEA. My father, Creon, is also a King.

CREON. I know. Go to Colchis then and complain.

MEDEA. All right, I shall return there. I will not frighten the matrons of your village any longer; nor will my horse steal the scanty grass of your land any longer. I shall return to Colchis, but let the one who brought me here take me back there.

CREON. What do you mean?

MEDEA. Give Jason back to me.

CREON. Jason is my guest, the son of a King who was my friend. And he is free to do as he chooses.

MEDEA. What are they singing in your village? Why these brilliant displays in the sky, these dances, this wine given so freely to all? If tonight is the last evening they allow me to stay, why do these honest Corinthians prevent me from sleeping?

CREON. I have come to tell you that as well. Tonight they are celebrating my daughter's betrothal. Jason will marry her tomorrow.

MEDEA. Long life and long happiness to them both.

CREON. They have no need of your wishes.

MEDEA. Why refuse them, Creon? Invite me to the wedding. Introduce me to your daughter. I can be useful to her, don't you know? For ten years now I have been Jason's wife. I have quite a lot to teach your daughter, who has only known him ten days.

CREON. It is to avoid this scene that I have decided you should leave Corinth tonight. Harness your horse and pack. You have one hour to cross the border. These men will show you the way.

MEDEA. And if I should refuse?

CREON. The sons of old Pelias, whom you murdered, have asked all the Kings of this shore for your head. If you remain, I will deliver you into their hands.

MEDEA. They are your neighbors, and they are strong. Kings do each other such good turns. Why are you waiting?

CREON. Jason asked me to let you go.

MEDEA. Kind Jason! I ought to thank him, don't you think? Can you imagine the Thessalians torturing me the very day of his wedding? Can you see me at the trial, only a few leagues from Corinth, saying aloud for whom I had Pelias killed? "For the son-in-law, honest judges, for the honored son-in-law of your kindly neighboring King, with whom you maintain the best possible relationship!" You take the task of Kingship very lightly, Creon. At my father's palace I had time to learn that one does not govern that way. Have me killed at once.

CREON [*in a hollow voice*]. Yes, I know I ought to. But I promised to let you go. You have one hour.

MEDEA [*stands in front of him*]. Creon, you are old. You have been King for a long time. You have seen enough men and slaves. You have played enough filthy tricks. Now look at me and recognize who I am. I am Medea. Medea, the daughter of Aeëtes, who had plenty of others slaughtered when it was necessary—and more innocent than myself, I can tell you that. I am one of your race.

Of the race of those who judge and who decide, without ever reconsidering and without remorse. You do not behave like a King, Creon. If you want to give Jason to your daughter, have me killed at once . . . with the old woman and the children who are asleep in there—and the horse. Have two trustworthy men burn all that on this plain and scatter the ashes afterward. Let there be only one thing left of Medea: a big black spot on this grass and a tale to frighten the children of Corinth at night.

CREON. Why do you want to die?

MEDEA. Why do you want me to live now? Neither you, nor I, nor Jason has anything to gain in having me live another hour. You know it well enough.

CREON [gestures vaguely and suddenly says in a hollow voice]. I am weary of blood.

MEDEA [shouts to him]. Then you are too old to be King! Let your son reign in your stead, let him do the work as it ought to be done. And you go and tend your vineyards in the sun. That is all you are good for!

CREON. Arrogance! Fury! Do you think I came here to seek your advice?

MEDEA. You did not come for it, but I give it to you. It is my right. And yours is to silence me if you have the strength for it. That is all.

CREON. I promised Jason that you would leave unharmed.

MEDEA. Unharmed! I will not leave unharmed, as you say. That would be too easy a thing if, on top of all that, I were not even harmed! I am to vanish! To be annihilated! A shadow, a memory, an unfortunate mistake, that Medea dragged along for ten years. All that is only Jason's dream! He may conjure me away, hide himself among your guards in your palace, bury himself in your daughter's innocence, and become King of Corinth when you die . . . he knows his name and mine are bound together for centuries. Jason-Medea! That will never be severed any more. Drive me away, kill me, it will be the same. In marrying him your daughter marries me, and you accept me with him whether you like it or not. [She shouts.] Creon, be King! Do what must be done. Drive Jason away. He bears half my crimes. His hands which are going to touch your daughter's skin are red from the same blood. Give us one hour; even less for both of us.

We are accustomed to flee after each of our evil deeds together. Believe me, it doesn't take long to pack.

CREON. No. Go alone.

MEDEA [*suddenly in a soft voice*]. Creon. I do not want to beg you. I cannot. My knees cannot bend, my voice cannot be humble. But you are human, since you could not bring yourself to have me killed. Do not let me go alone. Give the ship back to the exile. Give her companion back to her. I was not alone when I came. Why discriminate between us now? It is for Jason that I killed Pelias, betrayed my father, and slaughtered my innocent brother when I fled. I am Jason's woman. I belong to him, and so does each of my crimes.

CREON. You are lying. I have thought it all out. Jason is innocent without you. Separated from yours, his case is defensible. You alone have soiled yourself. . . . Jason is one of us, the son of one of our Kings. His youth, like many another, may have been wild; now he is a man who thinks as we do. You alone come from afar; you alone are a stranger here with your hatred and your witchcraft. Go back to your Caucasus, find a man among your race, a barbarian like yourself; and leave us in this rational land, on the shore of this even sea which has no need for your frenzied passion and your screams.

MEDEA [*after a pause*]. Very well, I will go. But my children, what is their race? The criminal's or Jason's?

CREON. Jason thought they would only hinder your flight. Leave them with us. They will grow up in my palace. I promise you they will have my protection.

MEDEA [*softly*]. I have to say thank you again, don't I? On top of everything you are human, you are just, all of you, and without hatred.

CREON. Keep your thanks. Go. The hour is almost past, and when the moon is high in the sky nothing will protect you here any longer. My order has been given.

MEDEA. Though a barbarian and a stranger, Creon, and however rough the Caucasus from where I come may be, mothers there hold their children tightly against themselves like other mothers. And so do the beasts in the forests. . . . They are asleep inside. These cries, these torches in the night, these unknown hands which take them and tear them from me—they may be too much to pay for their mother's crimes. Give me until tomorrow.

I will awaken them in the morning as I always do and I will send them to you. Believe Medea, King! They will have hardly passed the bend in the road and I shall be gone.

CREON [*looks at her for a moment in silence, then says suddenly*]. Agreed. [*He adds in a hollow voice, still looking at her.*] You see, I am getting old. One night is too much for you. It is enough time for ten of your crimes. I should deny your request. . . . But I too, Medea, have killed many. And children as well when I entered conquered villages at the head of my drunken soldiers. . . . In exchange I give the peaceful night of these two children to Fate. And if she so desires, let her use the night to ruin me.

He exits, followed by his men. The moment he disappears MEDEA's *face lights up and she spits toward him, shouting with all her might:*

MEDEA. Depend on it, Creon! Depend on Medea! Fate should be helped a little. You have lost your claws, old lion, if you are now reduced to making prayers and atoning for little dead children. . . . Ah! you want to let these two children sleep because something stirs in you when alone at night, in your empty palace after dinner you think of all those you killed. It is your stomach, old beast, which is decaying. Nothing else! Eat gruel, Creon, take medicines, and do not become soft over yourself . . . who are so kind, the old Creon whom you know so well, such a good man at heart—only misunderstood— but who, nevertheless, slaughtered his share of innocent ones when he still had his teeth and solid legs. The beasts kill their old wolves to keep them from these final tender tears. Don't expect them to count in your favor. I am Medea, old hyena! My scales are right, even if the gods let themselves be caught. I know what good and evil mean. I know one pays at once for what he does, and that all is fair, but that we have to help ourselves at once. And since your chilled blood and dead glands have made you cowardly enough to give me this night, you are going to pay for it! [*She shouts to the* NURSE.] Go and pack, old hag! Gather your pots and pans, roll the blankets, and harness the horse. We shall be gone in an hour.

JASON *appears.*

JASON. Where are you going?

MEDEA [*facing him*]. I am running away, Jason! Running away! There is nothing new for me in changing my abode. Only the cause of my flight is new, for until now it was for you that I fled.

JASON. I came behind them. I waited until they were far away to see you alone.

MEDEA. Have you still something to say to me?

JASON. I have. And, anyway, I must listen to what you have to say before you go.

MEDEA. And you are not frightened?

JASON. Yes.

MEDEA [*goes softly toward him*]. Let me look at you . . . I loved you! For ten years I slept next to you. Have I aged like you, Jason?

JASON. Yes.

MEDEA. I can still see you standing before me—like this— that first night in Colchis. That dark hero who had just landed, the spoiled child who wanted the gold of the Fleece and who was to be kept from dying. . . . Was it you, do you think?

JASON. It was I.

MEDEA. I ought to have let you face the monsters alone! Alone face the giants rising in arms from the earth, and the dragon who guarded the Fleece.

JASON. Perhaps.

MEDEA. You would be dead. How easy a world without Jason would be!

JASON. A world without Medea! I have also dreamed of it.

MEDEA. But this world includes both Jason and Medea, and we have to take it as it is. And you may ask your father-in-law for help and have me taken to the frontier by his men. One or two seas are not enough between us—you know that. Why did you prevent him from having me killed?

JASON. Because I loved you. Because you were mine for a long time, Medea.

MEDEA. And I no longer am?

JASON. No.

MEDEA. Happy Jason who is freed from Medea! Is it your sudden love for this little Corinthian goose, her young and sour smell and her locked maiden knees which have freed you from me?

JASON. No.

MEDEA. Who then?

JASON. You.

A pause. They stand face to face. Suddenly she shouts:

MEDEA. You will never be freed, Jason! Medea will always be your woman. You may have me exiled, may strangle me in a moment when you can no longer bear my shouting. Yet never, nevermore will Medea leave your memory. Look at this face in which you read only hatred. Look at it with your own hatred. Resentment and time may deform it; vice may leave its mark on it. One day it will be the face of a vile old woman whom everyone will loathe. But to the very end you will keep reading in it the face of Medea!

JASON. No! I will forget it!

MEDEA. You think so? You will go and drink in other eyes, suck life from other mouths, take your little man's pleasure wherever you can. Oh! you will have plenty of other women, you need not worry. Now you will have thousands of them, you who were exhausted by having only a single one! You will never have enough of them to find this gleam in their eyes, this taste on their lips, and this smell of Medea in them.

JASON. All that I want to flee!

MEDEA. Your head, your ugly man's head, may want to forget; in spite of yourself in the darkness your confused hands will seek on those strange bodies for the lost form of Medea. Your head will tell you they are a thousand times younger or more beautiful. Then do not close your eyes, Jason; do not let yourself go for even a second. In spite of yourself, your stubborn hands will seek for their remembered home. . . . And in the end you will take women who resemble me, new Medeas for old Jason's bed, when the real Medea will be nothing but an old unrecognizable bag of bones. Anything—a mere fold of a hip, or the tremble of a single muscle—will be enough for the young hands of your old arms to remember, and be surprised at not finding her again. Cut off your hands, Jason. Cut off your hands at once, and change them if you still want to love.

JASON. Do you think I am leaving you to look for another love? Do you think it is to start all over again? It is not only you that I hate—it is love.

A pause. They look at each other again.

MEDEA. Where do you want me to go? Where are you sending me? Shall I get to the Phasis, Colchis, my father's kingdom, the fields soaked with my brother's blood? You are driving me away. To what country do you order me without you? What free seas? To the Straits of Pontus, where I passed behind you, cheating, lying, stealing for you? Lemnos, where I am not likely to be forgotten? Thessaly, where they are waiting for me, to revenge their father, killed for you? All the paths I opened for you I have closed for myself. I am Medea, loaded with horror and crimes. You may not know me any longer, but *they* all know me still. What a burden an old accomplice is! You see you should have let them kill me.

JASON. I will save you.

MEDEA. You will save me! What will you save? This worn-out skin, this carcass of Medea only fit to drag along in its boredom and its hatred, no matter where? A little piece of bread and a house someplace, and let her grow old in silence, and at last let no one speak of her any more! Is that your wish? Why are you such a coward, Jason? Why do you not go to the very end? There is only one place, only one dwelling where Medea will be silent at last. This peace you want me to have so that you can live, give it to me. Go and tell Creon that you accept. It will only be a little hard moment to bear. You have already killed Medea today; you know it. Medea is dead. What more, then, can a little blood of Medea mean? A puddle on the ground, which will be washed away; a caricature petrified in a grin of horror, which will be hid someplace in a hole. Nothing. Have done with it, Jason. I cannot bear to wait any longer. Go and tell Creon.

JASON. No.

MEDEA [*more softly*]. Why not? Do you think a muscle which is torn, a skin which cracks is more?

JASON. I do not want your death either. Your death is still yourself. I want oblivion and peace.

MEDEA. You will never have them any more, Jason! You lost them in Colchis that night in the forest where you took me in your arms. Dead or alive, Medea is there, in front of your joy and your peace, standing guard. The dialogue you began with her will be finished now with your death. After the words of tenderness and love, it was insults and scenes. Now, true enough, it is hate, but it is still with Medea that you speak. The world is Medea for you, forevermore.

JASON. Has the world always been Jason for you?

MEDEA. Yes.

JASON. You forget quickly! I did not come back here for a last scene. But this couch to which you pretend we are bound forever, who was the first to desert it? Who was the first to accept other hands on her skin, the weight of another man on her body?

MEDEA. I.

JASON. I thought you had also forgotten why we fled from Naxos.

MEDEA. You were already escaping. Your body rested near mine each night, but in your head, in your ugly man's head, closed up, you were already conjuring another happiness without me. Then I did try to be the first to escape from you!

JASON. "Escape" is a convenient word.

MEDEA. Not so convenient, you see, for I have not been able to. I hated those hands, that other smell, even that pleasure you no longer gave me. . . . I hated them at once. I helped you kill him. I told you the time. I was your accomplice against him. I sold him to you. Have you forgotten the night I told you, "Come, he is here. You can take him"?

JASON. Never speak of that night again!

MEDEA. I was vile that night, wasn't I? Twice vile? And you despised me, you hated me with all your might, and I had nothing else to expect from you but that cold glance—yet all the same it was you I begged to take me away. Though you know, Jason, my shepherd from Naxos was handsome! He was young and he loved me!

JASON. Why did you not choose to tell him to kill me? I would be sleeping far from you now. I would have finished.

MEDEA. I was unable to. I had to glue myself to your hatred again, like a fly, to resume my way with you. The very next day I had to lie down again against your bored body so that I could finally go to sleep. You think that I have not despised myself a thousand times more than you have? I howled before my mirror alone! I have torn my-

self with my nails for being that bitch who came back to
sleep in her hole. Beasts forget each other and at least
leave each other once their lust dies. . . . Yet I know
you, hero for Corinthian girls! I weighed your worth. I
know what you can give. But you see I am still here.

JASON. Perhaps you had your shepherd killed too soon!

MEDEA [*suddenly says brusquely*]. I tried, Jason, didn't you
know that? I tried with others, too, since then. I simply
couldn't!

A pause. JASON *suddenly says more softly:*

JASON. Poor Medea . . .

MEDEA [*stands up before him like a fury*]. I forbid you to
pity me!

JASON. You allow me to feel contempt? Poor Medea, entangled with yourself! Poor Medea, for whom the world
reflects only Medea. You may forbid pity. Nobody will
ever have pity for you. Nor would I, were I to learn your
story today. The man Jason judges you with other men.
And your case is settled forever. Medea! It is a beautiful
name though; it will have been yours alone in this world.
Proud one! There will never be other Medeas on this
earth, ever: take that with you to the little dark corner
where you hide your joys. Mothers will never give their
daughters this name. You will be alone until the end of
time, as you are this moment.

MEDEA. I am glad!

JASON. You are glad! Stand up, clench your fists, spit, rage.
. . . The more we are able to judge you, to hate you, the
better it will be, will it not? The larger the circle around
you, the more alone you will be, the more you will suffer,
the better it will be. Well, you are not alone tonight, so
much the worse. . . . I who suffered most by you, I
whom you chose among all to devour, I pity you.

MEDEA. No!

JASON. I pity you, Medea, who know only yourself, who can
give only to take. I pity you, bound to yourself forever,
surrounded by a world seen through yourself. . . .

MEDEA. Keep your pity! Medea wounded is still a threat.
Rather, defend yourself.

JASON. You look like a little quartered beast who struggles
entangled in its own intestines and still crouches to attack.

MEDEA. It bodes no good, Jason, for hunters who allow

themselves feelings of pity instead of rearming. You know all that I still can do?

JASON. Yes, I know.

MEDEA. You know that I will not be moved, that I will not start having pity at the last minute! You have seen me face and risk everything many times for much less, haven't you?

JASON. Yes.

MEDEA [shouts]. Then what do you want? Why do you come so suddenly and confuse everything with your pity? I am vile; you know that. I betrayed you like the others. I only know how to do evil. You cannot endure me any more, and you sense what crime I am preparing. Beware then! Retreat! Call the others. Defend yourself instead of looking at me this way.

JASON. No.

MEDEA. I am Medea! I am Medea—you are making a mistake! Medea, who never gave you anything, ever, except shame. I lied, cheated, stole. I am dirty. . . . It is because of me that you are running away and that everything around you is stained with blood. I am your misery, Jason, and your ulcer. I am your wasted youth, your broken home, your wandering life, your solitude, your shameful sore. I am all the filthy gestures and all the filthy thoughts. I am pride, selfishness, lewdness, vice, and crime. I stink! I stink, Jason! They are all afraid and draw back before me. You know I am all of that, and that I soon will be decay and ugliness and old age full of hatred. All that is black and ugly on earth was entrusted to me. . . . Then, since you know all this, why do you not stop looking at me like that? I don't want your tenderness. I don't want the kindness in your eyes. [She shouts before him.] Stop! Stop, Jason! or I kill you at once so that you won't look at me like that any more!

JASON [softly]. Perhaps it would be best, Medea.

MEDEA [looks at him and says simply]. No. Not you.

JASON [goes to her and takes her by the arm]. Then listen to me. I cannot prevent you from being yourself. I cannot prevent you from doing the evil you bear within you. Besides, the die is cast. These unsolvable conflicts come to a head as others, and without doubt someone already knows how everything will end. I cannot prevent anything. I must simply go on playing the part which has fallen to me since the beginning of time. But what I can do is to say everything, once and for all. Words are nothing but they must be said all the same. And if to-night I must be among the dead in this story, then I want to die washed clean of my words. . . .

I loved you, Medea, at first as a man loves a woman. You undoubtedly knew and enjoyed only that love, but I gave you more than a man's love—perhaps without your knowing it. I lost myself in you, like a little boy in the woman who brought him into the world. For a very long time you were my country, my light. You were the air I breathed, the water I had to drink, and my daily bread.

When I took you in Colchis, you were only a girl more beautiful and harder than the others whom I had conquered together with the Fleece and was taking away. Is that the Jason you regret? I took you away as I did your father's gold . . . to spend you quickly and to use you as merrily as I would that gold. And then, well, of course I still had my ship, my faithful companions, and other adventures to pursue. At first I had the same kind of love as you, Medea; I loved you through myself. . . . The world was Jason, Jason's joy, his courage and his strength —his hunger. And if we were both greedy, well, we would see which of us would devour the other. . . .

And then one night, a night which looked like any other night, you fell asleep at the table like a little girl, your head against me. And that night, when perhaps you were only worn out from the long journey, I suddenly felt I had charge of you. A minute before I was still Jason and I had only my pleasure to follow in this world, as harshly as I liked. You had but to be silent, your head to slip on my shoulder, and all of that was finished. . . . The others would go on laughing or talking around me, but I had just left them. The young man, Jason, was dead. I was your father and your mother. I was the one bearing the sleeping Medea's head on him. What were you dreaming of in your little woman's brain while I was thus taking charge of you? I carried you to our bed, and I did not love you, did not even desire you that night. I only watched you in your sleep. The night was still. For a long time now we had left your father's pursuers far behind, my companions

in arms were standing guard around us, and yet I did not
dare close my eyes. I defended you, Medea—indeed,
against nothing—the entire night.

In the morning we resumed our flight and days resem-
bled each other. But little by little all those boys who had
been the first to follow me on the unknown sea, all those
young fellows from Iolcus who were ready to attack monsters with their fragile weapons if I lifted my finger, little
by little they grew afraid. They understood I no longer
was their leader, that I would never bring them to look
for anything anywhere again, now that I had found you.
Their glances were sad and maybe a little scornful, but
they never reproached me. We divided the gold and they
left us. Then the world took its shape. The shape I
thought it would always keep. The world became
Medea. . . .

Have you forgotten those days when we did nothing,
thought of nothing without each other? Two accomplices
before a life grown hard, two little brothers, both alike,
carrying their knapsacks side by side, sworn friends, sharing the load, each with his knife to protect the other,
each sharing the same fatigue and the same bread. I
would have made you ashamed had I offered you my
hand when the way was hard, had I offered to help you.
Jason was in command of only one small Argonaut. My
little fragile army with its hair raised in a kerchief, with
clear honest eyes—that was you. But I still could conquer
the world with my faithful little troop . . . ! The first
morning on the *Argo*, with my thirty sailors who had
given me their lives, I did not feel as strong. . . . And
at night, at bivouac, the soldier and the captain would
undress side by side, surprised at finding each other man
and woman again under their like tunics, and at loving
each other. We may be miserable now, Medea; we may
tear each other and suffer. Those days were given to us
and no shame or blood can ever stain them.

A pause. He dreams a little. MEDEA *has squatted down on
the ground while he was speaking, her arms around her
knees; her head is hidden. He sits near her on the ground
without looking at her.*

JASON. Afterward the little soldier took up her woman's face
again, and again the captain too had to become a man,

and we began to hurt each other. Other girls passed in the
street whom I could not help but look at. I was astonished
to hear for the first time your laughter ring with other
men, and then you began to lie. One lie at first, which
followed us a long time like a venomous beast whose eyes
we dared not meet when we looked back. Then others,
more numerous each day. And at night, when we took
each other silently, ashamed of our bodies, which were
still accomplices, the whole herd of your lies would swarm
and breathe around us in the darkness. Our hatred must
have been born then from one of those untender struggles.
But why talk again of what is dead? My hatred, too, is
dead. . . .

   He has stopped. MEDEA *says softly:*

MEDEA. If we are attending the wake of only dead things,
   Jason, why do both of us feel so much pain?
JASON. Because it is hard for all things to be born in this
   world and it is also hard for them to die.
MEDEA. Did you suffer?
JASON. Yes.
MEDEA. Doing what I did, I was no happier than you.
JASON. I know.

   A pause.

MEDEA [*in a hollow voice*]. Why did you remain so long?
JASON. I loved you, Medea. I loved our fierce life. I loved
   crime and adventure with you. And our embraces, our
   dirty and wild struggles, and this feeling of complicity we
   found again at night on the straw in the little corner of
   our wagon after our vileness. I loved your black world,
   your boldness, your revolt, your connivance with horror
   and death, your passion for destruction. I believed with
   you that one should always take and fight and that everything was permitted.
MEDEA. And you no longer believe it tonight?
JASON. No. I want to accept now.
MEDEA [*whispers*]. Accept?
JASON. I want to be humble. I want the world, the chaos
   through which you led me by the hand—I want it to take
   shape at last. You are probably right in saying there is no
   reason, no light, no resting place, that we always have to
   search with bloodstained hands, strangle and throw away
   all that we have torn apart. But *I* want to stop now and

be a man. Maybe behave without illusions, as those we
used to despise. Just as my father did and my father's
father and all those who accepted before us—and more
simply than we. To clear a little piece of ground where
man can stand in this confusion and this night.

MEDEA. You think you can do that?

JASON. Without you, without your poison drunk every day.
Yes, I can.

MEDEA. Without me. Then *you* were able to imagine a
world without me?

JASON. I am going to try with all my might. I am not young
enough now to suffer. I answer the appalling contradictions, the abysses, the wounds by the simplest gesture man
has invented in order to live: I discard them.

MEDEA. You speak softly, Jason, and you say terrible things.
How sure of yourself you are! How strong!

JASON. Yes, I am strong!

MEDEA. Race of Abel, race of the just, race of the rich, how
confidently you speak. It is good to have Heaven on your
side and the police as well, isn't it? It is good to find yourself thinking like your father and your father's father, like
all those who have been right since the beginning of time.
It is good to be good, to be noble, to be honest. And all
of that given to you one fine morning as if by chance, with
the first weariness, the first wrinkles, the first gold. Play
the game, Jason, give the signal. Say yes! *You* are preparing a splendid old age for yourself!

JASON. I would have loved to do that with you, Medea. I
would have given everything to grow old together with
you in an appeased world. You are the one who refused.

MEDEA. No!

JASON. Follow your way. Turn around and around, tear yourself to pieces, beat yourself, scorn everything, insult, kill,
deny all that is not yourself. As for me, I have had
enough. I am content. I accept these appearances with
the harshness and determination I had when I refused
them with you before. And if I must continue fighting, it
is for them I will fight now—and humbly too—leaning
against the futile wall I have built with my own hands
between the absurd nothingness and myself. [*A pause. He
adds.*] And when all is said and done, this is what it is to
be a man, this and nothing else.

MEDEA. Have no doubt, Jason. You are a man now.

JASON. I accept your contempt, with this name. [*He rises.*] That young girl is beautiful. Less beautiful than you when you appeared to me the first night in Colchis, and I will never love her as I loved you. But she is new, she is simple, she is pure. I am going to receive her without smiling from her father's and mother's hands, in the morning sun, with her white dress and her train of little children. . . . From the clumsy fingers of that little girl I expect humility and oblivion. And if the gods grant it, what you hate most in the world, what is farthest from you: happiness, poor happiness.

A silence. He has stopped. MEDEA *whispers:*

MEDEA. Happiness . . . [*Another silence. Suddenly she says with a little humble voice, without moving.*] Jason, this is hard to say, almost impossible. It chokes me and I am ashamed. If I told you that I am going to try with you now, would you believe me?

JASON. No.

MEDEA [*after a pause*]. You would be right. [*She adds in a toneless voice.*] Well . . . we have said everything, haven't we?

JASON. Yes.

MEDEA. You are finished. You have washed yourself clean. You can go now. Farewell, Jason.

JASON. Farewell, Medea. I cannot tell you: be happy . . . be yourself.

He has gone. MEDEA *murmurs again:*

MEDEA. Their happiness . . . [*Suddenly she stands tall and shouts to* JASON, *who has disappeared.*] Jason! Do not leave this way! Turn around! Shout something! Hesitate! Feel some pain! Jason, I beg you, all you need is a single moment of bewilderment or doubt in your eyes to save us all . . . ! [*She runs after him, stops, and shouts again.*] Jason! You are right, you are kind, you are just, and all the blame is mine forever. But doubt it! For just a second, for just a little second! Look back and perhaps I will be freed. . . . [*Her arm falls down wearily.* JASON *is now far away. She calls in another voice.*] Nurse.

The NURSE *appears on the threshold of the wagon.*

MEDEA. It will soon be daybreak. Awaken the children, dress

them as if for a feast day. I want them to bring my wedding gift to Creon's daughter.

NURSE. Your gift, poor child! What have you left to give?

MEDEA. In the hiding place, the black chest I brought from Colchis. Bring it.

NURSE. You had forbidden anyone to touch it! Even to let Jason know it existed.

MEDEA. Go fetch it, old hag, and without a word. There is no longer time to listen to you. Everything must go terribly fast now. Give the chest to the children and lead them within sight of the city. Let them ask for the King's palace and say that it is a gift from their mother, Medea, for the bride. . . . Let them deliver it into her hands and let them come back. Listen once more. The chest contains a gold veil and a diadem, remnants of the treasure of my race. But *they* must not open it! [*She shouts terribly at the hesitating old woman.*] Obey!

The old woman disappears into the wagon. Later she will come out again, silently, with the children.

MEDEA [*alone*]. It is now, Medea, that you must be yourself! O Evil! Great living beast who crawls on me and licks me, take me. I am yours tonight. I am your wife. Come into me, tear me, swell and burn in the middle of myself. You see, I welcome you, help you, open myself to you. . . . Weigh on me with your large hairy body; press me in your big calloused hands; your raucous breath on my mouth, choke me! At last I am alive! I am suffering and being born. This is my wedding. It is for this night of love with you that I have lived.

And you, night, weighty night, night rustling with suppressed cries and struggles, night swarming with the leaping beasts which chase after each other, which take and kill each other . . . please wait a little longer; do not go away too fast. . . . Oh, numberless beasts around me, obscure workers of this land, terrible innocences, killers. . . . That is what men call a quiet night, this gigantic swarming of silent matings and murders. But *I* feel you, I hear all of you for the first time tonight at the bottom of water and grass, in the trees, under the earth. . . .

A like blood beats in our veins. Beasts of the night, stranglers, my sisters! Medea is a beast like you! Medea is going to glow and kill like you! This plain touches other plains and those plains still others down to the limit of the shade, where millions of beasts who are alike take each other and slaughter at the same time. Beasts of this night! Medea is here standing among you, consenting, and betraying her race. I utter with you your obscure scream. I accept like you, without wanting to understand any more, the black command. I trample, I put out the little light. I give the shameful signal. I take upon myself, I assume, I claim. Beasts, I am you! All that is hunting and killing tonight is Medea!

The NURSE *enters suddenly.*

NURSE. Medea! The children must have reached the palace and a great clamor is rising from the city. I do not know what your crime is, but the air already re-echoes with it. Harness the horse to the wagon; let us run away and reach the border.

MEDEA. I run away? But if I had already gone I would come back to enjoy the sight.

NURSE. What sight?

The BOY *rushes in.*

BOY. All is lost! The kingdom, the state have fallen. The King and his daughter are dead!

MEDEA. Dead so quickly? How?

BOY. Two children came at dawn bearing a gift for Creüsa, a black chest containing a veil richly embroidered with gold and a precious diadem. Creüsa had hardly touched them, hardly adorned herself with them like a little anxious girl in front of her mirror, when she suddenly changed color and fell writhing in horrible sufferings, disfigured by the pain.

MEDEA [*shouting*]. Ugly? Ugly like death, was she not?

BOY. Creon rushed in, he wanted to take her, to tear off the veil and the gold band which were killing his daughter! But hardly had he touched them when he, too, grew pale. He hesitated a moment with horror in his eyes, then collapsed, howling with pain. Now they are lying against each other, dying in the convulsions and entangling their limbs, and no one dares to come near them. But the rumor is spreading that you are the one who sent the poison. The men have taken their staffs and their knives;

they are hurrying toward the wagon. I have run before
them. You will not even have time to defend yourself.
Run, Medea!

MEDEA [shouts]. No! [She shouts to the Boy, who has fled.]
Thank you, boy! Thank you for the second time! You
must run. It is better not to know me. As long as men will
remember, it will be better never to have known me!
[She runs toward the NURSE.] Take your knife, Nurse, cut
the horse's throat. Nothing must remain of Medea in a
moment. Put wood under the wagon. We are going to
make a bonfire as in Colchis. Come!

NURSE. Where are you dragging me?

MEDEA. You know where. Death, death is gentle. Follow me,
old hag, you will see. You have finished whining and
dragging your old bones which hurt you. You are going
to rest, at long last, for a long Sunday.

NURSE [frees herself, howling]. I don't want to, Medea! I
want to live!

MEDEA. How long, old bitch, with death on your back?

The two frightened CHILDREN *run in and throw themselves
into* MEDEA's *arms.*

MEDEA [stops]. Ah! So here you are, you two? Are you
frightened? All these people who are running and howling, these bells . . . All that will be quiet. [She pulls
their heads backward, looks into their eyes, and murmurs.]
Innocence! Trap of children's eyes, sneaky little brutes,
heads of men. Are you cold? I will not hurt you. I shall
be quick. Just time for the surprise of death in your eyes.
[She caresses them.] Come. Let me reassure you, let me
hug you a minute, warm little bodies. You feel good
against your mother. You are no longer scared. Warm
little lives that came out of my womb, little wills to live
and be happy. . . . [Suddenly she shouts.] Jason! Here
is your family, tenderly united. Look at it. And may you
always wonder whether Medea, too, would not have loved
happiness and innocence. Whether she, too, might not
have been faith and faithfulness. When you suffer in a
moment and until the day you die, think that long ago
there was a little girl, Medea, exacting and pure. A little
Medea tender and gagged in back of the other. Think
that she will have struggled all alone, unknown, without a

helping hand, and that *she* was your true woman! I would have wanted, Jason . . . perhaps I, too, would have wanted it to last forever and that it be the way it is in stories! I want, I want still in this moment—as strongly as I used to when I was a child—everything to be light and kindness! But innocent Medea was chosen to be the prey and the place of the struggle. . . . Others more frail or more mediocre can glide through the meshes of the net toward calmer waters or down to the slime; small fish do not concern the gods. Medea was game too big for the snare; she stays there. The gods do not have such a windfall every day—a soul strong enough for their battles, for their dirty games. They put the whole weight on my back and they look at me while I struggle. Look with them, Jason, at Medea's last efforts! I still have the innocence to slaughter in that little girl, who would have wanted so much, and in these two warm little pieces of myself. They are waiting for this blood above. They cannot bear to wait any longer! [*She drags the* CHILDREN *toward the wagon.*] Come, little ones, do not be frightened. You see, I am holding you, I am caressing you, and all three of us are going home now. . . .

They are inside the wagon. The stage remains empty for a moment. The NURSE *reappears, wild-eyed, like a beast in hiding. She calls out:*

NURSE. Medea! Medea! Where are you? They are coming! [*She draws back and suddenly shouts.*] Medea!

Flames are shooting forth from everywhere. They envelop the wagon. JASON *enters quickly at the head of his armed men.*

JASON. Put out the fire! Get hold of her!

MEDEA *appears at the window of the wagon and shouts:*

MEDEA. Do not come closer, Jason! Forbid them to move! JASON [*stopping*]. Where are the children? MEDEA. Keep asking yourself so that I can see your eyes really well. [*She shouts.*] They are dead, Jason! Both of them were slaughtered, and before you take a single step I will be struck by the same sword. Now I have found my scepter again. My brother, my father, and the Fleece of the golden ram are given back to Colchis. I have found my country again and the virginity which you tore from me. I am Medea at last and forever! Look at me before remaining alone in this rational world; look at me well, Jason. I touched you with these two hands, I put them on your burning brow so it would be cool, and sometimes I put them burning on your skin. I made you weep, I made you love. Look at them. I am your little brother and your wife! I, the horrible Medea! And now try to forget her!

She strikes herself and collapses in the flames, which increase and envelop the wagon. JASON *motions his men to stop as they go toward the flames, and says simply:*

JASON. Yes, I will forget you. Yes, I will live. And in spite of the bloody trace of your passage near me, tomorrow with patience I will reconstruct my poor and fragile human edifice under the indifferent eyes of the gods. [*He turns toward his men.*] One of you watch the fire till only ashes remain, until the last bone of Medea is burned. The rest of you come with me. Let us go back to the palace. Now we must live, secure order, give Corinth laws, and without illusions rebuild a world befitting us, in which to wait and die.

He goes out with his men except for one who starts chewing some tobacco and morosely stands guard before the fire. The NURSE *enters and timidly goes and sits down near him in the rising dawn.*

NURSE. Nobody had time to listen to me. And yet I had something to say. After the night, morning comes and there is the coffee to make and then the beds. And when you have swept, you have a nice little moment in the sun before peeling the vegetables. Then, if you have been able to gather a few coins, it's good to feel the little warm nip in the middle of your stomach. Afterward you eat the soup and you wash the dishes. In the afternoon there is the laundry, or the brass to polish, and you talk a little with the neighbors and supper comes along very gently. . . . Then you go to bed and you sleep.

GUARD [*after a pause*]. It will be a beautiful day.

NURSE. It will be a good year. There will be sun and wine. And the harvest?

GUARD. They mowed last week. They'll gather it in tomorrow or the day after if the weather keeps up.

NURSE. Will the crop be good around here?

GUARD. No need to complain. There will still be bread for everyone this year.

The curtain falls while they are talking.

CECILE, or THE SCHOOL FOR FATHERS

(*Cécile, ou l'École des Pères*)

A play in one act

English version by
LUCE *and* ARTHUR KLEIN

CHARACTERS

Monsieur Orlas
Cécile, *his daughter*
Araminthe, *governess of Cécile*
The Chevalier
Monsieur Damiens, *father of Araminthe*
Two Bodyguards
Two Footmen

CECILE

A garden framed by boxed orange trees. The house is on the left, a small Chinese pavilion on the right. MONSIEUR ORLAS is seated in the pavilion and ARAMINTHE is standing beside him. Costumes are either Louis XVth or perhaps Louis XVIth of the bourgeois class. In either case they are as false as possible.

MONSIEUR ORLAS. Araminthe, I am very disturbed. I have always thought you were too young and much too charming to take care of my daughter.

ARAMINTHE. If you remember, monsieur, there were four candidates for the position of governess. The three others were old and uglier than sin. Why then did you choose me, monsieur?

MONSIEUR ORLAS. Precisely because you were young and beautiful. And yet sometimes I fear that I chose you only for my own sake. I could not bear the thought of dining with an old hag at my table. Still I believe I have been a bad father. I ought to have confided Cécile to an old dragon of a woman and to have borne it stoically. I ought to have taken my meals apart or else read the newspapers while eating.

ARAMINTHE. Among other things, monsieur, you insisted that I teach Mademoiselle Cécile that nothing was more rude than to read while eating.

MONSIEUR ORLAS. I have been a fool! In the first place you are the same age.

ARAMINTHE. Mademoiselle Cécile is seventeen years old and I will soon be twenty-three.

MONSIEUR ORLAS. It is the same thing.

ARAMINTHE. Allow me to contradict you, monsieur. I feel I have learned very many things in five years. And particularly to be suspicious of men.

MONSIEUR ORLAS [*suddenly*]. Why do you say that to me?

ARAMINTHE. So that you will not be troubled by what seems to upset you. I am very capable of protecting Mademoiselle Cécile, whose youth and inexperience could so easily

91

be deceived by lovely words. You should at least give me credit, monsieur, for not being deceived myself.

MONSIEUR ORLAS. I wonder why you insist on being so disagreeable with me, Araminthe?

ARAMINTHE. Have I said anything disagreeable?

MONSIEUR ORLAS. "You should at least give me credit, monsieur, for not being deceived myself." Just what do you mean by that? That I try to deceive you? The rhetoric of young girls has always sounded Greek to me. It is true I have paid you several compliments. So what? You are no longer a child, Araminthe. You are twenty-three years old. I am a man for whom love has always been the chief interest, and although the father of Cécile I am still capable of loving. Thank God for that! Do you suppose it is easy to live in the same house with so ravishing a creature as yourself? To have you opposite me at table each day, to have you smile at me while Cécile is dreaming of heaven only knows what. . . . And then in the evening to have all three of us climb the stairs together to our respective rooms. And yours only next door to mine. I am a fool! I should have chosen a hag.

ARAMINTHE. You still have time.

MONSIEUR ORLAS. Yes, there is always time to make myself unhappy needlessly. I do not speak only of the grief Cécile would feel. You know how attached she is to you. But my entire existence would be saddened. I would gulp my meals to shorten the torture, and I would develop ulcers. . . . You know what that does to one's temper. Besides, I could never bear to know you were living in another home where you would be the prey to men's desires. You are a child, Araminthe. Do not forget you are only twenty-three. What do you know of life, my dear? Here you live with a well-bred gentleman who respects you. Imagine yourself governess of the Baron's daughter, who I know has suggested it. And on my life I wager two days would not pass before he came and knocked at your chamber door.

ARAMINTHE. Render unto Caesar the things which are Caesar's, monsieur. You waited an entire week before you did it yourself.

MONSIEUR ORLAS. I am a well-bred man. Besides, you did not open the door.

ARAMINTHE. As I would not open it for the Baron were I to
lose your confidence and find myself at his home.

MONSIEUR ORLAS. All the same you do not mean to compare
me with this old fogy, this graybeard?

ARAMINTHE. I thought I heard you say you studied together
and except for a year or so were the same age.

MONSIEUR ORLAS. Yes, but he looks it. I don't. Anyway,
that has no importance. Still if I had not paid you some
attention one way or another you would have been the
first to feel offended. I have come to know the contradictions in a woman's heart. [*He rises thoughtfully.*] I do not
mind telling you, Araminthe, that I am very upset by this
young chevalier. He comes here much too much.

ARAMINTHE. He loves your daughter and your daughter loves
him.

MONSIEUR ORLAS. What do they know at their age? In the
first place, he doesn't have a sou! His father is in strait-
ened circumstances, besides which he already supports
two older sons. And even if he made nuns out of his three
daughters, he still could not give the boy a sou! If his
great-uncle died in time, he might perhaps become a
Knight of Malta. But that is all he can expect. Therefore,
from every point of view the marriage is an impossibility
for him. I will not permit them to see each other!

ARAMINTHE. Then they will do so behind your back.

MONSIEUR ORLAS. Thunder and blazes, mademoiselle, are
you here to tell me that? You are here to prevent it!

ARAMINTHE. It would be beyond my powers even if I wanted
to. Their passion will overcome all obstacles. And besides,
monsieur, I would not want to. I cannot see anyone in
love unhappy.

MONSIEUR ORLAS. So you would find the suffering of this
silly fop unbearable if I prevent him from seeing Cécile?
And yet I have been pining away at your door these six
months past, and it does not trouble you in the least. Does
it?

ARAMINTHE. If I had opened my door to you, monsieur, do
you believe you still could have entrusted Mademoiselle
Cécile to me?

MONSIEUR ORLAS. Do not confuse the issue. I simply demand that you be very strict with Cécile who is still a
child, and . . .

ARAMINTHE. We are the same age.

MONSIEUR ORLAS. The same age? Ridiculous! You are
twenty-three and she is only seventeen. In five years a
young lady has the time to learn to know the world, to
judge the virtue of a man and the sincerity of a feeling.
I do not understand you, Araminthe. After all, you must
plainly see that I am madly in love with you.

ARAMINTHE. Indeed, I believe that one cannot help but see
it, monsieur. You are as indiscreet about it as possible. I
must exercise every ingenuity so that Mademoiselle Cécile
will not perceive it. And if you do not stop trying to touch
my knee under the table, one of these days you will surely
touch hers!

MONSIEUR ORLAS. A friendly caress from her father would
not astonish this child. I kiss her a hundred times a day.

ARAMINTHE. If she happened to suspect that this friendly
caress from her father was meant for another knee, I fear
she would be offended, monsieur. And more seriously than
your frivolousness is able to imagine.

MONSIEUR ORLAS [grumbling dreamily]. My frivolousness
. . . my frivolousness . . . [He asks in another tone.]
So according to you, Araminthe, I am a bad father? I
shall never get over it.

ARAMINTHE. You have the desire to be the best father in
the world, monsieur. And I believe it is my duty to see
that at least this one of your desires is fulfilled. I assure
you that is why I put my knees under my chair in the
most uncomfortable of positions. And I never hear your
little knocks on my door at night.

MONSIEUR ORLAS [approaching her with a lascivious look in
his eye]. And if I should put Cécile in a convent—and I
mean a very gay convent—or if I should send her to
spend some time with her aunt who is a canoness? She
would have many young cousins there with whom to
play. . . .

ARAMINTHE. Would you want to cause her this grief by
separating her from her young chevalier? And, further-
more, if Mademoiselle Cécile is gone, then my place will
no longer be in this home. I take care of her, monsieur,
but she takes care of me as well. We could not do without each other in the midst of all the dangers that sur-
round us.

MONSIEUR ORLAS [sighs]. Life is an abyss full of contradictions, Araminthe! I am going into my study and think of all that. I am unwilling to believe that there is no solution and that duty and happiness can not be reconciled.

ARAMINTHE. I believe that is what men have always been seeking, monsieur, ever since they left their caves to try and live in society. They have only invented marriage to try and reconcile these two notions for a time.

MONSIEUR ORLAS. For a very short time, Araminthe. Believe a man who has gone through the venture. Afterward it is like these chemical tests our neighbor Monsieur de Voltaire enjoys making. At first the mixture is very effervescent; then happiness, which is vaporous, vanishes like smoke, and the pipette contains only the large gray stone of duty. [*He asks thoughtfully.*] Is the chevalier coming again today?

ARAMINTHE. Just as every afternoon.

MONSIEUR ORLAS. Do not leave them alone for a minute! These children caress and embrace each other as soon as your back is turned.

ARAMINTHE. One does that at their age.

MONSIEUR ORLAS [*a bit dryly*]. One does it at mine and yet I do without. [*He starts to go, changes his mind, then goes to her.*] You are too cruel, Araminthe. Let me take you just once in my arms?

ARAMINTHE [*pushing him back firmly and with a smile*]. No, monsieur. Not even for the tiniest second.

MONSIEUR ORLAS [*feeling vexed, starts to leave*]. Be merciless with them. See that their chairs do not even touch! And keep a close eye on the tablecloth if they should take tea. It is so easy to stretch your leg under it. Listen, Araminthe, why not teach my daughter how to sit on a chair so that no knee could possibly touch hers?

ARAMINTHE [*smiling*]. I think such a gymnastic exercise is less important for her than for me, monsieur.

MONSIEUR ORLAS [*exits with a sigh*]. I am indeed an unhappy man, Araminthe.

The CHEVALIER *enters.*

CHEVALIER. Araminthe!

ARAMINTHE. Monsieur?

CHEVALIER. Do you think I have come too soon?

ARAMINTHE. You always come too soon, Monsieur le Chevalier. We have just finished eating.

CHEVALIER. And yet I have waited more than an hour in
the street before coming in. Such time lost, Araminthe!
I can see that you have never loved. Ah yes, Araminthe,
when you reach my age . . .

ARAMINTHE. I am afraid that will never happen again,
monsieur.

CHEVALIER [*protesting*]. What? To love and to be loved as
beautiful as you are? [*He takes her hands and kisses
them.*]

ARAMINTHE [*withdrawing her hands and laughing*]. No,
monsieur. To be your age. It is an experience I under-
went three years ago. I am told it happens only once.

CHEVALIER. I was twenty only three days ago, and I tell
you, Araminthe, it is a terrible thing.

ARAMINTHE. You will accustom yourself to it, I assure you.
And by the time you have done so, it will not be terrible
any longer.

CHEVALIER. Soon I will be old, Araminthe, and I have not
yet even lived. You say you reached my age without
loving. Does not your heart feel oppressed for having
wasted your life?

ARAMINTHE. To be truthful with you, Monsieur le Chevalier,
I still have hope.

CHEVALIER. And you are right. You are too pretty not to
have hope. Do you know that if I was not in love with
Cécile I would just die to kiss your hand. I trust you will
forgive my speaking so informally. After all, you are like
my sister.

ARAMINTHE [*withdrawing her hand*]. Speak informally if it
gives you pleasure, only I beg you to treat my hand with
more formality.

CHEVALIER [*suddenly*]. Do you know that I am desperate,
Araminthe?

ARAMINTHE. Really! As much as yesterday?

CHEVALIER. Much more. I had it out with my father this
morning and it was a stormy session. He forbade me to
see Cécile again. He made me swear that I had entered
this home for the last time.

ARAMINTHE. And you swore?

CHEVALIER. Yes . . . with all kinds of mental reservations.
But, you see, I was forced to do so.

ARAMINTHE. Your father has no heart.

CHEVALIER. I believe more particularly that he has no

money. And Cécile's dowry is meager. (You know, Araminthe, that fathers are the most extraordinary creatures I know. My father already had the most explicit information from her father's notary as to the amount of her dowry before I had kissed Cécile even once!) He says that he wants only my happiness, and I think he does. But he has my two older brothers whom he must first set up. Nothing will be left for me. I can choose between two things: either wait until my uncle dies and then become a Knight of Malta—which leaves Cécile out of the picture since the order insists on celibacy—or else marry a crock of gold, which equally leaves Cécile out of it.

ARAMINTHE. And has he found it?

CHEVALIER. What?

ARAMINTHE. The "crock"?

CHEVALIER. Yes. And it is overflowing. But she is like a skeleton, ugly as a witch, and old on top of all that. She will soon be twenty-five years old.

ARAMINTHE. So in two years I shall be old! You are not very gracious, Monsieur le Chevalier.

CHEVALIER [kissing her hands]. You do not understand. Naturally, if it concerns you, Araminthe, age would not count. . . . [He stops.] No . . . no, you see, even if it did concern you, I still love Cécile. . . . And yet I like to kiss your hands. You know so much about life, Araminthe, tell me, do you believe that everything always remains so entangled in one's heart?

ARAMINTHE. Always.

CHEVALIER. In any case, you won't leave us if I marry Cécile, will you? You are like her sister somehow, and I want to marry you as well—like a sister.

ARAMINTHE. You ask for Cécile's hand, but you also want my two hands from time to time, don't you? Monsieur le Chevalier gets on quite well for someone who was twenty years old only three days ago. But I am afraid you are not going to have either. How can you possibly marry Cécile since her dowry is too small and you have absolutely nothing?

CHEVALIER. Ah? I haven't told you yet. But I have come to a decision.

ARAMINTHE. Yes?

CHEVALIER. I am eloping with her this very night. To see

her again I am forced to do that since I swore never to set foot here any more. Naturally, I am taking you as well.

ARAMINTHE. I ought not to tell you but I believe Mademoiselle Cécile is crazy enough to follow you. However, I am here to dissuade her from it.

CHEVALIER. You would have the heart to prevent us from loving each other?

ARAMINTHE. To prevent you from doing something stupid? Why, of course. Have you even thought of the consequences of what you plan to do?

CHEVALIER. The consequences are quite simple. Thank heavens, Monsieur Rousseau has made it fashionable for fathers to be sympathetic. When Cécile and I are married, Araminthe, we will have to endure their scandalized reproofs—just for custom's sake—and then they will have nothing left to do but give us their blessing.

ARAMINTHE. Perhaps they will agree to give you their blessing since it costs nothing. But they certainly won't give you a sou.

CHEVALIER. Don't you think that if my father had my three sisters become nuns he could find it possible to do some little thing for me?

ARAMINTHE. I am not familiar with your father's state of affairs, but I do believe you decide your sisters' vocations a bit too easily!

CHEVALIER. Bah! They are ugly, Araminthe. They will never find a more indulgent husband than Jesus Christ. And then their eternal life would be assured. Everything passes so quickly here below. Look at yourself. You just said three years have hardly gone by since you were twenty and you are already disillusioned. We help them avoid I don't know how many opportunities for feeling bitter and how many temptations to sin in condemning them to Heaven. And then, I love Cécile so much!

ARAMINTHE [putting her finger on his chest]. This nice little heart, all brand-new, which beats so violently for everything seems to me, Monsieur le Chevalier, to be a pretty little stone.

CHEVALIER. Do not deceive yourself. I am sensitive. I have often wept torrents of tears. But one cannot weep for the entire world. It is beyond human strength. One must choose.

ARAMINTHE. Never mind; leave your sisters. It is wicked to think as you do. . . . And besides no good could come out of it. I am sure your father would not have the heart to sacrifice all three even if circumstances forced him to let you marry Cécile. You must weigh the consequences of your act. Are you willing to accept poverty?

CHEVALIER. What do you mean by that, Araminthe? All the same I would be able to have a new coat tailored from time to time, wouldn't I?

ARAMINTHE. Yes, I believe so. I am sure that no matter how poor Monsieur Orlas may be, he would not let Cécile nor you go without ribbons. But you are a handsome man, Chevalier, and come from a very good family. Have you never dreamt of having a great fortune? Dreamt of life at court, festive occasions, the King's favor, and perhaps a famous regiment with you as commander?

CHEVALIER [exclaiming miserably]. I have dreamt only of these things since I was fifteen! You know that very well! But I love Cécile. You are cruel, Araminthe. Why do you delight in putting salt on the wound?

ARAMINTHE. To see if I am able to give you my consent.

CHEVALIER. I would give everything in the world to lead my men on a horse and lead them to assault! The smell of gunpowder, the swords glimmering in the sun, death! . . . Ah! what a wonderful life!

ARAMINTHE. Well, my little horseman, you cannot take Cécile with you on your horse. You cannot lead an assault well when a woman you love rides with you. No, do not lower your head. Look at me. [She raises his head.]

CHEVALIER [taking her hands and covering them with kisses]. Oh! your hands! your hands! I adore your hands, Araminthe!

ARAMINTHE. You adore my hands, you adore to lead an assault, you adore Cécile, but at bottom I am afraid that you only adore yourself. I refuse to give my consent, monsieur. You will not elope with my pupil.

CHEVALIER. You are not serious, Araminthe? I would kill myself.

ARAMINTHE. My little finger told me no.

CHEVALIER. And you believe it? Show me your finger and I will give it a piece of my mind! [He takes the little finger and kisses it.]

MONSIEUR ORLAS *enters.*

MONSIEUR ORLAS. Chevalier!

CHEVALIER [*greeting him*]. I kiss your hands, monsieur.

MONSIEUR ORLAS. Mine as well? Does it seem perfectly
natural to you, Monsieur le Chevalier, that I cannot open
a single door in this house without finding you kissing
somebody?

CHEVALIER. I was merely greeting Araminthe.

MONSIEUR ORLAS. And in a moment you will merely be
greeting my daughter. Well, you are a young man who
greets too much. I have a great many things to do in this
house. In the future behave in such a manner that I can
open any door with peace of mind.

CHEVALIER [*bowing gravely*]. I promise to see to that,
monsieur. [MONSIEUR ORLAS *exits.*] Have I spoken to him
with sufficient respect? It seems to me that I have been
perfect with him.

ARAMINTHE. Perfect. Only he has just caught you kissing
the hands of a person he is courting, and you are going
to elope with his daughter tonight.

CHEVALIER. What are you saying? Monsieur Orlas is courting you? I will not permit it!

ARAMINTHE. Really? And why not?

CHEVALIER. Have I not told you that you are my sister? I
am going to find him at once and demand an explanation
of his behavior. I tell you, Araminthe, that I will not allow
anyone to bother you.

ARAMINTHE. How do you know that he bothers me? And as
for demanding an explanation of his behavior, wait until
tomorrow. He will have to demand an explanation from
you then, and that way you can kill two birds with one
stone.

CHEVALIER. It would be the height of absurdity to wait
until tomorrow. He would clearly have the upper hand
after what will take place tonight and I would be at a
distinct disadvantage. I am going at once.

ARAMINTHE [*stopping him*]. And if I should forbid you to
go?

CHEVALIER. Ah, so you are flattered by his attentions? The
attentions of a man almost forty who already has a foot
in his grave? You appall me, Araminthe. . . . You do
not know how to read your own heart. You cannot possibly love this old man.

ARAMINTHE. Who said that I loved him?

CHEVALIER. You love me, Araminthe. You love me like a brother because I love Cécile. But, still, you love me.

ARAMINTHE. That is news to me!

CÉCILE *enters.*

CÉCILE [*in a rage*]. I have been waiting for you, monsieur, at the appointed place for over an hour. I know you have been here a long time for I heard the front bell ring. And all this while you have been speaking to Araminthe!

CHEVALIER [*going to her*]. Cécile, my love, I was simply arranging the final details with her for tonight. My father forced me to swear that I would never come here again. Things are coming to a point. Tonight I must elope with you.

CÉCILE. If you are in so little hurry, monsieur, to see me when you come here, what will it be like when we are married and you can see me all the time? I must think this over again. I am not so sure I want to elope.

CHEVALIER [*trying to take her hands*]. Cécile, my love!

CÉCILE. No, monsieur. Tell these pretty words you say so well to others, monsieur. Kiss their hands!

CHEVALIER. This is scandalous! Who dared tell you? Your father, was it not?

CÉCILE. I have not seen my father since lunch, and he told me nothing at all. But I know enough about men to have understood everything while I was waiting for you.

CHEVALIER. Who could have been wicked enough to have told you that, Cécile? It is true that I kissed Araminthe's hands, but I was only thanking her for helping our love. . . .

CÉCILE. What are you saying, monsieur? Do my ears deceive me? You kissed Araminthe's hands? No, it cannot be true. . . .

CHEVALIER. But you have just said to me yourself that someone told you he had seen me!

CÉCILE. I told you that no one said anything to me, monsieur. You took the responsibility of disclosing this deed yourself, which at least is something in your favor. So then! You keep my esteem for this confession, as cruel as it may be, even if you have lost my love. Farewell, monsieur. Keep the oath you made to your father. Never show your face here again.   [*She exits.*

CHEVALIER [*throwing himself at Araminthe's feet*]. Araminthe, I perish before your eyes! Catch her. Tell her I love her. Tell her I don't love you. It is true your hands are like honey to my lips, but their sweetness is the fleeting pleasure of a moment. But as soon as Cécile leaves my side everything grows dark! Quickly, run after her and tell her I love only her, Araminthe, and I swear that I will always love you!

ARAMINTHE. All right, monsieur. But now we do not have much time. I do not want to waste time pointing out your contradictions, and I am going to try and arrange your affairs. Have everything ready for tonight.

CHEVALIER. You agree then to my elopement?

ARAMINTHE. I will see when the moment comes if I can allow everything to take its course. At least, I agree to your making believe to elope. You are right. Perhaps it is a way to make your fathers come to some agreement.

CHEVALIER. Oh, thank you! I adore you, Araminthe! Let me kiss your hands!

ARAMINTHE. Monsieur, you are completely irresponsible.

CHEVALIER. Yes, it is true. I forgot. I won't ask you any more. Or at least only after I have married Cécile, and will no longer risk losing her.

ARAMINTHE [*exits laughing*]. You can be sure of it. Shrewd young man!

CHEVALIER [*alone*]. Ah, how amusing life is! . . . I must go and warn my bodyguards. We may be forced to resort to violence tonight. I adore Cécile, I adore Araminthe, tonight I kidnap them both and only three days ago I was twenty years old!   [*He exits.*

The stage remains empty for a moment. Perhaps some soft music is heard. Then MONSIEUR ORLAS *and* CÉCILE *enter, returning from a walk.*

MONSIEUR ORLAS. Cécile, I must have a talk with you. I have wanted to for ever so long. Neither of us does so very much all during the day, and yet I simply haven't found the time. The problems in this house overwhelm me. You are very young, Cécile, and you will learn as you grow older that knowing how to live is quite a problem. "Ah, yes, Papa," you will tell me. "You merely have to get up in the morning and go to bed at night and with

a little patience the day goes by. . . . If only you enjoy
the delicacies of a well-set table and have a friend or two
come and chat with you during the afternoon, the trick
is done. Then it is time to go back to bed and to forget
everything." But unfortunately the brain keeps ticking
away.

CÉCILE. Yes, Papa.

MONSIEUR ORLAS. "Yes, Papa"! What kind of an answer is
that? I don't want you to listen to me politely while you
are thinking of something else, Cécile. I want you to
make an effort to understand what I am saying to you.
It is too easy to remain a child and think: "Fathers are
stupid, and definitely narrow-minded. They live with the
prejudices of their time. They know nothing of what is
good. Listen to them respectfully since that is the
custom. Yes, Papa. I promise indeed, Papa." . . . And
then as soon as my back is turned you do whatever you
like.

CÉCILE. No, Papa.

MONSIEUR ORLAS. "No, Papa"! It is the same thing. I demand a little less respect, Cécile, but instead a little
gleam in your eye which proves to me you are listening.
If I speak to you as a father and you listen as a young
daughter, when we have finished you will make me a
pretty curtsy and I will give you a little friendly pat on
the cheek, but we won't have accomplished a thing! I
would much prefer that you cast aside the privilege of
your age and that you grant me for a brief moment the
attention and consideration you would have for another
child.

CÉCILE. You know that I always respectfully obey you in
everything, Papa.

MONSIEUR ORLAS. Well! Now you are acting like a little
fool. You know very well I do not ask you that. Still there
is something in your glance that has betrayed you and I
think you understand me. You are a lively little creature,
cunning, with the wisdom of an old Chinese philosopher
under your wild youthfulness. But century-old conventions
have placed impenetrable barriers between us. Each of us
thinks he must act the ready-made part just because I am
your father and you are my daughter. Everything I want
to tell you is already branded in your mind as banal,

conventional, and boring. You are unjust, Cécile. . . .
Can't you imagine that I am not your father for a minute?
And that I am a witty and charming man.

Cécile. Yes, Papa.

Monsieur Orlas [bitterly]. "Yes, Papa"! It is better if you
do not answer at all. We will make headway more quickly.
I want to confess something first, Cécile: I am just about
as old as you. [He looks at her with satisfaction.] Well,
at least I have managed to surprise you all the same! . . .
But I see very well that you still do not trust me. You
are thinking it is an unusual beginning. But let us be
wary. All this will end as usual by lecturing. Everybody
knows nothing else can come from a father's lips. Do you
know what you look like this very moment, Cécile? Like
a little prisoner being questioned by an enemy general
staff . . . However, you are grown-up and beautiful. In
a year, in a month—who knows? perhaps even tomorrow
—you will have gone over to the other side. You as well
—you will be a woman. Then we shall be able to understand each other, but perhaps it will be too late. I would
have liked to find the way to your heart before.

Cécile. But my heart is yours, Papa.

Monsieur Orlas. Like a little closed-up box whose key one
has lost. I will never know what is inside.

Cécile [after a moment]. I do not know what you mean,
monsieur.

Monsieur Orlas. Ah, this time you did not say "Papa."
We are making headway. Now I confess a second thing,
Cécile. Not only are we the same age, but you please me
very much. We are lucky to have disentangled ourselves
from conventions. I would never have tried to attract
your attention had you been very ugly, bigoted, or stupid.
But for the past ten minutes I have been making witty
remarks to please you and I am not even sure that I have
astonished you. It is really sad, Cécile. You will see when
you are a bit older that there are not many interesting
men in the world. You had one close at hand. It is a pity
you paid no attention to him because he was your father.

Cécile [after a pause]. You urge me too quickly, monsieur.
This is our first meeting. We must see each other again.

Monsieur Orlas. Thank you, Cécile! You are a clever girl.
Thank God, I was not mistaken! And you are wisdom
itself. Indeed, I have rushed things a bit. One must be a

terribly young man to believe you can push matters of the heart. Well, we will take all the time that is necessary. You see, there are certain things you know much more about than I do. Let me kiss your hand as I would a lady's. I gather you have promised me another rendezvous. Shall we say this evening after dinner in the garden? We shall do as usual and seem to go to our rooms and then when everyone is asleep we will find each other here again, hmm? It is better if no one knows anything about our meetings.

CÉCILE [*stammers, bewildered*]. Did you say this evening, monsieur?

MONSIEUR ORLAS. Yes. Does it seem too soon to you? Do you want more time to think over matters? [CÉCILE *does not say a word.*] Well, answer me! What is wrong with you?

CÉCILE [*suddenly*]. Since you demand that we speak frankly . . . monsieur, this evening I have a rendezvous.

MONSIEUR ORLAS [*slumping*]. Have a rendezvous? After dinner? What do you mean? I cannot have heard correctly.

CÉCILE. Oh, but you have. I have a rendezvous. I cannot tell you more, monsieur.

MONSIEUR ORLAS [*beside himself*]. You cannot tell me more, mademoiselle? Do you realize that you are making a fool of me right now? And that I will not stand for it! With whom do you have a rendezvous this evening? Hmm? Well, answer! [CÉCILE *remains silent.*] Cécile, I am your father and I demand a reply! Now you are going too far! "Monsieur, this evening I have a rendezvous"! To have the audacity even to say that in front of me, her own father and only seventeen! Do you think of making me the accomplice in your debauchery, wretched child? What becomes of the respect you owe me in every matter? Do you forget who I am and is it necessary for me to remind you? Ah, believe me, I regret my credulousness and my confidence. But from now on I will treat you as you deserve. Now go to your room, mademoiselle. [CÉCILE *starts to speak.*] Not a word! I order you to stay there until you hear otherwise—and I assure you I shall do everything to prevent you from going out of your room tonight! Now go!

CÉCILE *curtsies and goes toward the house. She turns at the door and in a pitiful voice says simply:*

CÉCILE. You see how difficult it is, monsieur.   [*She exits.*

MONSIEUR ORLAS. "You see how difficult it is, monsieur"! And to her own father! Ah, nothing is sacred any longer! [*To* ARAMINTHE, *who has just entered.*] Araminthe, I am beside myself!

ARAMINTHE. What has happened, monsieur?

MONSIEUR ORLAS. I decided to have a heart-to-heart talk with Cécile. I did everything I could to inspire her with confidence, to make her understand that it was not the father but a friend who spoke to her. I thought I was on the point of solving the mystery of this little Sphinx and making myself understood for once. I proposed that we meet in the garden at night so that the moon and the stars might add a bit of romantic atmosphere to our conversation. I told her to be frank with me and forget who I was. And do you know what reply she made?

ARAMINTHE [*laughing*]. That she would be unable to because she had another rendezvous this evening?

MONSIEUR ORLAS [*jumping*]. Thunder and blazes, mademoiselle! Does everyone make a fool of me in this house! Did you know all about it?

ARAMINTHE. You wanted Cécile to speak to you as a friend, monsieur. I think the confidence she showed you terribly moving. She simply told you the truth. It is true. She has a rendezvous tonight.

MONSIEUR ORLAS. My daughter has a rendezvous tonight! And her governess herself tells me so to my face! We are in an insane asylum. Would it be indiscreet, mademoiselle, to inquire with whom my daughter has a rendezvous tonight?

ARAMINTHE. Yes, monsieur. It would be most indiscreet. It is a secret between the two of us.

MONSIEUR ORLAS. A secret between the two of you! That is really incredible. . . . I am deeply hurt, Araminthe. Cécile is only a little child with a child's brain. But I did hope that you at least would not make a fool of me. I am a very lonely man, Araminthe. I may seem gay, but most of the time I am sunk in despair. You all believe that I am working when I lock myself in my study, don't you? Working at God only knows what, since I have never

done anything in my life! The entire household goes
about on tiptoe so as not to disturb me. But do you know
what I actually do in this sanctuary of mine? I sit for
hours in front of my desk and look at the wall opposite
me.

ARAMINTHE. You should come and speak to us, monsieur.
Your daughter and I would be most happy to amuse you.

MONSIEUR ORLAS. I do not feel that either of you trusts me.
Something tells me that you always have some little secret
which belongs only to you both. You giggle over your
tapestries, whispering heaven only knows what in each
other's ear. As soon as I come, you stop! One would
really think that I turn you into stone.

ARAMINTHE. It is the respect we both owe you, monsieur,
that makes us pause. You are the master; you have serious
problems. We believe that you have no time for our silly
chatter.

MONSIEUR ORLAS. You are wrong. I have nothing to think
of, Araminthe, except my ennui. I have a modest income,
but it takes care of itself. And I have never had the good
fortune to take politics seriously as do most men of my
age. When I was twenty I lived as flippantly as you, and
time slipped through my fingers. As I grew older, I believed I had to strike an attitude to give myself importance. Yet each day that goes by enchains me more and
more to this ridiculous prison where I am my own jailer.
Why don't you free me, Araminthe, by loving me? It
would be a charitable act.

ARAMINTHE. I think the only reason one loves, monsieur,
is for his own pleasure. But you are still young and handsome. Why do you not take a mistress? That would keep
you busy.

MONSIEUR ORLAS. A fine thing to come from your lips!

ARAMINTHE. I know at least two or three young and beautiful women in the town who would be delighted to become your mistress.

MONSIEUR ORLAS. I know them too. They do not appeal to
me at all.

ARAMINTHE. Still, if you need them to cure you?

MONSIEUR ORLAS. But love is not a medicine! Once pleasure
passes, and it passes quickly—as you will learn one day,
my child—I wouldn't have anything to say to them and

I would simply die of boredom. I would rather sit in front of my wall. At least, I don't feel compelled to speak to myself.

ARAMINTHE. Do you believe, monsieur, in all frankness, that you would have very much more to tell me if I left my door ajar to you? Once pleasure passes—and it passes quickly, as you have just taught me—it would be exactly the same.

MONSIEUR ORLAS. With you?

ARAMINTHE. Yes, with me, monsieur, for you do not love me as I want to be loved one day. You are bored: I am young and fresh and I live here at your home. There is no more mystery than that. You spoke to me of the Baron a while ago. But tell me honestly, what man finding himself in your position would not try—just for the sake of trying—to knock softly on my door while going to bed at night? You simply conform to the most banal order of things, and for my part I do the same by not opening it. You can be sure that when I know that I love and am loved—I will hear. I have a sharp ear and I will hear, however softly he knocks.

MONSIEUR ORLAS [severely]. And if this young man who kissed your hand a while ago would softly knock, mademoiselle, would you hear him? I was not born yesterday, Araminthe. Other women were already playing this little game with me while you were still a child. So don't try to fool me. It isn't worthy of you—nor of me. My eyes are finally opening, you little schemer. Cécile is only a pretext which explains your entire attitude. This young fellow comes here to see you!

ARAMINTHE. And if it were so, monsieur? I am single. I am free. Who could find anything wrong in that?

MONSIEUR ORLAS. I could, heaven knows!

ARAMINTHE. You could? And by what right?

MONSIEUR ORLAS. By right of . . . Don't ask me so many questions! Your father entrusted you to me, Araminthe. The sacredness of your honor is in my hands. I am not a suspicious man—perhaps I should be more so—but woe to the one who trifles with me when it comes to honor. It will be my duty to warn your father if ever you are mad enough to open your door to this little puppy. And you can be sure he will be warned.

ARAMINTHE. And who would have warned my father then, had I opened it to you, Monsieur?

MONSIEUR ORLAS [*slightly embarrassed*]. Well, in such a case . . . Oh, stop joking, Araminthe! You are the only one who laughs at your jokes.

ARAMINTHE. Then stop living in a dream world, monsieur! The little chevalier comes here to see Cécile and not me. Everybody knows it, and you as well. I will even tell you a secret if you swear not to repeat it. But first you must swear. I do not trust you completely, monsieur. It is true you are a gentleman, but still you have two or three personalities and sometimes you are unable to tell one from the other.

MONSIEUR ORLAS. Enough, enough. I swear. But heaven alone knows if I understand you.

ARAMINTHE. Swear on what is most precious to you, and swear that you will never tell anyone. Well, go on and swear! And everything must be according to rules, so spit as well.

MONSIEUR ORLAS. Araminthe, you are making fun of me. But there, I swear. [*He holds up his hand.*] And I spit.

ARAMINTHE. Well, monsieur, the chevalier thinks so little of me that he is eloping with your daughter tonight.

MONSIEUR ORLAS [*at first astounded, bursts out laughing*]. Ah! Ah! That is a good one! What do you take me for? The stock father in a comedy? You think that I am going to masquerade in a dark cloak and catch a cold in the garden just to see if I don't find a hidden ladder, hmm? You are talking to the wrong person, mademoiselle.

ARAMINTHE. I believe it would be most prudent, monsieur. If Cécile told you she had a rendezvous tonight, it was not without reason.

MONSIEUR ORLAS. I will lock Cécile in her room, mademoiselle, and save that unfortunate child from playing I don't know what scandalous part in this affair between you and your lover. And I shall sleep soundly tonight, have no fear. After all, it is no business of mine if you have decided to ruin yourself!

ARAMINTHE. And you are right. But if I were in your place, monsieur, I would still keep a watch to see if anyone were kidnapped tonight.

MONSIEUR ORLAS. That's right, laugh at me. Now I see that

you never loved me and never will love me. I am going
to my study and think of ways not to suffer any more.
I am too old now to yield to despair. Tomorrow I will
tell you what I have decided. Adieu, Araminthe! I am
deeply wounded. [*He takes a step and turns back.*] Yet,
Araminthe, I want to tell you something. It is true I
knocked at your door. But I never really insisted. And although God knows how much I love making love, I was
almost happy that your door remained closed.

ARAMINTHE [*stammering, bewildered*]. What do you mean,
monsieur?

MONSIEUR ORLAS [*continuing*]. Yes, almost happy. You may
already be the mistress of this boy, and I am making
myself ridiculous by speaking to you as I do. I am not
easily respectful, Araminthe. There is something about a
skirt floating around a simple waist that does away with
the sense of respect in my mind. And yet there are such
strong contradictions in one's heart, that I was almost
happy in my bitterness to learn how to respect you before
your silent door. There it is. Ask that little man tonight
if he understands anything of this!   [*He exits.*

ARAMINTHE [*smiling happily to herself and whispering*]. It
only had to be said, monsieur. . . . You went through
so much trouble for nothing before! . . . And now, without even wanting to, you have found the words which
unlock a girl's door. . . . Poor little men! Poor little
strutting peacocks! They spread out their tails as con-
querors almost as soon as they are able to walk. . . . And
they could have such an easy victory if they knew they
only had to be a little wounded and sad. . . . But we
are certainly not going to teach them that! . . . I have
no fears for this one. He will be in the garden as soon as
night falls, with a dark, concealing cloak, pistols at his
side, and a taste for blood in his mouth. He may catch a
cold there, or he may find love. . . . Or perhaps even
both. Well, we shall see! . . . I will tell you a secret:
the playwright himself doesn't know. . . .

*She exits after a small curtsy. The stage remains empty and
night begins to fall while a mocking tune is being played.
When night has entirely fallen—quickly enough for this
time of year—a man appears wrapped in a dark cloak. He
advances cautiously. He beckons to someone and two men,*

*also in dark cloaks, come from a black corner of the garden
and join him.*

THE MAN. Ssssh!
THE MEN. Ssssh!

*Still another figure in a dark cloak comes from the house,
his face concealed in the folds of his cloak. It is* MONSIEUR
ORLAS. *The man who first appeared motions to his men to
go away.* MONSIEUR ORLAS *and the other man cautiously
survey each other before approaching.*

MONSIEUR ORLAS [*in a low voice*]. Monsieur Damiens?
MONSIEUR DAMIENS [*in the same voice*]. Monsieur Orlas?
MONSIEUR ORLAS. Yes. It is I.

They greet each other.

MONSIEUR DAMIENS. Many thanks, monsieur, for warning
me.
MONSIEUR ORLAS. Do not mention it, monsieur. It was only
my duty. I am a father like yourself, monsieur. [*He motions to the two men who are waiting.*] Are these gentlemen with you?
MONSIEUR DAMIENS. Two bodyguards whom I thought
worth while bringing. I thought that we might have to
meet force with force.
MONSIEUR ORLAS. You did wisely, monsieur. I myself am
armed with pistols. [*He points to them under his cloak.*]
MONSIEUR DAMIENS. How can I ever thank you, monsieur?
MONSIEUR ORLAS. It is the most natural thing in the world,
monsieur. You have entrusted Araminthe to my care. Her
honor is as precious to me as to you. But why are you
trembling? Have no fear.
MONSIEUR DAMIENS. I am a father, monsieur. And I will
also tell you without false shame that I am an old lawyer,
monsieur, and that I have little experience when it comes
to battles.
MONSIEUR ORLAS. I have no more taste for fighting than
you, monsieur. But when my daughter's honor is concerned or your daughter's—you see I place them both on
the same level—I am ready to take up arms. Besides, the
law is on our side.
MONSIEUR DAMIENS. Yes, it is. Still I don't hide from you
that I would have preferred a good lawsuit. Having
caught the opposing party *flagrante delicto*, I would have
crushed him! Alas! A lawsuit would have been too slow.

Lovers work more quickly than we do, monsieur. You are a father yourself. You know how difficult it is to protect your daughter!

MONSIEUR ORLAS. You're telling me, monsieur! I had fears for my own daughter before seeing through their intrigue. These young people no longer have respect for anything. It seems to me when we were their age we had more respect for family honor.

MONSIEUR DAMIENS. Oh, I don't know. We have also had our day. I can tell you a hundred stories in which I have been a little imprudent. I was hot-blooded when I was twenty.

MONSIEUR ORLAS. Yes, they were still speaking about it when I was old enough to understand. You were really hot-blooded, monsieur!

MONSIEUR DAMIENS. He! He! Yes, I suppose I was!

MONSIEUR ORLAS. Plenty of the ladies in this part of the country know a thing or two. They blushed every time your name was mentioned.

MONSIEUR DAMIENS. He! He! Yes, I suppose they did!

MONSIEUR ORLAS. I was still only a boy, monsieur, when I dreamed of following in your footsteps.

MONSIEUR DAMIENS. He! He! Yes, I suppose you were! You flatter me, monsieur. It is true that very few women treated me cruelly under the late King. But if I am not mistaken, monsieur, I believe that you yourself have established some reputation in our little town, haven't you?

MONSIEUR ORLAS. Well! I suppose I have broken several hearts, but I was paid back in time. One has to make hay while the sun shines.

MONSIEUR DAMIENS. And we made it, monsieur. But with good manners. We were not like these young fellows . . .

MONSIEUR ORLAS. Who respect nothing, monsieur!

MONSIEUR DAMIENS. We were satisfied with married women. After all, what is the difference between one cuckold more or less?

MONSIEUR ORLAS. Or even some servant, if need be. Or some wayward peasant. Hmm? But when it comes to young ladies of quality, monsieur . . .

MONSIEUR DAMIENS. Without caring for the father's honor . . . !

MONSIEUR ORLAS. We must be ruthless, monsieur! Sssh. Be careful. Let us hide. I think I saw a shadow at the end of the path by the linden trees. It must be our adventurer.

MONSIEUR DAMIENS. Do you think he is the kind of man who draws his sword easily? These young men of the nobility believe that everything is permitted them.

MONSIEUR ORLAS. The law is on our side, monsieur. And, besides, there are four of us with your bodyguards.

MONSIEUR DAMIENS. Yes. But we should take care not to be wounded. Let us hide far away. We will throw our men at him at the proper time.

MONSIEUR ORLAS. Do not be afraid. We will shame that boy before he even thinks of drawing his sword.

The CHEVALIER *enters, dressed in a dark cloak as well. He goes toward the house, gives a signal.* ARAMINTHE *appears at the window.*

CHEVALIER. Is it you, Araminthe?

ARAMINTHE. Yes, it is.

She appears at the door, wrapped in a cloak and goes to him.

CHEVALIER. And where is Cécile?

ARAMINTHE. She is coming. But there is a little difficulty I shall tell you about directly. You must hide here for a while. [*She leads him to the little Chinese pavilion and lets him in.*] Do not make a sound until I return, and no matter what you hear, do not make a move. [*She locks him inside.*]

CHEVALIER [*in the pavilion*]. Why do you lock the door?

ARAMINTHE. To be sure I will find you here at the proper time. Sssh! Not a word! Everything will be all right.

She returns to the house and gives a signal. CÉCILE *appears, hidden under a mantle.*

CÉCILE. Is it you, Araminthe?

ARAMINTHE. Yes. You can come now. Everything is going as we expected. I am going in to get our things. Wait for me there.

CÉCILE. Where is the chevalier? You know very well that I am afraid in the dark.

ARAMINTHE. One must not be afraid the night one elopes, mademoiselle! . . . The chevalier will join you in a minute. [*She disappears into the house.*]

MONSIEUR ORLAS, *hidden under his cape, walks around* CÉCILE, *who grows obviously worried and is not sure that she recognizes him.*

Monsieur Orlas [*in a whisper*]. Is it you?

Cécile [*in the same tone*]. Yes, it is. Is it you?

Monsieur Orlas. Yes. [*To himself.*] Aha, the bird is caught. I shall make believe I am the chevalier.

Cécile. I am a little afraid.

Monsieur Orlas. Do not be afraid of anything, my child. I am here.

Cécile. Are you sure at least that you love me? Because if you don't there still is time.

Monsieur Orlas. Do not doubt it, my sweet. I am yours forever.

Cécile. How strangely you speak! I do not recognize your voice.

Monsieur Orlas. It is because I speak low so that no one will hear us. . . .

Cécile. As soon as she comes, we'll run away quickly. Are your horses and bodyguards at the little gate?

Monsieur Orlas. As arranged. [*To himself.*] The scoundrels! They planned to take my daughter as well.

Cécile. What are you saying?

Monsieur Orlas. I said, "She is very nice but why bother to take that child?" Wouldn't we be better off without her?

Cécile. I may be mad, monsieur, but I shall not elope without my chaperon.

Monsieur Orlas. What! This infant your chaperon? And what will her father say?

Cécile. And what will mine say? You must put up with some little unpleasantness when you elope.

Monsieur Orlas [*to himself*]. "Some little unpleasantness"! Ah, how they dare trifle with serious matters!

Cécile. What are you always muttering about? I cannot see your face.

Monsieur Orlas. I was simply telling myself that she would get in our way, and that we would have been much better alone, my beloved.

Cécile. She is my sister, monsieur. I cannot do anything without her. But you must swear to me that you will never kiss her hands again.

Monsieur Orlas [*to himself*]. Ha! Ha! Now it comes out.

Cécile. You elope with us both, but I am the one you are marrying.

Monsieur Orlas. And do you doubt it, my love? [*To himself.*] I was right. The rascal intended to play with them both. [*To Cécile.*] My attentions toward her were only a convenient mask to hide my real feelings for you. Besides, why speak of marriage at all? Is not love, love alone, enough for us?

Cécile. I love you, monsieur, and it is indeed a sufficient reason to follow you. But must we not conform to law?

Monsieur Orlas. What an ugly word in such a pretty mouth! What other law is there but the law of our hearts?

Cécile. But what about my father, monsieur?

Monsieur Orlas. What does that suspicious old man matter? We will travel, my love. We will be like those glamorous persons hated by weakhearted ones who never dared give everything to love. We shall be lovers. Ah, lovers! Have you ever been able to hear that word without feeling disturbed? Have you, Araminthe?

Cécile [*draws back, murmuring*]. Araminthe?

Monsieur Orlas. Is it not better than a household with screaming children hanging on your apron strings, and servants with their pots and pans to order around? The drudge of daily life ruins the sense of love. But each morning will see our love blossom anew, ready to be defended and conquered anew. We will have frightful scenes, wound each other to the heart. Each of us will torment the other, and yet we won't ever be able to part. Each of us will be the slave and the tyrant of the other. Men, all men, will desire you at the sumptuous gatherings where we will spend our nights, and their desire will reveal you to yourself and you will make a game of torturing me. I will never know if you really love me nor what is concealed behind your smiles. And if one day you happen to be away from me for a single hour, anxiety will gnaw my heart away. Because you will always lie to me, and you will always be an everlasting mystery to me. . . . This is life, Araminthe! This is what it is to be a woman and to love!

Cécile [*who has recognized her father while he was speaking, has a little smile as she says*]. Good heavens, monsieur, how mistaken you are! I have no desire ever to leave you—even for an hour. Nor have I any desire to lie to

you. And how absurd to think I would torment you. Can't
you see that the least little sadness in your eye makes me
suffer so? I simply want to be yours and to know it will
always be that way. You certainly are very young and you
know nothing about women. Even the wildest among
them, monsieur, wish for nothing else.

MONSIEUR ORLAS. Have you not read the lives of famous
mistresses? They only love themselves, my poor child.
Men were clods of clay they molded according to their
whims. Men were simply instruments of their own triumph like their splendid gowns and their luxurious jewels.
Does it not tempt you to become one of these monstrous
goddesses, and to ravage all the hearts about you?

CÉCILE. Not at all, monsieur. Not in the least. How monoto-
nous it must be to love only oneself. And do you believe
that if any of those famous ladies had ever known real
happiness with one man they would have had any desire
to change? I never think of them, but if one day I should,
it would be to pity them for never having found love.

MONSIEUR ORLAS. Love . . . love . . . What do you know
about love at your age?

CÉCILE. Everything that cannot be taught, monsieur. That
is to say, almost everything.

MONSIEUR ORLAS [drawing nearer to her]. Very well, then,
I will teach you the rest. . . .

CÉCILE [drawing back]. Indeed, monsieur, these are strange
words coming from your mouth and they disturb me.
Throw off your disguise now. You know that I recognized
you in spite of the dark. What would your daughter who
loves and respects you say if she knew that you speak this
way to other girls at night?

MONSIEUR ORLAS [at first surprised, taking off his disguise].
Very well! Off with my disguise! Araminthe, you have
recognized me. I am the man who has desired you for so
long a time. I wanted to prevent this ridiculous elopement, because I know better than you that you cannot
love that little boy. And do not worry about Cécile. She
is a child who doesn't know anything. Don't give her
another thought. We shall put her in a convent or send
her to her aunt's. And tonight you will follow no one but
me. For I love you, Araminthe, you hear me, I love you,
love you madly, and I cannot live without you any longer!

Cécile [*in her true voice*]. I have known for a long time that you love Araminthe, but if you love her as much as you say, why don't you marry her, Papa?

Monsieur Orlas [*jumps and draws back, shouting*]. "Papa"! Who are you then? Unfortunate child! How could you possibly make fun of your father in this way?

Cécile. Did I approach you, monsieur? Did I take the initiative of beginning this strange conversation?

Monsieur Orlas. Wretched little girl! Forget at once everything I said to you. Not a word of it was true.

Cécile [*softly*]. But I have not heard a word, monsieur.

Monsieur Orlas. You must know that I recognized you myself and I only wanted to shame you.

Cécile. Then why all this comedy? It would have been so easy to tell Araminthe that you love her.

Monsieur Orlas [*sternly*]. Mademoiselle, it is your father's right to ask you questions and not yours! What were you doing in the garden so late at night, and in a traveling cloak as well? To whom did you think you were speaking before you recognized me?

Araminthe *appears, smiling.*

Araminthe. To the chevalier, monsieur, who loves her and wanted to elope with her this very night to marry her and make her happy. I warned you, remember?

Monsieur Orlas. You dare show your face, mademoiselle? You should know by now that there are laws in this country which protect a father's honor. It will rest with others to weigh your part in this escapade, for I intend to notify the proper authority of all this! You were going to make yourself the accomplice of a villainous act, mademoiselle! Let me tell you marriage is a sacred thing and it alone can sanctify love. You wanted my daughter to elope tonight, didn't you? You wanted to make her like one of those lost creatures who ruin themselves forever by placing love before duty, didn't you? Well, answer me!

Araminthe. I was at the window, monsieur, and I heard you when you thought you convinced me of the contrary a little while ago. You compromise yourself too much. You do better not to insist, and far better to leave your pistols alone. Your daughter and I have been able to keep our honor without you—and sometimes even in spite of

you! Haven't we? Cécile has parried your wily thrusts as
well as I could have done myself. Are you not willing to
grant us a bit of respect and confidence now?

MONSIEUR ORLAS. Come into my arms, my charming girl!
Cécile was right indeed. If I love you, why not admit it
and simply ask you to marry me? . . . I know now that
you love me too.

CÉCILE. You may kiss her, monsieur. I won't look.

MONSIEUR ORLAS. Thank you, Cécile. But I shall do it with
such tenderness that even you can be a witness.

MONSIEUR DAMIENS *rushes in with his bodyguards.*

MONSIEUR DAMIENS. Upon him, my brave men! We have
him now! [*They throw themselves on* MONSIEUR ORLAS.]
Caught in the act, monsieur. Kissing my daughter! And
eloping! You will surely be condemned to the galleys!
[*He recognizes* MONSIEUR ORLAS.] But what is this? A
betrayal? To find you, monsieur, kissing my daughter in
the dark?

MONSIEUR ORLAS. I can explain everything, monsieur. . . .

MONSIEUR DAMIENS. I thought you were a father, monsieur,
but you are only a vile seducer! Did you not swear a while
ago with pistols in your hands that you would protect the
honor of your ladies—or was I dreaming?

MONSIEUR ORLAS [*beginning to explain with embarrassment*]. Love, monsieur, is my only excuse. This feeling is
stronger than anything and——

MONSIEUR DAMIENS. To whom do you think you are talking,
monsieur? I was not born yesterday. Do you bandy the
most sacred things so lightly, monsieur? Are you one of
these thoughtless men who ruin ladies' reputations?

MONSIEUR ORLAS. No, monsieur. But sometimes there are
occasions where love——

MONSIEUR DAMIENS. Idle talk! Take care, monsieur, you are
speaking to a father! "Love" is a word they do not understand! I was greatly mistaken, monsieur, to put so much
confidence in you. You are nothing but a young puppy.

MONSIEUR ORLAS. But, monsieur——

MONSIEUR DAMIENS. Have respect for my age, monsieur! I
am old enough to be your father, monsieur!

ARAMINTHE [*in the arms of* MONSIEUR ORLAS]. Thank you,
Papa, for this charming phrase. Now I know I can love
him.

MONSIEUR DAMIENS. Love! Love! Don't any of you know any other word? Am I the only one too old to use it? I shall make you young people pay for it, and dearly too!

MONSIEUR ORLAS. You are unfair, monsieur. You have known love yourself. You confessed as much a little while ago. There is in love a force which triumphs over everything and it is why . . . [*He sees* CÉCILE *being kissed by the* CHEVALIER *whom* CÉCILE *has freed with* ARAMINTHE'S *key.*] One minute, monsieur. Here is our young rascal! [*He approaches them with indignation.*] Monsieur! Am I dreaming? Do you dare kiss my daughter, in my own garden, at night, and before my very eyes?

CHEVALIER. I love her, monsieur!

MONSIEUR ORLAS. A good excuse, monsieur!

CHEVALIER. But you just said yourself, monsieur, that love——

MONSIEUR ORLAS. It is too easy a word for you to use, young man. It has an entirely different meaning in my mouth. Yes, my young libertine, I know what dark designs you were contriving. But, God be praised, I came in time. The law will take care of you. And do you know the price you will pay? Hmm? The galleys, monsieur, the galleys! . . .

CHEVALIER. But, monsieur, you would not have the heart to——

MONSIEUR ORLAS. You are speaking to a father, monsieur, the protector of his daughter's honor. A father, do you hear? There is something in the majesty of the word "father" which should have made you pause.

MONSIEUR DAMIENS [*taking hold of him*]. A fine thing for you to be saying! What about me, monsieur? I am also a father, monsieur. Do not try to change the issue by talking of your daughter's honor. I want you to account for my own daughter's honor, monsieur!

MONSIEUR ORLAS. But since I tell you that I love her, monsieur!

CHEVALIER [*to* MONSIEUR ORLAS]. But since I tell you that I love her!

ARAMINTHE [*coming forward*]. This little comedy is beginning to be too long. Don't you think we have all spoken enough? Papa, Monsieur Orlas is marrying me. [*To* MONSIEUR ORLAS.] The chevalier, monsieur, has the honor to ask for your daughter's hand. Don't you think we can set our dark cloaks aside and continue this discussion in another place than the garden? The night is cool, we risk catching a cold, and besides I have had a midnight table laid for us. [*She claps her hands.* Two FOOTMEN *appear with candelabras. Other candles are lit inside the house.*] If you will only take the trouble to enter the house, you will find everything ready. . . . I even had musicians come secretly, and had an enormous engagement cake made for dessert with our four names engraved in silver icing.

MONSIEUR ORLAS. Did you know, then, that everything would end this way, precious girl?

ARAMINTHE. I was in on the secret of this comedy, monsieur. And there must always be a happy ending for this kind of play.

MONSIEUR ORLAS [*taking* MONSIEUR DAMIENS' *arm*]. Come, Monsieur Damiens, let us go and dine! Everything ends this way in France—everything. Weddings, christenings, duels, burials, swindlings, diplomatic affairs—everything is a pretext for a good dinner. Besides my cook is a genius. She would be reason enough, monsieur, for your entering my family. . . . You may as well tell your bodyguards to go and have a drink in the kitchen. [*To the* CHEVALIER.] Tell yours as well, monsieur, who, it seems, are waiting at the little gate.

CHEVALIER. A thousand thanks, monsieur! But it so happens that we have the same bodyguards.

MONSIEUR DAMIENS. What do you mean, the same? I shall have them hanged!

MONSIEUR ORLAS [*drawing him toward the house*]. Forgive them, monsieur. We only have two bodyguards in our little town and work is so scarce.

They go in a procession into the now illuminated house. One can hear music playing. CÉCILE *remains behind and appears to be sulking.*

CHEVALIER [*going to her*]. Well, Cécile, here you stand sulking while happiness stares you in the face. What are you waiting for?

CÉCILE. I am making a very important decision, monsieur.

CHEVALIER. I swear to you, my love, that I will never kiss Araminthe's hands again. Never!

CÉCILE. I should hope so, monsieur. But I have been think-

ing about everything my father has just told me. . . .
How really naïve I was. . . . When all is said and done,
monsieur, I think that I will make you suffer.

She enters the house, the worried CHEVALIER *following her.*
The music grows clear and brisk as the curtain falls.

TRAVELER WITHOUT LUGGAGE

(Le Voyageur Sans Bagages)

A play in three acts

Translated by
LUCIENNE HILL

CHARACTERS

GASTON, *a victim of amnesia*
GEORGES RENAUD, *his presumed brother*
MADAME RENAUD, *Gaston's presumed mother*
VALENTINE RENAUD, *Georges' wife*
THE DUCHESS DUPONT-DUFORT, *patroness of Gaston*
MONSIEUR HUSPAR, *lawyer in charge of Gaston's interests*
THE LITTLE BOY
MR. TRUGGLE, *the little boy's lawyer*
THE BUTLER ⎤
THE CHAUFFEUR ⎥ *servants of*
THE VALET ⎥ *the Renaud family*
THE COOK ⎥
JULIETTE ⎦

TRAVELER WITHOUT LUGGAGE

ACT ONE

SCENE I

The drawing room of a well-appointed house in a provincial town in France, with an extensive view over gardens. When the curtain rises the stage is empty. Then the BUTLER *ushers in the* DUCHESS DUPONT-DUFORT, MONSIEUR HUSPAR, *and* GASTON.

BUTLER. What name shall I say?

DUCHESS. The Duchess Dupont-Dufort, my lawyer, Monsieur Huspar, and Monsieur . . . [*She hesitates.*] . . . Gaston. [*To* HUSPAR.] We'll have to call him that, for the time being.

BUTLER [*who seems aware of the situation*]. I hope your Ladyship will excuse Monsieur and Madame Renaud, but Monsieur and Madame Renaud were not expecting your Ladyship until the eleven fifty train. I will tell Monsieur and Madame Renaud that your Ladyship is here. [*He goes.*

DUCHESS [*watching him go*]. Perfect butler, that. Oh, Gaston, my dear, I'm so wildly happy. I was positive you'd be the son of an excellent family.

HUSPAR. Don't get too carried away. We have five other possible families besides these Renauds, remember.

DUCHESS. No, no, Huspar. Gaston will recognize these Renauds as his own people, I know it! He will rediscover the flavor of his past here, in this house. Something tells me this is where he'll get his memory back. That something is my feminine intuition and it has seldom let me down.

HUSPAR [*bowing before such irrefutable logic*]. In that case . . .

125

GASTON *has been moving around the room, oblivious of them, and looking at the pictures, like a child out visiting.*

DUCHESS [*calling to him*]. Well, Gaston? You're excited, I hope?

GASTON. Not much.

DUCHESS [*sighing*]. Not much. Ah, my dear boy, I wonder sometimes if you realize quite how poignant your case is.

GASTON. But, Duchess——

DUCHESS. No, no, no. Nothing you can say will make me alter my opinion. You don't realize, you just don't realize. Now you don't, do you? Admit it.

GASTON. Perhaps I don't, not very well.

DUCHESS [*satisfied*]. That's better. You're a charming person and you'll always admit you're wrong, I will say that for you. But that doesn't alter the fact that this casual attitude, this total lack of interest on your part, is extremely reprehensible. Isn't it, Huspar?

HUSPAR. Why, I——

DUCHESS. It is, it is, it is! You really must back me up and make him see that he's got to be excited. [GASTON *has turned back to the pictures on the wall.*] Gaston?

GASTON. Duchess?

DUCHESS. Are you made of stone?

GASTON. Stone?

DUCHESS. Yes. Is your heart harder than granite?

GASTON. I—I don't think so, Duchess.

DUCHESS. A very good answer! I don't think so either. And yet, to a less well-informed observer than either of us, your behavior would lead one to believe that your heart is made of granite.

GASTON [*flatly*]. Oh.

DUCHESS. Gaston, perhaps you don't grasp the gravity of what I'm saying. I forget sometimes that I'm speaking to an amnesia case and that there are some words you may not have relearned in the last seventeen years. Do you know what granite is?

GASTON. It's a kind of stone.

DUCHESS. Quite right. But do you know what kind of stone? The hardest stone there is, Gaston. Do you understand?

GASTON. Yes.

DUCHESS. And don't you care that I'm comparing your heart to the hardest stone there is?

GASTON [*embarrassed*]. Well . . . no . . . [*A pause.*] It's
a bit of a giggle really.

DUCHESS. Did you hear that, Huspar?

HUSPAR [*pouring oil*]. He's a child.

DUCHESS [*peremptorily*]. Child, rubbish! He's an ingrate.
[*To* GASTON.] I see. Here you are, one of the most dis-
quieting cases in psychiatric history, one of the most heart-
rending enigmas of the war—and if I translate your vulgar
phraseology correctly, it makes you laugh? You are—as
one clever journalist so aptly put it—the living unknown
warrior, and it makes you laugh. Are you quite incapable
of respect, Gaston?

GASTON. But it's me, isn't it, so——

DUCHESS. Never mind! In the name of what you represent,
you ought to forbid yourself to laugh at yourself. This may
sound like a witty sally, but it fully expresses what I
mean. When you see yourself in the glass, Gaston, you
ought to take your hat off to yourself.

GASTON. Me—to myself?

DUCHESS. Yes, you, to yourself. We all do, when we think
of what you stand for. Who do you think you are, that
you should be exempt?

GASTON. Nobody, Duchess.

DUCHESS. Wrong answer! You think you're someone very
important. The fuss the papers have made over your case
has turned your head, that's all. [*He tries to say something.*] Don't answer me back, you'll only put me in a
rage! [*He drops his head and goes back to the pictures.*]
How does he strike you, Huspar?

HUSPAR. Him? Indifferent.

DUCHESS. Indifferent. That's the word. It's been on the tip
of my tongue for a week. Indifferent. That's it exactly.
Yet, good God, it's *his* future that's at stake, not ours!
We haven't lost our memory, *we* aren't searching for our
family! Are we, Huspar?

HUSPAR. Definitely not.

DUCHESS. Well then!

HUSPAR [*with a worldly-wise shrug*]. You're new to it all,
your illusions are still fresh. He's been meeting all our
efforts with this apathy for years now.

DUCHESS. It's unpardonable of him not to realize the trouble
my nephew is taking on his behalf. If you knew how

beautifully he's taking care of him, what devotion he's put into this whole enterprise! I hope he told you about the great event before you left?

HUSPAR. Dr. Jibelin wasn't at the hospital when I went to collect Gaston's case history. Unfortunately I wasn't able to wait for him.

DUCHESS. What's this, Huspar? You mean you didn't see my little Albert before you left? Then you don't know the good news.

HUSPAR. What news?

DUCHESS. At the last pentothal injection he gave him, he succeeded in getting Gaston to talk in his delirium. Oh, he didn't say much. He said, "Fartarse."

HUSPAR. Fartarse?

DUCHESS. Yes, fartarse. You may say that's not much, but the interesting thing is that it's a word nobody has ever heard him utter when he's awake, a word nobody remembers ever using in his hearing, a word which therefore has every likelihood of belonging to his past.

HUSPAR. Fartarse.

DUCHESS. Fartarse. It's a very tiny clue, but it *is* something. His past isn't just a black hole any more. Who knows if that "fartarse" won't set us on the right track? [*Dreamily.*] Fartarse. A friend's surname perhaps. A common swear-word, who knows? We have a small basis to build on now.

HUSPAR [*ruminatively*]. Fartarse.

DUCHESS [*repeating it delightedly*]. Fartarse. When Albert came to announce this unhoped-for result, he flung open the door and he cried "Aunt! My patient has said a word from out of his past. It was a term of abuse." I shook from head to foot, my dear. I was expecting some piece of filth. Such a charming lad, I should have been deso-lated if he turned out to be of low extraction. A pretty waste of effort it would be for my little Albert to spend nights on end—he's lost pounds over it—asking him questions and sticking needles in his rump, if the fellow recovers his memory only to tell us that before the war he was a plumber's mate! But something tells me differ-ent. I'm a romantic, my dear Huspar. Something tells me that my nephew's patient was an extremely famous man. A playwright, for preference. An eminent playwright.

HUSPAR. Eminent—it's unlikely. He would have been recognized by now.

DUCHESS. The photographs of him were all terrible. Besides, war takes such a toll on a man, doesn't it?

HUSPAR. I don't recall a well-known playwright ever reported missing during the hostilities. People of that sort always announce their slightest movements to the press . . . let alone their disappearance.

DUCHESS. Ah, Huspar, you're very cruel! You're destroying such a lovely dream. But he *is* a man of breeding, I'm quite sure of that. See how distinguished he looks in that suit. I sent him to Albert's tailor.

HUSPAR [*putting on his pince-nez*]. Why yes, I was going to say that doesn't look like a hospital suit.

DUCHESS. You surely don't expect me to put my nephew's patient up in my own house, and parade him around myself to all the families who are claiming him, dressed in putty-colored flannelette!

HUSPAR. An excellent idea, I think, these house-to-house visits.

DUCHESS. Aren't they? My little Albert said to me, the moment he took up his case, "What he needs to do, in order to find his past," he said, "is to saturate himself in the atmosphere of that past." The next step was obvious: take him along to the five or six families who had produced the most telling evidence. But Gaston isn't his only patient. Albert couldn't take time off from the hospital to conduct these visits himself—that was out of the question. So what was to be done? Ask the Bureau of Missing Persons for funds to carry out an official investigation? You know how stingy those folk are. What would you have done? I shouldered arms and jumped into the breach. As in 1914!

HUSPAR. Very laudable.

DUCHESS. When I think that in Dr. Bonfant's day, families came in hordes to the asylum every Monday, saw him for a few minutes each, and then went home by the next train! How could you find your nearest and dearest under those conditions, I ask you? Dr. Bonfant is dead, I know, and we must hold our peace. But the least one could say about him, if silence over a grave weren't a sacred duty, is that the man was an idiot and a criminal.

HUSPAR. A criminal—oh, come . . .

DUCHESS. Don't exasperate me, Huspar. I just wish he weren't dead so I could fling the word in his face. A criminal! It's all his fault if this poor unfortunate boy has been languishing in mental homes ever since 1918! When I think that he kept him at Pont-au-Bronc for nearly fifteen years without getting him to say one word about his past, and my little Albert has had him for three months and he's already made him say "fartarse"—well, I'm speechless! He's a great psychiatrist, Huspar, is my little Albert.

HUSPAR. And a charming young man, too.

DUCHESS. The dear lad. Things are changing fast now he's in charge, thank heaven. Identification parades, graphological evidence, chemical analyses, police investigations—nothing that's humanly possible will be spared to help Gaston find his rightful family. On the clinical side too, Albert insists on the most up-to-date methods. Just think —he's already given him seventeen pentothal injections!

HUSPAR. Seventeen! But that's an enormous lot!

DUCHESS [delightedly]. Enormous! And it's extremely brave of my little Albert too. Because—we have to face the fact —it's risky.

HUSPAR. What about Gaston?

DUCHESS. What could he have to complain about, pray? It's all for his own good. He'll have a bottom like a pincushion but he'll get his past back. And our past is the best part of all of us! What right-thinking man would hesitate between his past and the skin of his behind?

HUSPAR. It's not a question that arises much.

DUCHESS [to GASTON as he passes by her]. Isn't that so, Gaston? Aren't you grateful to Dr. Jibelin, after all those wasted years with Dr. Bonfant, for taking such trouble to give you back your past?

GASTON. Very grateful indeed, Duchess.

DUCHESS [to HUSPAR]. There, you see! He says it himself! Oh, Gaston my dear, isn't it moving—don't you find?—to think that on the other side of that door there may be a mother's heart beating, an old father waiting to open his arms to you!

GASTON. Well, you know, I've been through it so many times; so many deluded old women kissing me with their damp noses, so many fond old men rubbing their beards on me. . . . Imagine having four hundred families, Duchess. Four hundred families all avid to clasp you to their bosom. That's a lot of families.

DUCHESS. But children, Gaston, dear little children! Little babies waiting for their father! Will you dare to say you don't long to kiss the little darlings—to bounce them on your knee?

GASTON. That would be a bit awkward, Duchess. The youngest couldn't be much under twenty.

DUCHESS [sighing]. Oh, Huspar . . . He feels a need to defile all that's most sacred in life!

GASTON [lost in thought suddenly]. Children . . . I should have some of my own now, real ones, if they'd let me live.

DUCHESS. You know that was impossible.

GASTON. Why? Because I couldn't remember anything before that spring evening in 1918, when they found me on a railway siding?

HUSPAR. Quite so, alas . . .

GASTON. Yes, I daresay it frightened people to think of a man living without a past. Foundlings aren't too well thought of, as it is. . . . But at least there's time to instill a few little notions into them. But a man, a grown man, who scarcely had a country, no place of birth, no background, no name . . . Good God, the fellow's a bleeding outcast.

DUCHESS. In any case, Gaston, my dear, everything points to the fact that your education wasn't all it might have been. I've already forbidden you to use that word.

GASTON. What—outcast?

DUCHESS. No . . . [She hesitates.] The other one.

GASTON [continuing his reverie]. And a police record too, maybe. . . . Have you thought of that, Duchess? You trust me with your silver at table; my room is a step away from yours. . . . Supposing I'd already killed three men?

DUCHESS. Your eyes tell me you haven't.

GASTON. You're lucky they honor you with their secrets, then. I stare into them until I'm dizzy sometimes, trying to find out a little of all the things they've seen. They give me nothing.

DUCHESS [smiling]. You haven't killed three men though, don't you worry. One needn't know your past life to know that.

GASTON. They found me in a trainload of returning prisoners from Germany. So I'd been to the front. Like the others, I must have hurled lumps of lead and iron at other men. Oh, I'm a bad shot, I know that much about myself. But during the war, the High Command reckoned more on the number of bullets than on the skill of those who fired them. Let's hope, anyway, that I didn't manage to hit three men.

DUCHESS. Gracious me, the very idea! On the contrary, I fondly hope you were a hero. I meant killing people in peacetime!

GASTON. A hero is fairly vague in wartime too. The backbiter, the miser, the thief, the coward even—they were all condemned alike by regulations to be heroes, cheek by jowl, and in the same way almost.

DUCHESS. Don't worry. A little voice inside me tells me—and it's never wrong—that you were a very well-brought-up young man.

GASTON. That's a slender basis for asserting that I never did an evil thing. I must have hunted. Well-brought-up young men always hunt. So let's hope I was a hunter everybody laughed at; let's hope I didn't hit three animals.

DUCHESS. My dear boy, it takes all my fondness for you not to laugh, to listen to you talk. Your scruples are exaggerated.

GASTON. I was so content in the asylum. I'd grown used to myself. I knew that self well, and now I have to leave it and find another me and put that on like an old coat. Will I recognize myself tomorrow, I who drink nothing but water, in the lamplighter's son who had to have his four full jugs of red wine every day? Or—me with my tiny store of patience—in the haberdasher's son who collected, and graded according to size, twelve hundred different sorts of buttons?

DUCHESS. Exactly! That's why I was set on visiting these Renauds first. They're a better class of people altogether.

GASTON. That means they have a grand house and a grand butler, but what kind of son did they have?

The BUTLER appears in the doorway.

DUCHESS [*seeing him*]. We'll know in a second. [*Raising her hand to stop the BUTLER.*] Wait a second, my good man, before you show in your master and mistress. Gaston,

would you go out into the garden for a little while? We'll
send for you.

GASTON. Very well, Duchess.

DUCHESS [drawing him aside]. Oh, and do stop calling me
"Duchess." It was different when you were only my
nephew's patient.

GASTON. Right.

DUCHESS. Go along. And don't peep through the keyhole!

GASTON [as he goes]. I can wait. I've already seen three hundred and eighty-seven of them.   [He goes out.

DUCHESS. Delightful boy! Ah, Huspar, when I think that
Dr. Bonfant used to put him to planting cabbages, I
shudder from top to toe. [To the BUTLER.] You may show
in your master and mistress, my good fellow. [She takes
HUSPAR's arm.] Oh, my dear Huspar, I'm so terribly
wrought up! I feel as if I'm embarking on a pitiless struggle against fate, against death, against all the dark forces
in the world. I came in black, I thought the occasion
called for it.

The three RENAUDS *come in. They are upper middle class
and clearly rich.*

MADAME RENAUD [in the doorway]. You see! I told you! He
isn't here.

HUSPAR. We just asked him to leave the room for a moment.

GEORGES. Let me introduce myself. I'm Georges Renaud.
[Introducing the two ladies who came in with him.] My
mother. And my wife.

HUSPAR [bowing]. Lucien Huspar. I am the patient's solicitor. [Indicating the DUCHESS.] Madame la Duchesse Dupont-Dufort, president of various charitable bodies con-
nected with the mental home at Pont-au-Bronc. The
Duchess very kindly consented to accompany the patient
here, in the absence of her nephew, Dr. Jibelin, who is
detained at the hospital.

They exchange bows.

DUCHESS. Yes, I have allied myself, as far as my feeble
strength allows, to my nephew's good work. He has put
such enthusiasm, such burning faith, into the task at
hand!

MADAME RENAUD. We will always be deeply grateful for

the way he's taken care of our darling Jacques. It would have given me great joy to tell him so personally.

DUCHESS. Thank you.

MADAME RENAUD. Oh, but do sit down, won't you? Please forgive me—this is such a moving moment. . . .

DUCHESS. I do feel for you, believe me.

MADAME RENAUD. You can imagine how impatient we are to see him. It's two whole years since we first saw him at the asylum.

GEORGES. And despite repeated applications, we haven't set eyes on him since.

HUSPAR. There were so many similar cases. You must bear in mind that there are four hundred thousand men listed as missing in France alone. Four hundred thousand families, and very few of them have given up hope, believe me.

MADAME RENAUD. Yes, but two years! And if you knew in what conditions they showed him to us! I'm sure you aren't to blame, nor your nephew either, since he wasn't in charge of the asylum then. But the patient swept past us in a great crush of people—we couldn't even get near him! There were over forty people there.

DUCHESS. Those identification parties of Dr. Bonfant's were a downright scandal.

MADAME RENAUD. They certainly were! Of course, we didn't give up. My son had to get back to his business. But we took rooms in a nearby hotel, my daughter-in-law and I, in the hope that we might get in to see him again. After repeated bribes, an attendant let us see him alone for a few minutes—without any results, I'm afraid. Another time, my daughter-in-law contrived to take the place of a sewing woman who was ill. She saw him on and off for a whole afternoon, but they weren't alone, so she couldn't say anything to him.

DUCHESS [to VALENTINE]. How very romantic! But suppose they'd unmasked you? I hope you can sew!

VALENTINE. Yes.

DUCHESS. And you didn't manage to be alone with him at all?

VALENTINE. No, not for a second.

DUCHESS. Ah, that Dr. Bonfant has a lot to answer for!

GEORGES. But why, seeing the amount of proof we've given you, were any other families even considered? That's what I can't understand.

HUSPAR. Yes, it seems extraordinary, I know. But do you realize that after our last cross-check, which was extremely thorough, there still remain five families—apart from yourselves—with more or less equal chances?

MADAME RENAUD. Five! But there can't be!

HUSPAR. I'm afraid there are.

DUCHESS [*consulting her list*]. The families Bougran, Brigaud, Grigou, Legropâtre, and Madensale. But I want you to know that I insisted we should see you first, because I like you so very much.

MADAME RENAUD. Thank you, that's very kind.

DUCHESS. No, no, don't thank me! I mean it. From the very first, your letter gave me the impression that you were charming people, and meeting you confirms that in every way. After you, Lord knows what kind of people we're going to stumble on! There's a milkman, a lamplighter——

MADAME RENAUD. A lamplighter?

DUCHESS. A lamplighter, yes, madame, a lamplighter! We live in impossible times! These people all have ideas far beyond their station. But they won't give Gaston to a lamplighter, not while I'm alive they won't!

HUSPAR [*to* GEORGES]. Yes, you see, we had announced that claimants would be visited in alphabetical order—which was logical enough—but as that would have made you the last, her Ladyship insisted, a little unwisely perhaps, that we should waive the rules and come and see you first.

MADAME RENAUD. Why unwisely? Those in charge of the patient are entitled to please themselves, I should have thought!

HUSPAR. Possibly. But you have no idea what a hornet's nest of feeling—often mercenary, alas—Gaston has stirred up. His pension as a wounded serviceman, which he has never been able to draw, comes to quite a tidy sum, you know. Arrears and compound interest amount today to more than two hundred and fifty thousand francs.

MADAME RENAUD. How can money enter into a situation as tragic as this?

HUSPAR. It does, unfortunately. And while we're on the subject, I'd like to say a word or two on the patient's legal position.

MADAME RENAUD. Later, Monsieur Huspar, later, if you wouldn't mind.

DUCHESS. Monsieur Huspar has a lawbook where his heart should be. But he's a dear fellow [*She pinches him.*] so he's going to fetch Gaston for us right away, aren't you, Huspar?

HUSPAR [*bowing to superior force*]. Very well, ladies. But I must ask you not to get too emotional. Don't rush at him the moment he appears. He's been through that sort of thing so many times, it puts him in a most distressing nervous state.   [*He goes out.*

DUCHESS. You must be terribly anxious to see him again.

MADAME RENAUD. A mother could hardly feel otherwise, surely.

DUCHESS. I'm quite overcome myself, in sympathy! [*To* VALENTINE.] You knew our patient too, madame—at least, the man you believe our patient to be?

VALENTINE. Yes, of course. I told you, I went to the asylum.

DUCHESS. So you did! What a featherbrain I am!

MADAME RENAUD. Georges, my elder son, married Valentine when she was very young. She and Jacques were great friends. They were devoted to each other, weren't they, Georges?

GEORGES [*shortly*]. Very.

DUCHESS. Yes, a brother's wife is almost a sister, isn't she?

VALENTINE [*oddly*]. Quite.

DUCHESS. You must be insanely happy at the thought of seeing him again.

VALENTINE, *ill at ease, looks at* GEORGES.

GEORGES. Very happy indeed. As a sister.

DUCHESS. I'm such a romantic soul! Do you know, I always dreamed that a woman he'd been passionately in love with would be there to recognize him and give him a lover's kiss—his first kiss on emerging from that sepulcher! I see it isn't to be.

GEORGES [*shortly*]. No, I'm afraid not.

DUCHESS. So much for my dream! [*She goes to the window.*] Monsieur Huspar is taking a long time. Your grounds are very big, and he's rather nearsighted. I expect he's got lost.

VALENTINE [*aside to* GEORGES]. Why are you looking at me like that? You aren't going to rake all that up again?

GEORGES [*gravely*]. I put it out of my mind when I forgave
you.

VALENTINE. Then don't look daggers at me each time that
old lunatic opens her mouth.

MADAME RENAUD [*who has heard none of this and apparently knows nothing*]. Darling Valentine. Look, Georges,
she's quite upset. It's nice to think she remembers our
little Jacques so kindly, isn't it, Georges?

GEORGES. Yes, Mother.

DUCHESS. Here he comes!

Enter HUSPAR alone.

DUCHESS. I knew it! You couldn't find him?

HUSPAR. Yes, I did, but I didn't like to disturb him.

DUCHESS. What do you mean? What was he doing?

HUSPAR. Standing in front of a statue.

VALENTINE [*with a cry*]. A hunting goddess, with a circular
stone seat, at the far end of the garden?

HUSPAR. Yes. Look, you can see it from here.

They all look.

GEORGES [*abruptly*]. Well, what does that prove?

DUCHESS [*to HUSPAR*]. My dear, isn't this exciting!

VALENTINE [*softly*]. I don't know. I seem to remember he
was very fond of that statue, that seat.

DUCHESS [*to HUSPAR*]. We're getting warmer and warmer!

MADAME RENAUD. You surprise me, Valentine dear. That
corner of the garden used to be part of the Dubantons'
property. True, we'd already bought it in Jacques' day, but
we didn't knock the wall down until after the war.

VALENTINE [*flushing*]. I don't know, yes, I expect you're
right. . . .

HUSPAR. He looked so odd standing there, by that statue,
I didn't dare interrupt him before I'd inquired whether
this might have some special significance. Apparently it
doesn't, so I'll go and fetch him.   [*He goes out.*

GEORGES [*quietly, to VALENTINE*]. Is that where you used to
meet? On that seat?

VALENTINE. I don't know what you mean.

DUCHESS [*to MME. RENAUD*]. I'm sure you're feeling very
wrought up—and who can blame you?—but I must ask
you to keep absolutely calm.

MADAME RENAUD. You can rely on me.

HUSPAR *comes in with* GASTON.

MADAME RENAUD [*murmuring*]. Yes, it's he, it's Jacques. . . .

The DUCHESS *goes to* GASTON *with a sweeping dramatic gesture and screens the others from him.*

DUCHESS. Gaston, try not to think, let yourself go, don't make any effort at all. Now look carefully at all these faces. . . .

Silence. They all stand there motionless. GASTON *comes to* GEORGES, *looks at him, then passes on to* MADAME RENAUD. *Before* VALENTINE, *he stops for a second. She murmurs, barely audibly:*

VALENTINE. My darling . . .

He looks at her, surprised; then he passes her, goes back to the DUCHESS, *and spreads his arms in a helpless gesture of regret.*

GASTON [*kindly*]. I'm very sorry. . . .

Curtain.

SCENE II

A big ornate double door, closed. The RENAUDS' *servants are grouped around it, whispering. The* COOK *is bent double at the keyhole. The others crowd around her.*

COOK. Wait, wait! They're all staring at him like a monkey in the zoo. The poor boy doesn't know where to put himself.

CHAUFFEUR. Let's have a look.

COOK. Wait a minute! He just jumped up off his chair. Knocked his cup over too. Had enough of their questions by the look of it. Master Georges is taking him over to the window. He's holding his arm, very kindly, just as if nothing had happened. . . .

CHAUFFEUR. Well, I'll be——

JULIETTE. My word, you should have heard him when he found their letters after the war! He looks mild as a lamb, does Master Georges, but the sparks flew then, I can tell you!

VALET. And I'll tell *you* something. He was right.

JULIETTE [*furiously*]. What? Right, was he? Saying nasty things about the dead—is that right? Do you think it's a decent thing to do—picking quarrels with the dead?

VALET. The dead had no call stealing other men's wives in the first place.

JULIETTE. Oh, you and your wife-stealing! You haven't stopped bleating about it ever since we got married! It's not the dead who do you wrong, much good they'd be at it, poor things. It's the living. And the dead have nothing to do with the carryings-on of the living.

VALET. Very convenient, that is! You mess around with someone's wife and flip-flip, out of sight, out of mind, and everything's lovely. All you have to be is dead.

JULIETTE. It's no fun being dead, you know!

VALET. Being a cuckold's no fun either!

JULIETTE. On and on and on! It'll happen to you one of these days the way you keep harping on it.

The CHAUFFEUR *tries to push the* COOK *aside.*

COOK. Wait, wait! They're all going over to the bookcase. They're showing him some photographs. [*She gives him her place.*] With the old-style keyholes you could see something. But these new-fangled things . . . Eyestrain, that's all they're good for.

CHAUFFEUR [*peering through the keyhole*]. It's him! It's him! The bastard. I'd know his ugly little snout anywhere!

JULIETTE. Here! What do you want to say that for? You shut your own ugly snout.

VALET. Why are you sticking up for him?

JULIETTE. I liked him, he was nice, was Master Jacques. And what do you know about him, anyway? You never knew him. I liked him a lot.

VALET. Well, what of it? He was your master. You cleaned his boots for him.

JULIETTE. What's that got to do with it? I liked him.

VALET. Huh! Like his brother, I'll bet. A first-class swine.

The CHAUFFEUR *gives up his place to* JULIETTE.

CHAUFFEUR. Worse, man, worse! God, the times he's kept me hanging about till four in the morning outside night clubs. And then, at dawn, when you were frozen stiff, out he'd come, red in the face and stinking of drink from five yards off, and he'd throw up all over the back seat—the pig!

COOK. You can say that again. The times I've stuck my hands into it, as true as I stand here! And all of eighteen years old!

CHAUFFEUR. And the abuse you'd get! Language as made *me* blush, even!

COOK. And a brute with it! Do you remember, there was a little potboy in the kitchens then. Gave him a kick or a clout whenever he saw him, poor little devil.

CHAUFFEUR. And for no reason, too. A regular little thug, that's what he was. And when we heard he'd caught it, back in 1918—we're no worse-natured than most—but we all drank to it, remember?—and said serve him right.

BUTLER. Come along now, that's enough. Back to work.

CHAUFFEUR. What? Don't tell me you don't think the same as us, Monsieur Jules?

BUTLER. I could tell you a thing or two, don't you worry! I've heard their scenes at table. I was there when he raised his hand to his mother! What about that?

COOK. His own mother! A boy of eighteen!

BUTLER. And as for his bits of nonsense with Madame Valentine, they're known to me, I may say, in every detail.

CHAUFFEUR. Well! Very good of you to have shut your eyes to it, Monsieur Jules, if I may say so.

BUTLER. Abovestairs is abovestairs, my lad. That's their affair.

CHAUFFEUR. Yes, but with a little villain, like him . . . Here, let's have another look at him.

JULIETTE [*moving away for him*]. It is him, I'm sure it is! Master Jacques. . . . He was a lovely-looking boy, you know, in those days. Really handsome. And so genteel.

VALET. Oh, shut up about him, girl. There's a heap of handsome fellows besides him, and younger too.

JULIETTE. That's true. Twenty years nearly. It's a long time. Do you think he'll think I've changed a lot?

VALET. What's it to you if he does?

JULIETTE. Oh, nothing. . . .

The VALET *thinks a minute, while the others make faces behind his back.*

VALET. Here . . . why have you been mooning about the place ever since you heard he might come back?

JULIETTE. Me?

The others giggle.

VALET. Why do you keep looking at yourself in the mirror and asking if you've changed?

JULIETTE. What—me?

VALET. How old were you when he went to the front?

JULIETTE. Fifteen.

VALET. The postman, was he your first?

JULIETTE. You know he was! He gagged me and gave me a sleeping pill—I told you!

VALET. You're sure he *was* your first?

JULIETTE. What a thing to ask! It's not something a girl forgets! He flung his sack down in the kitchen, the brute, and all his letters fell out onto the floor!

CHAUFFEUR [*still at the keyhole*]. Look at that Valentine; she can't take her eyes off him. If he stays here, old Georges will sprout another pair of horns, I'll bet you anything you like!

The BUTLER takes his place at the keyhole.

BUTLER. Disgusting, that's what it is.

CHAUFFEUR. Perhaps he likes it that way, Monsieur Jules!

They all snicker.

VALET. They make me laugh, with their "amnesia." If they were his real family, he'd have recognized them by now, it stands to reason. He's been here all day. Amnesia nothing. Eyewash, the lot of it.

COOK. I don't know so much. As God is my judge, there are times when I can't even remember if I've put salt in my sauces.

VALET. Yes, but—a family!

COOK [*shrugging*]. For all the interest he took in them. Little gallivanter!

BUTLER [*at the keyhole*]. It's him all right, though. I'll bet my head on it.

COOK. Yes, but they say there are five other families besides! And all with the same amount of things to prove it.

CHAUFFEUR. I'll tell you my opinion if you want to know.

There's no sense even hoping that little swine isn't dead, not for our sakes, not for anybody's, and that's a fact.

COOK. You're right!

JULIETTE [*witheringly*]. Oh, it's lovely being dead—you should try it!

BUTLER. Nor for his sake either, if you ask me. He's better off dead. Start off life the way he did and you come to no good anyway.

CHAUFFEUR. Besides, what if he's got attached to his quiet life in the asylum? Look at the pile of things he'll have to know about. That trouble with the Grandchamps boy, the Valentine business, that to-do over the five hundred thousand francs—and a whole lot more that we don't know about.

BUTLER. You're right. I'd rather be in my shoes than his.

VALET [*looking through the keyhole*]. Look out, they're getting up. They'll be coming out in a minute.

The servants scatter.

JULIETTE [*dreamily, as she goes*]. That Master Jacques, though . . .

VALET [*suspiciously, as he follows her out*]. Master Jacques what? What about him?

JULIETTE. Oh, nothing.

They have gone out.

Curtain.

ACT TWO

SCENE I

Jacques Renaud's room and the long, ill-lit corridors of the old mansion which lead into it. On the opposite side, a paved hallway and a big stone staircase, with a wrought-iron handrail leading down from it. MADAME RENAUD, GEORGES, and GASTON appear at the top of the stairs and cross the hall.

MADAME RENAUD. Excuse me, I'll lead the way. Now this, you see, is the passage you used to walk through to your room. [*She opens the door.*] And this is your room. [*They all three go inside.*] Oh really, how careless! I particularly said to open the shutters!

She opens them. Light floods into the room. It is furnished in the elaborate style of 1910.

GASTON [*looking around him*]. My room.

MADAME RENAUD. You wanted it decorated and to your own plan. You had such advanced ideas!

GASTON. Apparently I was fond of morning-glories and buttercups to the exclusion of everything else.

GEORGES. Yes, very bold you were in your tastes!

GASTON. So I see. [*He notices an absurd-looking piece of furniture.*] What's that? A tree in a thunderstorm?

GEORGES. It's a music stand.

GASTON. Was I a musician?

MADAME RENAUD. We wanted you to learn the violin, but you just wouldn't. You flew into insane rages if we tried to make you practice. You kicked all your instruments to pieces. Only that music stand survived.

GASTON [*smiling*]. Very silly of it. [*He goes to look at a portrait.*] Is that him?

MADAME RENAUD. Yes, that's you, when you were twelve.

GASTON. I always pictured myself as shy and fair.

143

GEORGES. You had dark hair, almost black. You used to kick a ball around all day, you smashed everything to bits.

MADAME RENAUD [*showing him a big trunk*]. Look what I had brought down from the attic.

GASTON. What's that—my old trunk? You're beginning to make me think I lived in the Second Empire!

MADAME RENAUD. No, silly! It's your Uncle Gustave's trunk and it's full of your toys.

GASTON [*opening the trunk*]. My toys! Did *I* have toys too? Yes, of course I must have. . . . I'd forgotten about the toys.

MADAME RENAUD. Look. Your slingshot.

GASTON. A slingshot. It looks as if it meant business, too.

MADAME RENAUD. My God, the birds you killed with that thing! A real fiend, you were. And you weren't content with the birds in the garden either. I had an aviary full of prize songbirds. One day you went into it and slaughtered them all.

GASTON. Birds? Little birds?

MADAME RENAUD. Yes.

GASTON. How old was I?

MADAME RENAUD. Seven—nine perhaps.

GASTON [*shaking his head*]. That wasn't me.

MADAME RENAUD. Yes, it was, it was!

GASTON. No. At seven I'd go into the garden with bread crumbs and coax the sparrows to peck out of my hand.

GEORGES. What? You'd have wrung their necks, poor things!

MADAME RENAUD. Yes, look at that dog whose paw he broke with a stone!

GEORGES. And the mouse he led about on the end of a string.

MADAME RENAUD. And the squirrels, later on, and the ferrets and the weasels. The amount of little creatures you killed! You'd stuff the best specimens. There's a whole collection of them upstairs. I must have them brought down. [*She rummages in the trunk.*] Here are your knives, your first shotguns . . .

GASTON [*searching too*]. Are there no Teddy bears, no Noah's arks?

MADAME RENAUD. Even as a tiny boy, all you ever wanted

were scientific toys. Look, your gyroscopes, your test tubes, your magnets, your mechanical crane.

GEORGES. We wanted to turn you into a brilliant engineer.

GASTON [*spluttering with laughter*]. Me?

MADAME RENAUD. But the things you liked best of all were your geography books. You were always top of your class in geography.

GEORGES. At ten years old you could place any city in the world on the map blindfolded.

GASTON. Blindfolded. . . . True, I've lost any memory I had. . . . But I tried to learn the capitals of Europe again in the asylum. Well, even with my eyes open . . . Let's shut this treasure chest. I doubt if it will teach us anything. I don't see myself like that as a child at all. [*He shuts the trunk, wanders around the room, touches various objects, sits in the chairs. Then he asks suddenly.*] Did he have a friend, that little boy? Another boy who went everywhere with him, who shared his secrets and his stamp collection?

MADAME RENAUD [*volubly*]. Of course, of course! You had dozens of playmates. All the boys at school, and then at college, why——

GASTON. Yes, but . . . not playmates. A friend. . . . You see, before I ask you who my women were——

MADAME RENAUD [*shocked*]. Oh, but, Jacques, you were so young when you went away!

GASTON [*smiling*]. I'll ask about them just the same. . . . But before I do, it seems to me far more urgent to ask who was my friend.

MADAME RENAUD. Why, you can see them all in the school photographs. I'll show them to you. Then, later, there were the boys you went out with in the evenings.

GASTON. But the boy I liked going out with most, the one I told everything to?

MADAME RENAUD [*hastily, with a quick glance at* GEORGES]. There wasn't any one boy you preferred, not really.

GASTON [*looking at her*]. Your son didn't have a best friend, then? Pity. I mean it's a pity if we find out that I was he. I don't think there's anything more comforting for a grown man than seeing the reflection of one's childhood in the eyes of another grown-up little boy. It's a pity. I'd even hoped, you see, that this imaginary friend would give me back my memory—as a good turn, the way friends do.

GEORGES [*after a slight hesitation*]. Well, you did have a friend, yes. One you were very fond of. You even stayed friends until you were seventeen. . . . We didn't want to mention it, it was such a painful business. . . .

GASTON. Did he die?

GEORGES. No, no. He didn't die, but you stopped seeing each other, you fell out—for good.

GASTON. For good? At seventeen? [*A pause.*] Did you ever know why?

GEORGES. Vaguely. . . .

GASTON. And neither your brother nor that other boy ever tried to make it up?

MADAME RENAUD. There was the war, remember. Besides . . . Well, I'll tell you. You quarreled over some futile thing or other. You had a fight, as boys do at that age. And—without meaning to, I'm sure—you . . . did something violent, something—unfortunate, let's say. You pushed him down some stairs. His spine was injured. He was in plaster for a long time, and he's been a cripple ever since. Now you can see how awkward, how painful, it would have been if you'd attempted to see him again.

A pause.

GASTON. I see. And where did we have this fight? At school? At his house?

MADAME RENAUD [*quickly*]. No, here. But let's not talk about it, it's too dreadful. That's one of the things you'd do best not to remember, Jacques.

GASTON. If I remember one thing, I'll have to remember them all, you know that. A past comes wholesale, not by the piece. Where are those stairs? I'd like to see them.

MADAME RENAUD. There. Just outside your room. But what's the point, Jacques?

GASTON [*to* GEORGES]. Will you show me?

GEORGES. If you like, but I really don't see why you should want to see that spot again. . . .

They go out into the hall.

MADAME RENAUD. There.

GASTON *looks around, then leans over the handrail.*

GASTON. Whereabouts were we fighting?

GEORGES. Oh, we never knew exactly. One of the maids told
us about it afterward. She saw the whole thing.

GASTON. It's not an everyday occurrence. I imagine she
described it in considerable detail. Where were we fighting? This landing is so wide. . . .

MADAME RENAUD. Right on the edge, I should imagine. He
must have lost his footing. Who knows, you may not
have pushed him even!

GASTON [going back to her]. If that's the case, if it was just
an accident, then why didn't I sit with him every evening
in his room? Give up my Saturdays to keep him company,
instead of going out into the sunshine, so he wouldn't
feel the unfairness of it all too much? Why?

GEORGES. Everybody gave a different version of it, you know.
. . . And then, local gossip made things worse, as you
can imagine. . . .

GASTON. Which maid was it who saw us?

MADAME RENAUD. What's the use of your knowing that?
Anyway, she isn't with us any more.

GASTON. There must be other servants in the house who
were here at the time. I'll ask them.

MADAME RENAUD. I trust you won't listen to backstairs
gossip. They'll tell you some tales, you may be sure, if
you start questioning the servants! You know what that
class is like!

GASTON [turning to GEORGES]. You must know how I feel.
So far I haven't recognized one single thing in your house.
What you've told me about my brother's boyhood seems
about as remote from my own temperament as it could
possibly be. But—perhaps because I'm tired, or perhaps
it's something else—I feel, for the first time, a strange
stirring inside me as I listen to people telling me about
their child.

MADAME RENAUD. There! Oh, darling Jacques, I knew it!
I knew——

GASTON. No! Don't be affectionate. Don't call me "darling
Jacques" too soon. We're investigating a case, like the
police, as toughly—as callously, if possible—as the police.
This contact with a total stranger, whom I may have to
accept in a minute as a part of me, this uncanny betrothal with a ghost—all that's painful enough without
having you to struggle with on top of it. I'll bow to all the
evidence, I'll listen to all the anecdotes, but something

tells me that before anything else, I must know the truth about that fight. The truth, however cruel.

MADAME RENAUD [*hesitantly*]. Well now . . . you came to blows over some stupid little thing—you know how quick-tempered one is at that age——

GASTON [*interrupting*]. No, not you. That servant *is* still here, isn't she? You were lying just now?

A *pause*.

GEORGES [*shortly*]. Yes. She's still here.

GASTON. Send for her, please. Why temporize? You know I'll find her anyway.

GEORGES. It's too stupid—stupid and horrible.

GASTON. I'm not here to learn something pleasant. And, anyway, suppose that's the one episode that brings my memory back? You've no right to keep it from me.

GEORGES. All right, if you insist, I'll call her. [*He rings the bell.*]

MADAME RENAUD. Why, Jacques, you're trembling! I hope you're not going to become ill.

GASTON. Am I trembling?

MADAME RENAUD. Perhaps there's a glimmer of light inside you now—is there?

GASTON. No. Darkness. The darkest night.

MADAME RENAUD. Then why are you trembling?

GASTON. It's silly. But of all the thousands of memories there could have been, it was the memory of a friend I yearned for most. I've built a whole edifice on that imaginary friend. Our long walks, the books we read together, the girl we both loved and I gave up for his sake, and even—you'll laugh at this—the time I saved his life on a sailing trip. So you see, if I really am your son, I shall have to get used to a reality so very different from that dream. . . .

JULIETTE *comes in.*

JULIETTE. You rang, madame?

MADAME RENAUD. Master Jacques would like to speak to you, Juliette.

JULIETTE. To me?

GEORGES. Yes. He wants to ask you about that unfortunate accident of Marcel Grandchamps'.

MADAME RENAUD. You know the truth, my dear. Master

Jacques may have been a violent boy, but you know he could never have done anything deliberately evil.

GASTON [*interrupting again*]. Don't say anything to her, please. Where were you, mademoiselle, when the accident happened?

JULIETTE. On the landing, with the two young gentlemen, Master Jacques.

GASTON. Don't call me "Master Jacques" yet. How did the quarrel begin?

JULIETTE [*with a glance at the* RENAUDS]. Well . . .

GASTON [*going over to them*]. Would you mind letting me speak to her alone? I feel you're embarrassing her.

MADAME RENAUD. I'll do anything you want if only you'll come back to us, Jacques.

GASTON [*seeing them out*]. I'll call you. [*They both go.* GASTON *turns to* JULIETTE.] Sit down, won't you?

JULIETTE [*flustered*]. May I?

GASTON. How old are you?

JULIETTE. Thirty-three. You know I am, Master Jacques; I was fifteen when you went to the front. So why ask?

GASTON. In the first place, because I didn't know. In the second place, I tell you I may not be Master Jacques at all.

JULIETTE. Oh yes, you are. I'd recognize you anywhere, Master Jacques.

GASTON. Did you know him well?

JULIETTE [*bursting into tears*]. You can't have forgotten *everything!* Don't you remember anything at all, Master Jacques?

GASTON. Absolutely nothing.

JULIETTE [*wailing*]. Asking me a thing like that after what happened! Torture it is, torture for a woman!

GASTON [*dazed for a second, then suddenly realizing*]. Oh . . . Oh, I see. I'm sorry. So then, Master Jacques was . . .

JULIETTE [*sniffing*]. Yes.

GASTON. I'm very sorry. . . . And you were how old?

JULIETTE. Fifteen. He was my first.

GASTON [*smiling suddenly, all tension gone*]. Fifteen and he was seventeen. . . . Why, that's a very sweet story. It's the first thing I've heard about him that strikes me as a little endearing. And how long did it last?

JULIETTE. Until he went away.

GASTON. And I tried so hard to guess what his sweetheart looked like. Why, she was charming.

JULIETTE. Charming she may have been, but she wasn't the only one, don't think it!

GASTON [still smiling]. Oh, really?

JULIETTE. I should say not!

GASTON. Well, that isn't so dislikable either.

JULIETTE. I suppose you think it's funny! But you must admit, for a woman, it's——

GASTON. Yes, of course, for a woman . . .

JULIETTE. It's agony for a woman, I can tell you, bearing the cruel pangs of thwarted love!

GASTON [blinking]. The cruel pangs of . . . Yes, I suppose it is. . . .

JULIETTE. I was only a worthless little kitchenmaid, but that didn't stop me draining the bitter cup of sorrow to the dregs.

GASTON. Bitter cup of . . . er—yes. . . .

JULIETTE. Haven't you ever read *Ravished on her Wedding Night?*

GASTON. No.

JULIETTE. Oh, you should. There's a situation almost exactly like ours in it. Bertrande's dastardly seducer goes away too—to America actually, to his millionaire uncle. And that's when she tells him—Bertrande does—that she's drained the bitter cup of sorrow to the dregs.

GASTON. Oh, I see! It's something out of the book!

JULIETTE. Yes, but it applied so terribly well to me!

GASTON. Yes, of course. . . . [He rises abruptly and asks.] And he loved you very much did he—Master Jacques?

JULIETTE. Passionately. Well, I'll tell you, he used to say he'd kill himself for my sake.

GASTON. How did you come to be his mistress?

JULIETTE. Oh, it was my second day in this place. I was doing his room, and he pushed me onto the bed. I was laughing like a mad thing. Well, can you wonder, at that age! It all happened in spite of myself, as you might say. But afterward he swore he'd love me all his life.

GASTON [looking at her with a smile]. Funny Master Jacques.

JULIETTE. Why funny?

GASTON. No reason. Anyway, if I become Master Jacques,

I promise I'll talk this whole situation over with you very seriously.

JULIETTE. Oh, I'm not asking for any sort of amends, you know. I'm married now.

GASTON. Even so, even so . . . [*A pause.*] But I'm playing truant, I'll never pass my exams this way. Let's get back to that fight—that whole horrible story I'd give anything in the world not to have to know.

JULIETTE. Oh yes, the fight with Master Marcel.

GASTON. Yes. You were there?

JULIETTE [*proudly*]. Of course I was there!

GASTON. You saw the quarrel right from the start?

JULIETTE. I certainly did!

GASTON. Then perhaps you can tell me what unlikely nonsense they were fighting about so savagely?

JULIETTE [*calmly*]. What do you mean, unlikely nonsense? They were fighting over me.

GASTON. Over you?

JULIETTE. Of course it was over me. What's so surprising about that?

GASTON [*reiterating, stunned*]. Over you!

JULIETTE. Yes, I tell you! You see, I was Master Jacques' girl—I'm telling you this because you've got to know, but don't go blurting it out, will you? I don't fancy losing my place over something that happened twenty years ago. Yes, I was Master Jacques' mistress and—I may as well admit it—Master Marcel used to run after me a bit, too.

GASTON. And?

JULIETTE. Well, one day he tried to kiss me in the passage. Of course, I didn't let him, but you know what a man's like when he's got that sort of thing in mind. Just at that moment Master Jacques came out of his room and saw us. He made a grab at Master Marcel, and Master Marcel hit back. They started fighting, then they both went down and rolled around on the floor.

GASTON. Where were they?

JULIETTE. On the first-floor landing. Just outside this room.

GASTON [*with a sudden mad cry*]. Where? Where? Where? Show me! Come and show me! I want to see the exact spot! [*He drags her out by the wrist into the hall.*]

JULIETTE. You're hurting me!

GASTON. Where? Where?

JULIETTE [*snatching her wrist away and rubbing it*]. Here,
I tell you! They fell just here, half in the hallway and
half on the landing. Master Marcel was underneath.

GASTON [*shouting*]. But they weren't anywhere near the
edge! How could he possibly fall down the stairs? Did
they both roll over as they were fighting?

JULIETTE. No. Master Jacques managed to get to his feet
and he took hold of Master Marcel's leg and dragged him
over to the stairs.

GASTON. And then?

JULIETTE. Then he pushed him over! And he shouted,
"There, you little swine, that'll teach you to mess around
with someone else's girl!" [*A pause.*] Oh, he was quite a
lad, was Master Jacques.

GASTON [*dully*]. And he was his best friend.

JULIETTE. I should say so! They'd been going to school together ever since they were six years old.

GASTON. Since they were six years old . . .

JULIETTE. Yes, it was a frightful thing, I know. But there!
Love conquers all!

GASTON [*looking at her and murmuring*]. Love, yes, of
course, love . . . Thank you, mademoiselle.

GEORGES *knocks on Jacques' far door, opens it, and seeing
the room empty, goes out into the hall.*

GEORGES. Excuse my coming back. You didn't call us.
Mother was getting anxious. Well, did you find out what
you wanted to know?

GASTON. Yes. Thank you. I found out what I wanted to
know.

JULIETTE *has gone out.*

GEORGES. I know, it isn't a pretty story, is it? But no matter
what anybody said, I'm still convinced it was an accident,
basically . . . and you were only seventeen, one mustn't
forget that. . . . A prank, that's all it was—a sinister
prank. [*A pause. He looks uneasy.*] How did she describe
it?

GASTON. Just as she saw it, I imagine.

GEORGES. She told you it was over your rowing club
championships, did she? You were in rival crews—and
keen sportsmen, both of you—well, it's understandable,
you . . . [GASTON *says nothing.*] Anyway, that's the
version I chose to accept. Of course the Grandchamps

family spread a different tale, but I for one have always refused to believe it. Don't try to find out; it was stupid and foul.

GASTON [*looking at him*]. Were you fond of him?

GEORGES. He was my brother. In spite of everything. Because there was a great deal more besides that. Oh, you were terrible.

GASTON. So long as I still can, I shall ask you to say, "He was terrible."

GEORGES [*with a wan smile as he thinks back*]. Terrible. . . . You caused us a lot of worry, I can tell you. If you do come back to us, I'm afraid there's a lot more you'll have to know about, things worse even than that wretched fight. At least you can keep the benefit of the doubt about that.

GASTON. So there's still more I have to know.

GEORGES. Well, what can you expect? You were a child. A boy left to his own devices in a disrupted world. Mother, with her rigid principles, pitted herself against you in her clumsy way without achieving anything— except to drive you farther back into yourself. I didn't have enough authority. . . . You did one very silly thing, among others—something that cost us a great deal. . . . Well, we older ones were all away at the front. Youngsters of your age did as they liked. . . . You tried to set up a company. Now, whether you ever believed in the scheme, or whether you used it as a pretext for reasons of your own, I don't know. Only you can tell us that, if you ever get your memory back. The fact remains that you bewitched an old woman, a friend of the family—and "bewitched" is the word—into giving you a large sum of money. Nearly five hundred thousand francs. You were the so-called go-between. You had some letterheads printed, of some fictitious place of business, you signed fake receipts, and so on. . . . One day the whole thing came out. But it was too late. There were only a few thousand francs left. You'd spent the rest in bars and night spots, with women and odd drinking friends. . . . We paid her back, naturally.

GASTON. Your delight at the prospect of your brother's homecoming is positively saintlike.

GEORGES [*avoiding his eyes*]. More so than you think, Jacques.

GASTON. What? Is there more to come?

GEORGES. We'll talk about it some other time.

GASTON. Why not now?

GEORGES. Better not, I think. I'll call Mother. She must be getting anxious.

GASTON [stopping him]. You can tell me. I'm almost sure I'm not your brother.

GEORGES looks at him for a moment in silence. Then he says dully:

GEORGES. You look very like him. . . . It's the same face, only as if a kind of storm had swept across it.

GASTON [smiling]. Eighteen years . . . Yours too, no doubt, although I was never privileged to see it without lines.

GEORGES. It isn't only the lines. It's a worn look you have. A wearing away. But one that instead of furrowing your face and hardening it, has, as it were, softened it and rubbed it smooth. It's as if a turmoil of kindness and good will had swept across your face.

GASTON. Yes, I can see there's every chance that your esteemed brother's face wasn't particularly stamped with kindness.

GEORGES. No, no, you're wrong about him. He was hard, yes—and frivolous and irresponsible. But . . . I cared for him a lot, with all his faults. He was better-looking than I was. Not cleverer perhaps—the cleverness you need at school or in business—but more sensitive, more brilliant definitely. . . . [He adds heavily.] More . . . attractive. He was fond of me too, you know, in his own way. He even had—as he grew out of childhood, anyway —a sort of grateful tenderness that touched me very much. That's why it was so hard when I found out. [He hangs his head as if he were in the wrong.] I hated him then, yes, I hated him. And then, very quickly, I just couldn't go on holding it against him.

GASTON. But for what?

GEORGES lifts his head and looks at him.

GEORGES. Are you Jacques? [GASTON moves his hand in a gesture of helplessness.] I keep telling myself he was young, and weak underneath like all violent people. . . . I keep telling myself it's all too easy for a handsome pair of lips on a summer's night when you're about to leave

for the front. I keep telling myself that I was miles away,
that she was only a little girl herself. . . . But . . .

GASTON. I don't follow, quite. He stole a girl from you?
[*A pause.*] Your wife? [GEORGES *nods dumbly.* GASTON
says tonelessly.] The bastard.

GEORGES [*with a rueful little smile*]. It may be you.

A pause.

GASTON [*hoarsely*]. Georges—that is your name, isn't it?

GEORGES. Yes.

GASTON *looks at him a moment, then makes an awkward
gesture of affection.*

GASTON. Georges . . .

MADAME RENAUD *comes into the hall.*

MADAME RENAUD. Are you there, Georges?

GEORGES [*gruffly, ashamed of his emotion*]. Excuse me, will
you?   [*He goes out quickly.*

MADAME RENAUD *comes into the room.*

MADAME RENAUD. Jacques?

GASTON [*motionless*]. Yes.

MADAME RENAUD. Guess who's just arrived? The effrontery
of it!

GASTON [*wearily*]. I can't remember anything as it is. So as
for guessing games . . .

MADAME RENAUD. Aunt Louise, my dear! Aunt Louise!

GASTON. Aunt Louise? And that's effrontery, is it?

MADAME RENAUD. I should think so indeed! After what
happened! I hope you'll do me the favor of refusing to
speak to her if she ever tries to see you behind our backs.
She behaved in a way that . . . ! Not that you ever liked
her anyway. My word, if there's someone in the family
you really loathed, my dear, and with good reason, it was
your cousin Jules.

GASTON [*still motionless*]. So I have a genuine loathing for
someone and I didn't know it?

MADAME RENAUD. What—for Jules? Why, don't you know
what he did to you, the little wretch? He gave you away
to the Board of Examiners for having some logarithm
tables. It's true! I have to tell you these things or you
might be nice to all those people, since you don't remember anything. There's Gerard Duboc, who's sure to
come fawning over you in that sugary way of his. He did

you out of a very good job in the Fillière Company—
and you had a much better chance of getting it than he
did, with your uncle in the firm. He told lies about you
to the managing director. We found out later that he
was behind it. I hope you'll slam the door in his face,
and the same with certain others I'll tell you about, too,
who stabbed you in the back.

GASTON. It's full of pretty things, a past, isn't it?

MADAME RENAUD. On the other hand, you'll have to be
very nice to old Madame Bouguon, although she's rather
repulsive since she had her stroke, poor thing. She helped
to bring you into the world.

GASTON. That doesn't seem a good enough reason.

MADAME RENAUD. And she nursed you through pneumonia
too—I was ill myself at the time. She saved your life, my
dear.

GASTON. Yes, that's true, there's gratitude too. I'd forgotten
gratitude. [A pause.] Obligations, hatreds, injuries . . .
What did I expect memories to be? [He stops and then
adds thoughtfully.] And I was forgetting remorse. I have
a complete past now. [He smiles a funny little smile and
goes to her.] But you see how demanding I am. I should
have preferred a different model, one with a few joys in
it. A spark of feeling too, if possible. Have you nothing
to offer me?

MADAME RENAUD. I don't understand you, my child.

GASTON. It's simple enough. I would like you to tell me
about one of my old delights. My hatreds and my remorse
have taught me nothing. Give me something that delighted your son, so I can test the ring of it inside me.

MADAME RENAUD. That's easy enough. You had a lot of
enjoyment, you know. You were so pampered.

GASTON. Tell me one thing, just one.

MADAME RENAUD. All right. . . . It's annoying having to
remember on the spur of the moment. . . . I don't
know which to choose from.

GASTON. Say any one thing you think of.

MADAME RENAUD. Well, let's see. . . . Yes, when you were
twelve——

GASTON [interrupting]. A man's joy. The others are too
remote.

MADAME RENAUD [suddenly ill at ease]. The thing is . . .
you didn't tell me much about those. Well, goodness, a

grown-up son! You went out such a lot. Like all boys.
You were gods in those days. You went to the races, you
went out to parties. You had fun with your friends, but
with me . . .

GASTON. Did you never see me happy?

MADAME RENAUD. Well, of course I did, good heavens!
Why, on your graduation day, I remember——

GASTON [*interrupting*]. No! Not graduation day. Later on.
Between the time I put away my schoolbooks and the day
they put a gun into my hands, during those few months
which were to be, without my knowing it, my entire life
as a man.

MADAME RENAUD. I'm trying to think. You were out such
a lot. . . . You acted the man so much.

GASTON. Yes, but however much he plays the man, a boy of
eighteen is still a child! There must have been a burst
pipe in the yard that nobody could stop, or a day when
the cook uttered some frightful barbarism, or we met a
comic bus conductor . . . and you saw me laugh. A day
when I was gladdened by a gift, a ray of sunshine. I'm
not asking for an overwhelming joy. Just a tiny moment
of delight. I wasn't neurotic, was I?

MADAME RENAUD [*suddenly ill at ease*]. Well, you see,
Jacques dear . . . I was going to tell you all that later,
when we had more time. . . . But the fact is, you and
I weren't on very good terms just then. Oh, it was
nothing, childish sulks that's all. I'm sure it will seem
much more serious now, after all these years, than it was
at the time. Yes, as I was saying, at the particular time
you mentioned, between your leaving school and the army,
we weren't speaking to each other.

GASTON. Oh?

MADAME RENAUD. Yes. Oh, for quite futile reasons really.

GASTON. And did this . . . feud last for very long?

MADAME RENAUD. Almost a year.

GASTON. A year! We had some staying power, both of us.
Who stopped speaking first?

MADAME RENAUD [*hesitating slightly*]. Oh, I did, I suppose.
But you were to blame for it. You were so stupidly pigheaded over something.

GASTON. What youthful pigheadedness could possibly have
induced you not to speak to your son for a whole year?

MADAME RENAUD. You did nothing whatever to end this state of affairs. Nothing!

GASTON. But when I left for the war, we did make it up then, didn't we? You didn't let me go without kissing me good-by?

A pause.

MADAME RENAUD [*abruptly*]. Yes. [*A pause.*] It was your fault. I waited for you in my room. You waited in yours. You expected me to make the first move—me, your mother! After the way you'd behaved toward me. The others pleaded with you. It was no good. Nothing would make you give in. Nothing! And you were going to the front!

GASTON. How old was I?

MADAME RENAUD. Eighteen.

GASTON. Perhaps I didn't know where I was going. At eighteen war is a gay adventure. But it wasn't 1914 any more, when mothers hung garlands on the rifles. You must have known where I was going.

MADAME RENAUD. I was sure the war would be over before you'd left the training camp. I thought I'd see you again on your first leave. Besides, you were always so curt, so hard with me.

GASTON. But couldn't you have come to me and said, "Don't be so silly, kiss me"?

MADAME RENAUD. I was afraid of your eyes. Of how you'd stiffen in that proud way you had. . . . Suppose you'd told me to get out? You easily might, you know.

GASTON. Then you'd have come back again, wept at my door, gone down on your knees, and begged me to kiss you before I went away. You did wrong, you did wrong not to go down on your knees.

MADAME RENAUD. But, Jacques, your own mother!

GASTON. I was eighteen and they were sending me away to die. I may have behaved like a boor, shut myself up like a fool in my own ridiculous pride, but even so—I'm a little ashamed at saying this—but you should have gone down on your knees, all of you, and begged my pardon.

MADAME RENAUD. Pardon for what? *I* hadn't done anything.

GASTON. And what had I done, for that great gulf to open up between us?

MADAME RENAUD [*speaking suddenly as she had all those years ago*]. Oh, you'd taken it into your head to marry some little shopgirl you'd picked up, and who refused to sleep with you no doubt. . . . Marriage isn't a fairy tale. Were we supposed to let you ruin your life—bring this girl into the family? Don't tell me you loved her. How can you be in love at eighteen—I mean, deeply, lastingly enough to marry on and raise a family—with a little shopgirl you'd met at a dance three weeks before?

GASTON [*after a pause*]. Yes, of course, it was folly. . . . But my class was going to be called up in a few months, you knew that. Suppose that was the one piece of folly I was ever to commit? It was calf love and couldn't last —but suppose the boy who clamored for it had only a few months to live, not even time enough for it to fade?

MADAME RENAUD. But we didn't think you were going to be killed! And I haven't told you everything. Do you know what you shouted, right into my face, with your mouth all twisted and your hand raised to strike me— me, your own mother? "I hate you! I hate you!" That's what you screamed at me. [*A pause.*] Now do you understand why I stayed in my room hoping you would come up, right until the street door banged behind you?

GASTON [*quietly, after a pause*]. And I died at eighteen, without my moment of joy, because it was a piece of foolishness, and without your speaking to me again. I lay on the ground for a whole night with a wound in my shoulder and I was twice as lonely as the others who cried out for their mothers. [*A pause. He says suddenly, as if to himself.*] Yes, it's true. I do hate you.

MADAME RENAUD [*terrified*]. Jacques, what is it?

GASTON [*coming back to himself*]. What? I'm sorry. . . . Please forgive me. [*He moves away, hard and impenetrable.*] I'm not Jacques Renaud. I recognize nothing here of what was his. Just for a second, yes, as I stood listening to you, I merged with him. I'm sorry. But you see, for a man without a memory, an entire past is too heavy to take onto one's back at one go. If you want to please me, if you want what's best for me, you'll let me go back to the asylum. I grew lettuces, I polished floors, the days went by. . . . But even after eighteen years—the second half, exactly, of my life—those days, added one to the

other, never managed to make up that devouring thing
you call a past.

MADAME RENAUD. But, Jacques——

GASTON. Don't call me "Jacques" any more. He's done too
many things, that Jacques. Gaston is all right. He's no
one in particular, but I do know *what* he is. But this
Jacques, with his name already swamped with the bodies
of so many dead birds, this Jacques who betrayed and
murdered and went away all alone to the war with nobody to see him off, that Jacques who never even loved
—he frightens me.

MADAME RENAUD. But, my dear child——

GASTON. Go away. I'm not your child.

MADAME RENAUD. You're talking to me just as you used to
in the past!

GASTON. I have no past. I'm talking as I talk today. Go
away.

MADAME RENAUD [*stiffening as she did long ago*]. Very
well, Jacques! But when all the others have proved to you
that I really am your mother, you'll have to come to me
and beg my pardon.

She goes out without seeing VALENTINE, *who has overheard
the last few remarks, out in the passage.*

VALENTINE [*coming into the room*]. You say he never loved.
How do you know, when you know nothing?

GASTON [*looking her up and down*]. Go away. You too. Go
away.

VALENTINE. Why are you talking to me like that? What's
the matter?

GASTON [*shouting*]. Go away! I'm not Jacques Renaud.

VALENTINE. You're shouting it as if you were afraid you
were.

GASTON. It's partly that.

VALENTINE. Fear I can understand. The shadow of Jacques
at eighteen is a frightening burden to take on. But why
should you hate me?

GASTON. I don't like the little smiles you've been giving me
ever since I arrived here. You were his mistress.

VALENTINE. Who dared to say so?

GASTON. Your husband.

A *pause.*

VALENTINE. Well, if you're my lover, and I want you back
—are you absurd enough to think that's wrong?

GASTON. You're talking to a sort of aborigine. I'm a man of
mature years, yet I'm landing wide-eyed and fresh into
this world. Perhaps it isn't so wrong after all to take my
brother's wife, a brother who was fond of me and wished
me well.

VALENTINE [quietly]. When we met on holiday at Dinard,
I swam and played tennis with you much more than
with your brother. I went for more walks along the sea-
shore with you. It was you, only you, who shared my
kisses. I came to your mother's house, later, to parties
and your brother fell in love with me, but it was you I
came to see.

GASTON. It was him you married though, wasn't it?

VALENTINE. You were a child. I was an orphan, a minor,
without a penny to my name. And with a charitable
aunt who'd already made me pay dearly for the first few
offers of marriage I'd refused. Should I have sold myself
to some other man rather than to him, who brought me
nearer you?

GASTON. There's a column in women's magazines that
deals with problems of that sort.

VALENTINE. We became lovers—when I returned from my
honeymoon.

GASTON. Oh, so we did wait a little while.

VALENTINE. A little while? Two months, two horrible
months! Then we had three years all to ourselves, because
the war came and Georges went on the fourth of August.
And now, after these eighteen years, Jacques——

She touches his arm. He recoils.

GASTON. I am not Jacques Renaud.

VALENTINE. Even if you aren't . . . Let me look at the
ghost of the only man I ever loved. [*She gives a little
smile.*] Oh, you're curling your lip! [*She looks into his
face. He turns away, ill at ease.*] Does nothing in me
strike a chord in you—a look, a tone in my voice?

GASTON. Nothing.

VALENTINE. Don't be harsh with me. It means a great deal,
you see, for a woman who was once in love to find one
day, after an interminable absence, if not her lover, at

least in the faintest curl of his upper lip the scrupulously
exact copy of his ghost.

GASTON. I may be a highly exact ghost, but I am not Jacques
Renaud.

VALENTINE. Look at me.

GASTON. I am looking at you. You're a charming woman,
but I am not Jacques Renaud.

VALENTINE. Do I mean nothing at all to you—are you sure?

GASTON. Nothing.

VALENTINE. Then you'll never get your memory back,
ever.

GASTON. I'm beginning to hope I shan't. [A pause. He adds,
a little anxiously.] Why will I never get my memory back?

VALENTINE. Because you don't even remember someone you
saw two years ago.

GASTON. Two years ago?

VALENTINE. A sewing maid, a temporary sewing maid.

GASTON. A sewing maid? [A pause. He asks abruptly.] Who
told you about that?

VALENTINE. Nobody. I put on that disguise—with my
mother-in-law's full approval, by the way—so I could get
really near you. Look at me, man without memories.

GASTON [disturbed in spite of himself]. That girl in the
laundry who only stayed for a day—was that you?

VALENTINE. Yes, that was me.

GASTON. But you didn't say anything that day?

VALENTINE. I didn't want to say anything before we . . .
I hoped—you see what faith I have in love, in your love—
I hoped that in taking me you'd get your memory back.

GASTON. But afterward?

VALENTINE. Afterward, just as I was going to tell you, we
were interrupted, don't you remember?

GASTON [smiling at the memory]. Oh, the housekeeper.

VALENTINE [smiling too]. Yes, the housekeeper.

GASTON. But you didn't tell anybody that you'd recognized
me.

VALENTINE. Yes I did, but there were fifty other families
all doing the same thing.

GASTON [with a quick, nervous laugh]. Why yes, that's right,
how stupid of me; everybody recognizes me! That doesn't
prove I'm Jacques Renaud at all!

VALENTINE. But you did remember your sewing maid with
her big pile of sheets to mend?

GASTON. Yes, of course I remembered her. Apart from my amnesia, my memory's very good.

VALENTINE. Do you want to hold her in your arms again?

GASTON [*pushing her away*]. Let's wait until we find out if I'm Jacques Renaud.

VALENTINE. And if you are?

GASTON. If I am, I won't hold her in my arms again for anything in the world. I don't want to be lover to my brother's wife.

VALENTINE. But you already have been!

GASTON. It was so long ago and I've been so miserable since, I've washed my youth away.

VALENTINE [*with a triumphant little laugh*]. You're forgetting your sewing maid. If you're Jacques Renaud, you were your brother's wife's lover as little as two years ago. You yourself, as you are now, not some remote boy of eighteen.

GASTON. I'm not Jacques Renaud.

VALENTINE. Listen, Jacques, you really will have to give up this wonderfully simple life of yours. It's too easy to live without a memory. You'll have to accept yourself, Jacques. Our entire life, with our fine moral code and our precious freedom, consists ultimately in accepting ourselves as we are. Those seventeen years in the hospital, during which you kept yourself so pure, that's the exact length of adolescence, your second adolescence, and to-day you've come of age. You're about to become a man again, with everything that entails in the way of failures and blemishes—and moments of happiness too. Accept yourself and accept me, Jacques.

GASTON. If some conclusive proof forces me into it, I shall have to accept myself. But I'll never accept you!

VALENTINE. But you've already done it, whether you like it or not, two years ago!

GASTON. I won't take my brother's wife.

VALENTINE. When will you drop your fine phrases? You'll see, now that you're going to be a man, none of your new problems will be simple enough to sum up in a formula. You took me from him, yes. But he took me from you before that, merely because he was a man and master of his actions before you were.

GASTON. Besides, there isn't only you. I don't care to have swindled old ladies and violated maids.

VALENTINE. What maids?

GASTON. And another little thing . . . I don't much care
to have raised my hand against my mother, nor any of
the other eccentricities of my appalling little double.

VALENTINE. Listen to you shouting! Why, not ten minutes
ago, you very nearly did exactly that yourself.

GASTON. I told an inhuman old woman that I hated her.
But that old woman wasn't my mother.

VALENTINE. She was, Jacques. And that's why you said that
to her so vehemently. And, you see, it was enough for
you to rub shoulders for an hour with the characters out
of your past for you to drop unconsciously into your old
attitudes with them. Listen, Jacques, I'm going up to
my room, because you're about to get very angry. In ten
minutes, you'll call me down again, because your rages
are terrible, but they never last longer than ten minutes.

GASTON. How do you know? You're beginning to get on
my nerves. You talk as though you knew me better than
I know myself.

VALENTINE. But I do! Listen, Jacques, listen. There is one
definite piece of proof which I've never been able to
tell the others. . . .

GASTON [shrinking]. I don't believe you!

VALENTINE [smiling]. Wait. I haven't told you yet.

GASTON [shouting]. I won't believe you! I won't believe
anybody! I won't listen to any more about my past!

The DUCHESS *bursts in, followed by* HUSPAR. VALENTINE
hides in the bathroom.

DUCHESS. Gaston, Gaston, something terrible has happened.
Some people have just arrived, fighting mad and yelling
their heads off. It's one of your families. I had to receive
them. They screamed abuse at me. It was dreadfully rash
of me not to keep to the schedule we announced in the
press, I see that now. They think they've been tricked.
They're going to make a scandal, accuse us of all sorts
of terrible things!

HUSPAR. I'm sure nobody would dare question your Ladyship's good faith.

DUCHESS. They're blinded by those two hundred and fifty
thousand francs, can't you see that? They're talking of
favoritism, of wirepulling, and the Lord knows what.
Give them a bit longer and they'll be saying my little

Albert is conspiring to give Gaston to the Renauds so they can all share out his money!

Enter the BUTLER

BUTLER. Begging your Ladyship's pardon, but some more persons have arrived and are asking for your Ladyship and Monsieur Huspar.

DUCHESS. Their names?

BUTLER. They gave me this card, which I did not presume to present to your Ladyship straight away, as it pertains to trade. [*He reads it with great dignity.*] "Butter, eggs, cheeses. Bougran and Son."

DUCHESS [*consulting her list*]. Bougran? Bougran, you say? It's the milkman!

The VALET *knocks and comes in.*

VALET. I beg your pardon, madame, but there's a gentleman, or rather a man, asking to see your Ladyship. Judging by his attire, I'm afraid I didn't dare to ask him in.

DUCHESS [*looking at her list*]. What name? Legropâtre or Madensale?

VALET. Legropâtre, your Ladyship.

DUCHESS. Legropâtre, that's the lamplighter. Show him in with all due ceremony. They've all come on the same train. The Madensales will be arriving at any minute. I've just telephoned Pont-au-Bronc. I'll try to keep them quiet.

She goes quickly out, followed by HUSPAR.

GASTON [*in a harassed murmur*]. You, all of you, have proof, photographs that look like me, memories as cut and dried as crimes. I listen to you all and I can feel looming up behind me a monstrous hybrid creature, with a little bit of all your sons in it and nothing of me. Because your sons have nothing of me. [VALENTINE *has come in again.*] Me! Me! I exist, in spite of all your stories. You talk of the blissful simplicity of life without a memory. That's very funny. . . . You try taking all the virtues, all the vices, and loading them onto your back!

VALENTINE. Life will be much simpler for you if you'll only listen to me for a minute, Jacques. I'm offering you a past —a rather heavy one perhaps, but it will seem quite light because it frees you from all the others. Will you listen?

GASTON. Well?

VALENTINE. I've never seen you naked, have I? Well, you
have a scar, a very small scar which none of the doctors
who examined you ever discovered, I'm sure—just under
your left shoulder blade. It was made by a hatpin—the
things we wore in 1917!—and I gave it to you one day
when I thought you'd been unfaithful to me.

[*She goes out.*

GASTON *stands there stunned for a moment, then slowly
takes off his jacket.*

Curtain.

SCENE II

The CHAUFFEUR *and the* VALET *are standing on a chair
in the passage, looking through a small inner window.*

VALET. Hey, look! He's taking his clothes off!

CHAUFFEUR [*elbowing him out of the way*]. Go on! He's
mad as a hatter, that one! What's he doing? Looking for
fleas? Wait, wait! He's climbing onto a chair to look in
the mantelpiece mirror.

VALET. Don't be daft, man! Climbing onto a chair?

CHAUFFEUR. I'm telling you!

VALET [*taking his place*]. Let's have a look! Well, would
you believe it! And just so he can look at his back! I tell
you he's cracked. He's getting down now. He's seen what
he wanted to see. He's putting his shirt on. Now he's
sitting down. . . . Hullo? Well, I'll be damned!

CHAUFFEUR. Why, what's he doing?

VALET [*turning around and goggling*]. He's crying!

Curtain.

ACT THREE

Jacques' room. The shutters are closed, the russet gloom is streaked with light. It is morning. GASTON *is lying on the bed, asleep. The* BUTLER *and the* VALET *are bringing in the stuffed animals, which they set around the bed. The* DUCHESS *and* MADAME RENAUD *are directing operations from the passage outside. All this is performed on tiptoe and in whispers.*

BUTLER. Shall we put these round the bed too, your Ladyship?

DUCHESS. Yes, yes, all round his bed, so he'll see them the moment he wakes up.

MADAME RENAUD. Oh, if only the sight of these little creatures could bring him back to us!

DUCHESS. It may affect him very deeply.

MADAME RENAUD. He did so love trapping them! He'd climb trees up to giddy heights to put glue on the branches.

DUCHESS [*to the* BUTLER]. Put one on his pillow. Yes, go on! Right on his pillow.

BUTLER. Don't you think it might frighten him, your Ladyship, seeing this creature right by his face?

DUCHESS. An excellent thing, fright, in his case, my good man. An excellent thing. [*She goes to* MADAME RENAUD.] I'm sick with worry, you know, quite sick! I managed to quiet those people down last night, by telling them that Huspar and my little Albert would be here first thing this morning. But God knows if we'll ever get rid of them without a riot.

The VALET *comes in again.*

VALET. Monsieur Gaston's presumptive families have arrived, your Ladyship.

DUCHESS. There, you see! I told them nine o'clock, and they're here at five minutes to. That class never give an inch.

MADAME RENAUD. Where have you put them, Victor?

VALET. In the drawing room, madame.

167

DUCHESS. Are there as many as yesterday? Safety in numbers—that's the peasant mentality all over.

VALET. There are more of them, your Ladyship.

DUCHESS. More? How is that?

VALET. Yes, your Ladyship, three more. They came together.
A gentleman of good appearance, with a little boy and
his nurse.

DUCHESS. Nurse? What sort of nurse?

VALET. An English one, your Ladyship.

DUCHESS. Ah, those are the Madensales. Charming people,
I believe. It's the English branch of the family who are
claiming Gaston. Very touching to come all this way to
find a loved one, don't you find? Please ask them to wait
for a few minutes, will you?

MADAME RENAUD. But these people aren't going to take
him away before he's decided about us, are they?

DUCHESS. No, no, don't distress yourself. The experiment
began with you; we'll have to conclude it properly whether
they like it or not. My little Albert promised he would
be adamant on that point. However, we'll have to be
extremely diplomatic if we're to avoid the faintest sniff
of scandal.

MADAME RENAUD. I do feel you're exaggerating the danger
of that, really!

DUCHESS. Not a bit of it! The Left Wing press has its eye
on my young Albert, I know it has. I have my spies.
That lot will pounce on this like vultures on a carcass.
And I cannot allow that to happen—much as I should
like to see Gaston joining an enchanting family like
yours. You're a mother—well, I'm an aunt. My flesh and
blood come first. [*She squeezes her hand.*] But, believe
me, I'm just as lacerated as you are by the strain, the
torment of it all! [*The* VALET *comes in with some stuffed
squirrels. She watches him as he goes by.*] Why, it's
ravishingly pretty, that squirrel fur. Why on earth has
nobody thought of making coats out of it?

MADAME RENAUD [*dazed*]. I don't know. . . .

VALET. Too small, I expect.

BUTLER [*by the door, watching*]. Hush! He's just moved.

DUCHESS. He mustn't see us, whatever happens! [*To the*
BUTLER.] Open the shutters.

Light floods into the room. GASTON *opens his eyes. He
sees something close to his face. He recoils and sits up.*

GASTON. What's that? [*He looks around at all the stuffed squirrels, ferrets, and weasels, his eyes starting out of his head, and shouts.*] What are all these animals? What do they want with me?

BUTLER [*stepping forward*]. They're stuffed, sir. They're the little creatures you used to kill, sir. Great fun you had. Don't you recognize them, sir?

GASTON [*hoarsely*]. I've never killed any animals!

He has got up. The VALET *rushes over with his dressing gown. They both go out to the bathroom.* GASTON *comes back a second later and goes over to the animals.*

GASTON. How did he catch them?

BUTLER. Don't you remember, sir, the steel traps you used to pore over in the catalogues? For some of them though, sir, you preferred to use glue.

GASTON. So they weren't dead when he found them?

BUTLER. Mostly not, sir, no. You used to finish them off with your knife. Very handy with it you were, sir.

A pause.

GASTON. What can one do for dead animals? [*He goes to them with a timid gesture, too shy for a caress, and looks at them, murmuring.*] How can one stroke these tight, leathery skins? I'll throw bread and nuts to other squirrels every day. I'll forbid anyone, on any land I own, to do the slightest harm to ferrets. But how can I comfort these for the long night when they were afraid and in pain and didn't know why, with their paws held in those cold steel jaws?

BUTLER. Oh, you mustn't fret yourself like that, sir. They don't matter much, not these little things. Besides, it's all over now.

GASTON. It's all over now. . . . And even if I were powerful enough to make all little woodland creatures happy ever after, as you say—it's all over now. [*Going into the bathroom.*] Why am I wearing a different dressing gown this morning?

BUTLER. This one belongs to you too, sir. Madame told me to see you tried them all on, sir, in case you recognized one.

GASTON. What's this in the pockets? More souvenirs, like yesterday?

BUTLER. No, sir. This time it's mothballs.

The bathroom door shuts. The DUCHESS *and* MADAME
RENAUD *come out of their hiding place.*

BUTLER [*as he goes*]. You heard what he said, madame. I
don't think he recognized anything at all.   [*He goes out.*

MADAME RENAUD [*tight-lipped*]. If you ask me, he's doing
it on purpose! He isn't even trying!

DUCHESS. If that were so, I should speak to him very
severely, I promise you. But I'm afraid it goes deeper
than that.

GEORGES *comes in.*

GEORGES. Is he awake?

DUCHESS. Yes. But our little plan didn't work, I'm sorry
to say.

MADAME RENAUD. He was surprised and pained at seeing
those dead animals, but that's all.

GEORGES. Would you mind leaving me alone with him?
I'd like to talk to him if he'll let me.

MADAME RENAUD. Pray God you succeed, Georges! I'm
beginning to lose hope.

GEORGES. No, no, Mother, you mustn't do that. We must
keep hoping, whatever happens. However hopeless it
looks.

MADAME RENAUD [*rather crossly*]. Well, I'm getting rather
tired of his attitude. Do you know what? I think he's
sulking with me as he did in the old days.

GEORGES. But he hasn't even recognized you.

MADAME RENAUD. He was such a bad-tempered boy. Lost
memory or no lost memory, why should he be any different now?

DUCHESS [*as they both move to go out*]. I think you're
exaggerating his hostility toward you. Of course, it's not
for me to give you any advice, but you do act rather
coldly toward him, if you don't mind my saying so.
Gracious me, you're a mother, aren't you? Be pathetic,
weep at his feet, grovel a little!

MADAME RENAUD. It is my dearest wish to see Jacques take
up his rightful place here, madame. But I really cannot
go as far as that! Especially after what happened.

DUCHESS. That's a pity. I'm sure it would have a great effect
on him. Why, if anyone was threatening to take my
little Albert away from me, I'd be as savage as a tigress,
I know I should. Did I ever tell you?—when he failed

his matriculation, years ago, I marched in to the professor
of the faculty and nearly tore his beard off.

They go out. Meanwhile, GEORGES *knocks on the bedroom
door and goes in timidly.*

GEORGES. May I speak to you, Jacques?

GASTON [*from the bathroom*]. Who is it now? I said I
wanted to be left alone! Can't I even take a bath without somebody firing questions at me and shoving their
reminiscences down my throat?

The VALET *pops his head through the bathroom door.*

VALET. Monsieur Jacques is in his bath, sir. [*To the in-
visible* GASTON.] It's Monsieur Georges, sir.

GASTON [*off, a little more affably*]. Oh, it's you.

GEORGES [*to the* VALET]. Leave us for a moment, will you
Victor? [*The* VALET *goes out.* GEORGES *moves nearer
to the door.*] I want to say I'm sorry, Jacques. . . . I
quite realize we're annoying you with all our dramas.
But what I want to tell you is important. If it doesn't
bother you too much, I'd just like to say that——

GASTON [*interrupting*]. What new filth in your brother's
past are you going to rub my nose in this time?

GEORGES. It's not filth, Jacques, on the contrary. It's something I've been thinking. I'd like to tell you about it if
you'll let me. [*He pauses for a second and then goes on.*]
You see, just because one's honest, and always has been,
just because one never did anything bad—which is easy,
after all, for some—one tends to think one can say what
one likes to people. . . . One talks down to them, blames
them for things, feels sorry for oneself. . . . Are you
angry with me about yesterday?

*The answer comes after a slight pause, gruffly, almost re-
luctantly.*

GASTON [*off*]. Angry about what?

GEORGES. All the things I said. Acting the injured party,
making it out to be worse than it was. . . . The sort of
moral blackmail I treated you to, with my pathetic little
tale. [*A sound from the bathroom.* GEORGES *jumps up
hastily.*] Wait! Don't come out yet! Let me finish, it's
easier. If I see you, I'll put on my elder brother voice
again and I'll never be able to drop it. You see, Jacques,
I thought it all over very carefully last night. What

happened wasn't very pretty, I know, but you were just
a child—and so was she. And then again, at Dinard, before we got married, it was you she always wanted to
be with, not me. Perhaps you were already in love by
then and couldn't help yourselves, poor things. . . . I
came along and stepped between you with my clumsy
great feet, my position, my age. . . . I played the serious-minded suitor. . . . Her aunt must have pressed her
into accepting me. Anyway, the conclusion I came to last
night was that I had no right to reproach you as I did,
and I take it all back. That's all.

GEORGES *drops into a chair, exhausted with the effort.*

GASTON *comes out of the bathroom, goes to him, and lays
his hand gently on his shoulder.*

GASTON. How could you love that worthless little brute
as much as that?

GEORGES [*almost apologetically*]. He was my brother. . . .

GASTON. He never once acted like a brother. He robbed
you, he betrayed you. . . . You would have hated your
best friend if he'd done half of what he did.

GEORGES. A friend is different; he was my brother. . . .

GASTON. And, anyway, how can you want him back, even
altered as he is, and older, and see him come between
you and your wife again?

GEORGES [*simply*]. Even if he were a murderer, he's one of
the family. He belongs here.

GASTON [*repeating, after a pause*]. He's one of the family,
he belongs in the family. It's so simple, isn't it? [*He goes
on, as if to himself.*] He thought he was a kind man; he
isn't. He thought himself honest, and he's hardly that.
I'm alone in the world, he thought, and free—in spite of
the asylum walls—and instead the world is full of people
to whom he is committed, and who are waiting for him.
And his humblest acts and gestures can only be ex-
tensions of acts and gestures in the past. So simple! So
very simple! [*He seizes* GEORGES *roughly by the arm.*]
Why did you have to come along with your tale of woe
into the bargain? Why did you have to throw your affection in my face? To make it simpler still, I suppose? [*He
drops onto the bed, strangely weary.*] You've won.

GEORGES [*bewildered*]. But, Jacques, I don't understand.
What have I done wrong? I came to tell you all this—

and it wasn't easy, believe me—so that you'd feel a little warmer in the loneliness you must have known ever since yesterday morning.

GASTON. That loneliness wasn't the worst of my enemies.

GEORGES. You may have caught looks from the servants, sensed a kind of embarrassment around you. But you mustn't think nobody loved you. . . . Mother—— [GASTON *looks at him. He cannot finish. Instead, he says.*] And, anyway, there was me; I was very fond of you.

GASTON. And apart from you? Who?

GEORGES. Well—er . . . [*Embarrassed.*] Well, Valentine, I expect.

GASTON. She was in love with me, that's different. No, there was only you.

GEORGES [*his head bent*]. Perhaps, yes.

GASTON. Why, though? I simply can't understand why.

GEORGES [*gently*]. Did you never dream of a friend, a friend who was first a little boy who'd hold your hand and go for walks with you? You care about friendship—just think what a boon it can be to have a friend so new that he owes the secret of his first carefully spelled-out letters to you, his first shaky rides on a bicycle, his first floundering strokes in the water. A friend so defenseless that he needs you there all the time to protect him.

A pause.

GASTON. Was I very young when our father died?

GEORGES. You were two.

GASTON. And you?

GEORGES. Fourteen. So I had to look after you, didn't I? You were so little. [*A pause. He tells him his real reason.*] You've always been so little—for everything. For the money we gave you far too soon, fools that we were. For Mother's harshness and for my own weakness too, for my incompetence. That pride, that violence in you, which you wrestled with even at two years old—they were devils you couldn't be blamed for and it was up to us to save you from them. Not only were we incapable of doing so, but we condemned you to them and we let you go off all alone to the front. With your rifle and your kitbag and your gas mask, you must have made such a little soldier, standing there on the station platform.

GASTON [*shrugging*]. The ones that looked so fierce with

their big mustaches were just little soldiers too, I imagine.

GEORGES [*with a cry of pain almost*]. Yes, but you were eighteen! And apart from Latin verbs and the multiplication tables, the very first thing grown men were going to require of you in life was mopping up the trenches with a kitchen knife.

GASTON [*with a hollow laugh*]. What of it? Dealing out death strikes me as an excellent initiation into life for a young man.

The BUTLER *comes in.*

BUTLER. Her Ladyship requests you to be so kind as to join her in the drawing room as soon as you are ready, sir.

GEORGES [*getting up*]. I'll leave you. But, please, despite all they may have told you, don't hate that Jacques too much. I think he was, more than anything else, a poor little lad. . . .   [*He goes.*

The BUTLER *helps* GASTON *to dress.*

GASTON [*abruptly*]. Butler?

BUTLER. Sir?

GASTON. Have you ever killed a man?

BUTLER. You're joking, I trust, sir. If I had ever killed anybody, I certainly shouldn't be in Madame's service, sir.

GASTON. Not even during the war? A sudden tussle in a shell hole, man to man, during the second wave of an attack?

BUTLER. I fought the war as a corporal in the quartermaster corps, sir, and I must say, sir, we had very few opportunities of that sort in the supply depot.

GASTON, *motionless and very pale, says very quietly:*

GASTON. You're a lucky man. Because it's an appalling sensation to kill somebody so that one can live.

BUTLER [*not knowing whether to laugh*]. Appalling is right, sir. Especially for the victim.

GASTON. You're wrong, Butler. It's all a question of imagination. And the victim often has much less imagination than the murderer. [*A pause.*] Sometimes even, he's no more than a shadow in the murderer's dream.

BUTLER. In that case, I can see he wouldn't suffer much, sir.

GASTON. But the murderer has the privilege of two lots of suffering. Do you like living, Butler?

BUTLER. As much as the next man, sir.

GASTON. Imagine that in order to live you had to hurl a

young man into oblivion forever. A young man of eighteen. A young thug, a young swaggerer, but even so, a poor
little lad. You will be free, the freest man on earth, but
in order to be free, you have to leave that innocent little
corpse behind you. What are you going to do?

BUTLER. I must confess I've never asked myself the question,
sir. But if detective stories are anything to go by, the last
thing you want to do is leave a corpse behind.

GASTON [bursts out laughing]. But what if nobody except the
murderer can see the corpse anyway? [He goes to him and
says kindly.] There. The deed's done. He's there, at your
feet. Do you see him?

The BUTLER looks down at his feet, jumps aside, looks
around, and then scuttles out in terror, as fast as his dignity
will allow. VALENTINE comes quickly into the passage. She
runs into the room.

VALENTINE. What's this Georges tells me? Haven't you told
them yet? I didn't like to come into your room before the
others this morning, but I was expecting they'd call me
any minute with the good news. Why didn't you tell
them? [GASTON looks at her and says nothing.] Are you
trying to send me out of my mind? That scar—you saw it
in the mirror yesterday—you must have!

GASTON [quietly, without taking his eyes off her]. I saw no
scar.

VALENTINE. What did you say?

GASTON. I said I looked at my back very carefully and I saw
no scar on it at all. You must have made a mistake.

VALENTINE looks at him for a second, dazed; then she
understands and cries:

VALENTINE. Oh, I hate you! I hate you!

GASTON [very calmly]. I think it's better that way.

VALENTINE. But do you realize what you're doing?

GASTON. Yes. I am refusing my past and all the characters
in it—myself included. You may all be my family, my
loves, the true story of my life. But, you see . . . I don't
like you. I'm rejecting you, all of you.

VALENTINE. But you're mad! You're a monster! One can't
reject one's past! One can't reject oneself!

GASTON. Yes, I expect I'm the only man who's ever had the
God-given chance to do what must be everybody's secret

dream. I'm a grown man, and if I choose to, I can be as
new and unmarked as a child. It would be criminal not to
use that privilege. I refuse you. I have too many things to
forget about myself as it is since yesterday morning.

VALENTINE. And my love, my love for you, what are you
going to do with that? You aren't interested enough to
want to find out about that either, I suppose?

GASTON. All I can see of it just now is the hatred in your
eyes. It must be one of the aspects of love that only a man
without a memory could wonder at. In any case, it's a very
useful one. I don't want to see another. I am a lover who
doesn't know his mistress' love, a lover who doesn't remember the first kiss, the first tear, a lover who's shackled
by no memories, who'll have forgotten everything tomorrow. That's a rare enough gift too. I mean to make full
use of it.

VALENTINE. And what if I shout it to the world that I recognized that scar?

GASTON. I've envisaged that possibility. From the point of
view of love: I think the old Valentine would have done it
long ago and it's a fairly cheering sign that you've become
so cautious. From the legal point of view: you are my
sister-in-law, you claim to be my mistress. What court of
law would make a decision as serious as this one on an
unsavory bedroom intrigue which only you can vouch for?

VALENTINE [with clenched teeth]. I see. Congratulations,
you must be feeling very pleased with yourself. But don't
imagine, apart from all that claptrap about your lost memory, that your behavior is particularly unusual for a man.
Why, I'm sure you're secretly quite proud of your grand
gesture. It's so flattering, isn't it, to repulse a woman who's
waited for you for so long? Well, I'm sorry if this hurts
you, but I *have* had other lovers, you know, since the war!

GASTON [smiling]. Thank you. It didn't hurt.

The VALET *and the* BUTLER *appear in the passage. From
their dumb show, it is clear they consider it safer to approach*
GASTON *together.*

VALET [in the doorway]. Her Grace the Duchess Dupont-
Dufort requests me to request you to hurry and join her in
the drawing room as soon as possible, sir, as your families
are getting restive.

GASTON *has not moved. The servants go out again.* VALEN-
TINE *bursts out laughing.*

VALENTINE. Your families, Jacques! Oh, I have to laugh, it's
too silly! Because, you see, you're forgetting one thing. If
you refuse to come to us, you'll have to go to them, won't
you? Whether you like it or not. You'll have to sleep in
their dead son's sheets, wear their dead son's flannel waist-
coats, put on his reverently kept old slippers. Your families
are getting restless. Come. You're so afraid of your past—
come and see their screwed-up little tradesmen's faces,
come and ask yourself what a past of avarice and penny
pinching they have to offer you.

GASTON. They'll find it difficult to outdo you, at any rate.

VALENTINE. You think so? Those ill-gotten five hundred
thousand francs spent on laughter and gay living may
seem very light beside certain tales of stolen widows'
savings and greasy bank notes hoarded in old stockings.
Come along. Since you don't want us, you owe yourself
to your other families now. [*She tries to pull him out.*]

GASTON. No. I won't go.

VALENTINE. Oh. What are you going to do, then?

GASTON. I'll go away.

VALENTINE. Where?

GASTON. Where? Anywhere.

VALENTINE. That's an amnesia word. The rest of us, who
have a memory, know that one always has to pick a desti-
nation at the railway station and that one never goes any
farther than the price of one's ticket. If you had money,
the world would be open to you, but you haven't a penny
in your pocket. So what are you going to do?

GASTON. Upset your plans, leave on foot, across country, and
make for Châteaudun.

VALENTINE. Do you feel so free since you got rid of us? To
the police you're only an escaped lunatic from an asylum.
They'll arrest you.

GASTON. I'll be miles away. I walk very fast.

VALENTINE [*shouting in his face*]. Do you think I won't
give the alarm if you take one step out of this room? [*He
goes abruptly to the window.*] Don't be absurd. The window's too high up and that isn't a solution. [*He turns back
to her like a trapped animal. She looks at him and says*

softly.] You may get rid of us, but you won't rid yourself of your habit of letting your thoughts flit across your eyes as you think them. No, Jacques, even if you killed me to gain one hour's start, they'd catch you. You can't escape. [*He drops his head and stands at bay in the corner of the room*.] Besides, you know perfectly well that I'm not the only one who's on your trail and wants to keep you. All women do, and all men. Even the right-minded dead, who can sense in some vague way that you're trying to let them down. One can't escape so many people, Jacques. And whether you want to or not, you'll have to belong to somebody or go back to your asylum.

GASTON [*dully*]. Then I'll go back to my asylum.

VALENTINE. You forget I worked for a whole day in your asylum. I saw you hoeing lettuces very happily, but I saw you emptying slops and washing dishes too; hustled by the attendants; begging the kitchen staff for a pinch of tobacco for your pipe. . . . You're acting proud with us— you snarl at us, you mock us—but without us you're nothing but a helpless little boy who isn't allowed to go out by himself and who has to hide in the lavatories if he wants to have a smoke.

GASTON [*when she has finished*]. You can go. I haven't the smallest rag of hope left now. You've done your work.

She goes out without a word. GASTON *remains alone. He casts a weary glance around the room. He stops in front of the mirror and gazes at himself for a long while. Suddenly he picks up an object from the table, without taking his eyes off his reflection, throws it at the mirror, and shatters it. Then he slumps down on the bed and buries his head in his hands. Then, very quietly, the music starts, rather sad at first, then gradually, despite* GASTON, *despite us, it grows gayer. After a while, a* LITTLE BOY *in an Eton suit opens the door of the little hall, casts a furtive glance around, then carefully closes the door, and ventures into the passage on tiptoe. He opens all the doors as he passes and casts an inquiring look inside the rooms. He gets to the bedroom door and does likewise. He finds himself face to face with* GASTON, *who looks up in surprise at the apparition.*

LITTLE BOY. Excuse me, sir. I'm sorry to disturb you, but could you tell me where the little place is?

GASTON [*coming out of a dream*]. Little place? What little place?

LITTLE BOY. The little place where you can be by yourself.

GASTON *looks at him and then bursts into a sudden, good-natured laugh.*

GASTON. Well, isn't that funny? Do you know, that's just what I'm looking for, a little place where I can be my myself.

LITTLE BOY. I wonder who we could ask, then?

GASTON [*still laughing*]. I wonder, too.

LITTLE BOY. Anyway, you haven't got much chance of finding it if you stay there. [*He sees the broken glass.*] Oh dear, was it you broke the glass?

GASTON. Yes.

LITTLE BOY. I can see why you look so worried, then. But if I were you, I'd own up straight away. You're a grownup, they can't do much to you. They say it means seven years' bad luck, though. . . .

GASTON. They do say that, yes.

LITTLE BOY [*going out*]. I think I'll walk along the passage —I might meet one of the servants. I'll ask him and then I'll come back and tell you where it is. [GASTON *looks at him.*] The little place we're both looking for, I mean.

GASTON [*smiling and calling him back*]. Wait a second. Your little place, where you can be by yourself, is much easier to find than mine is. You have one right here, in the bathroom.

LITTLE BOY. Thank you very much, sir.

He goes into the bathroom. The music takes up its mocking little theme again. The LITTLE BOY *comes back after a second or two.* GASTON *has not moved.*

LITTLE BOY. I'd better get back to the drawing room now. Is it this way?

GASTON. Yes. Are you with the families?

LITTLE BOY. Yes. It's full of all sorts of strange people who've come to identify a man who lost his memory in the war. That's what I've come for, as a matter of fact. We rushed over by plane, because it seems there's some funny business going on. Of course, I don't really know what it's all about. You'll have to talk to Uncle Job. Have you ever been up in an airplane?

GASTON. Which family do you belong to?

LITTLE BOY. The Madensales.

GASTON. Madensales. Ah yes, the English people. I remember the file very well. "Next of kin: uncle." Why, I even copied the name down on the list. There *is* an uncle among the Madensales, am I right?

LITTLE BOY. Yes, sir. . . .

GASTON. Yes, of course, Uncle Job. Well, you can tell Uncle Job that if he takes my advice he won't hold out too much hope over his nephew.

LITTLE BOY. Why do you say that?

GASTON. Because there's every chance that the said nephew may never recognize Uncle Job.

LITTLE BOY. But there's no reason why he should. It isn't Uncle Job who's looking for his nephew.

GASTON. Oh. Is there another uncle then?

LITTLE BOY. Yes, of course there is. And it's rather funny, actually. You see, it's me.

GASTON [*blinking*]. You? You mean your father, don't you?

LITTLE BOY. No. Me. And it's very awkward for a small boy to be a grown-up person's uncle, I can tell you. It took me ages just to grasp it. But my grandfather had children very late in life, you see, so that's how it happened. I was born twenty-six years after my nephew.

GASTON *bursts out laughing and draws the* LITTLE BOY *onto his knee.*

GASTON. So you're Uncle Madensale?

LITTLE BOY. Yes. But don't make fun of me, it's not my fault.

GASTON. But, then, that Uncle Job you were talking about—who's he?

LITTLE BOY. Oh, he's an old friend of my father's. He's the lawyer who deals with all the business about my heirs. I just call him "uncle"; he isn't really.

GASTON. But how do you come to be the sole representative of the Madensale family?

LITTLE BOY. It's because of a dreadful disaster at sea. Have you ever heard of the sinking of the *Neptunia*?

GASTON. Yes. Years ago.

LITTLE BOY. Well, my entire family went for a cruise in her.

GASTON *looks at him in wonder.*

GASTON. So all your relations are dead?

LITTLE BOY [*kindly*]. Yes. But you needn't look at me like that, you know. It's not so sad really. I was only a baby when it happened. To tell the truth, I didn't even notice it.

GASTON *sets him on the ground, looks at him, then pats him on the back.*

GASTON. Little Uncle Madensale, you're a great character without knowing it.

LITTLE BOY. I'm not bad at cricket, actually. Do you play cricket?

GASTON. What I don't understand is why Uncle Job should come all the way from England to find a nephew for his young client. A nephew who'll complicate his finances more than somewhat, I should think.

LITTLE BOY. Oh, you can't know much about the rights of succession then. It's very involved, but I think it goes like this. If I don't find my nephew, then most of my money gets whisked away from under our nose. I'm very worried about it because among the property that's supposed to come to me there's a lovely house in Sussex with some marvelous stables with ponies. Do you like riding?

GASTON [*suddenly thoughtful*]. So Uncle Job must be very keen indeed to find your nephew?

LITTLE BOY. I should just say he is! For his sake as well as mine. He won't admit it, but my nurse told me that he gets a percentage on all my income.

GASTON. Ah, I see. And what sort of a man is this Uncle Job?

LITTLE BOY. He's rather round, with white hair.

GASTON. No, I didn't mean that. But I don't suppose you can really tell me what I want to know. Where is he at the moment?

LITTLE BOY. Smoking his pipe in the garden. He didn't want to wait in the drawing room with the others.

GASTON. Good. Will you take me to him?

LITTLE BOY. If you like.

GASTON *rings the bell. The* VALET *appears.*

GASTON. Tell her Ladyship that I have an announcement of vital importance to make to her. Do you get that? Of vital importance. Will you ask her to be so good as to come up here, please?

VALET. Of vital importance. Very good, sir. You can rely on

me. [*He goes out, highly excited, muttering.*] Of vital importance . . .

GASTON *leads the* LITTLE BOY *toward the other door.*

GASTON. Let's go this way. [*He gets to the door, stops and asks.*] Tell me, you're quite sure everybody's dead in your family?

LITTLE BOY. Yes, everybody. Even their best friends. They all went on that cruise together.

GASTON. That's perfect.

He ushers him ahead and follows him out. The music starts again, mocking. The stage is empty for a while; then the DUCHESS *comes in, followed by the* VALET.

DUCHESS. What do you mean, he wants to see me? But he knows I've been waiting for him downstairs for the last twenty minutes! An announcement, you said?

VALET. Of vital importance.

DUCHESS. Well, where is he?

GASTON, *followed by* UNCLE JOB *and the* LITTLE BOY, *comes solemnly into the room. The orchestra performs a tremolo or something like it.*

GASTON. Duchess, may I introduce Mr. Truggle, solicitor to the Madensale family. And this is their sole surviving member. Mr. Truggle has just told me something very disturbing. He maintains that his client's nephew had a slight scar, an inch or so below the left shoulder blade, which nobody knows about. An old letter he came across in a book recently informed him of this fact.

TRUGGLE. The letter in question will of course be at the disposal of the hospital authorities as soon as I get back to England.

DUCHESS. But this scar, Gaston—have you ever seen it? Has anybody?

GASTON. Nobody.

TRUGGLE. It's so small, madame, that I guessed it might have gone unnoticed until now.

GASTON [*taking his coat off*]. We'll soon find out. Would you care to look?

He pulls up his shirt. The DUCHESS *takes her lorgnette.* MR. TRUGGLE *puts on his thick glasses.* GASTON *leans forward to talk to the* LITTLE BOY *while the others examine his back.*

LITTLE BOY. That scar really is there, isn't it? I'd be terribly disappointed if it wasn't you.

GASTON. Don't you worry. It's me all right. Tell me, don't you really remember anything about your family? Not a single face? Not even a little story?

LITTLE BOY. No stories at all. But if that bothers you, I might try to find out.

GASTON. No. Don't.

DUCHESS [peering at his back, cries out suddenly]. There! There! There it is! Oh, my God, it's there!

TRUGGLE. So it is! So it is!

DUCHESS. Kiss me, Gaston! I insist you kiss me! Oh, it's such a marvelous adventure!

TRUGGLE [quite straight-faced]. And so unexpected.

DUCHESS [sinking into a chair]. Oh, the shock! I think I may be going to faint.

GASTON [helping her to her feet with a smile]. I don't think you will.

DUCHESS. Nor do I. I'll telephone Pont-au-Bronc instead. But tell me, Monsieur Madensale, there's something I should so like to know. At the last pentothal injection he gave you, my little Albert managed to make you say "fartarse" in your delirium. Is that a word which connects you to your past life now?

GASTON. Shush. Don't tell a soul. That was my pet name for him.

DUCHESS [horrified]. My little Albert! [She hesitates, then changes her mind.] Never mind, we forgive you. [She turns to TRUGGLE, simpering.] It's his English sense of humor, I realize that now.

TRUGGLE. Precisely.

DUCHESS [as the thought strikes her]. But what a terrible blow for the Renaud family! However am I going to break it to them?

GASTON [cheerfully]. I'll leave it to you. I'll be out of this house in five minutes and I won't be seeing them again.

DUCHESS. Haven't you even a message for them?

GASTON. No. No message. Oh, yes, on second thought . . . [He hesitates.] Tell Georges Renaud that his brother's light ghost lies sleeping in a common grave somewhere in Germany. He was never anything but a child deserving all forgiveness, a child he can love now without fear of reading anything vile on his man's face. There. And now . . . [*He opens the door wide and ushers them out with a kind little wave of the hand. He holds the* LITTLE BOY *close.*] Leave me alone with my family. We have to compare our memories. . . .

Triumphant music. The DUCHESS *goes out with* MR. TRUGGLE.

Curtain.

THE ORCHESTRA

(*L'Orchestre*)

A play in one act

Translated by
MIRIAM JOHN

The Orchestra by Jean Anouilh, translated by Miriam John.
Copyright © 1967 by Jean Anouilh and Miriam John.

*All applications for permission to perform this play, whether
by amateurs or professionals, must be made to Dr. Jan van
Loewen, Ltd., International Copyright Agency, 81-83
Shaftesbury Avenue, London W.1. No performance may
take place unless a license has first been obtained.*

CHARACTERS

PATRICIA, *first violin*
PAMELA, *second violin*
MADAME HORTENSE, *double bass and leader of the orchestra*
SUZANNE DÉLICIAS, *cello*
EMMELINE, *viola*
LÉONA, *flute*
MONSIEUR LÉON, *piano*
MONSIEUR LEBONZE, *manager of the brasserie*
THE WAITER
THE DOCTOR

THE ORCHESTRA

Sparkling music from behind the lowered curtain, which then rises on an all-female orchestra on the platform of a spa town brasserie. The restaurant is not visible. The women are dressed in exactly similar bespangled black gowns with a single pink rose as ornament.

At the piano, with his back to the audience, is a rather wan, skinny little man, hardly noticeable at first. To one side is a stand with a card bearing the number 3. The lively piece comes to an end shortly after curtain rise. As soon as they finish playing, the musicians start talking.

PATRICIA. Then I add some shallots and leave it to marinate. Just two minutes—no longer. When I have my sauce ready, I cut the veal in small cubes. . . .

PAMELA. I put bacon with mine.

PATRICIA. For real *timbale Poitevine* you *never* use bacon, if you don't mind my saying so.

PAMELA. Well, I do, always.

PATRICIA [*thin-lipped*]. Then it isn't *timbale Poitevine*, it's pig swill. I come from Loudun; I should know.

They hand their music sheets back to MADAME HORTENSE, *who plays double bass and is leader of the orchestra.*

PAMELA. Who's boasting? I come from Batignolles.

PATRICIA [*sourly*]. Oh—Paris!

MADAME HORTENSE, *still gathering up music, is speaking to* SUZANNE DÉLICIAS, *who is knitting away quietly between pieces behind her cello. They are continuing a conversation.*

MADAME HORTENSE. Three plain, three purl, slip three, and the same again.

SUZANNE D. That's Japanese stitch.

MADAME HORTENSE. No. Japanese stitch has a wrong side, my dear; this stitch has two right sides.

SUZANNE D. [*with a sour little laugh*]. Excuse me, but if you loop it like that, your work has quite simply got two wrong sides! It must look horrible for a man's pull-over.

187

MADAME HORTENSE. Just as you like. Anyway, Japanese stitch looks vulgar.

EMMELINE [*finishing a conversation with* LÉONA, *who is slightly hunchbacked*]. So I said to him, "Edmond," I said, "you can't make a woman suffer like this with impunity."

LÉONA. And what did he say to that?

EMMELINE. A foul word.

MADAME HORTENSE [*turns on the* PIANIST *as she continues her rounds*]. Monsieur Léon in the clouds, as usual! Come along now, quickly. Ready with your "Gay Reverie," or we shall get all our parts mixed up again! What a dreamer you are! I think your dandruff's getting worse and worse.

PIANIST. All artists have it.

MADAME HORTENSE. Why don't you use that Pope's Lotion I advised you to try?

PIANIST. It smells oriental. I don't think it's very virile.

MADAME HORTENSE [*with a smile*]. When I was with Monsieur Hortense, he used to use it. And I flatter myself that in all our twelve years of marriage I was the best-loved woman in the world. Monsieur Hortense performed three times a day—once in the afternoon. Ah! How he spoiled me!

PIANIST [*modestly*]. He was a violinist, and violinists are . . .

MADAME HORTENSE [*significantly*]. I've also known pianists with a fiery temperament.

PIANIST [*still modest*]. It's rarer, though.

MADAME HORTENSE *has gone to take her music back to the heap of sheet music on a table at the back of the stage.* SUZANNE D. *leaves her knitting and her cello and goes over to the piano.*

SUZANNE D. She never stops, does she?

PIANIST. We were just chatting.

SUZANNE D. If you don't shut her up, I will.

PIANIST. It's difficult to stop her while the customers are here. After all, she's the leader, isn't she?

SUZANNE D. Coward! Coward! [*She sits down again.*]

PATRICIA [*continuing a conversation with* PAMELA *of which we have not heard the beginning*]. Then I rub it with a bit of Kleenall and a really dry, soft rag.

PAMELA. I prefer a drop of ammonia.

PATRICIA [*acid*]. Ammonia removes the varnish, not the mark.

PAMELA [*also aggressive*]. Each to her own method.

PATRICIA. Yes, but some methods are bad. Certain women have no pride in their homes.

PAMELA. My home looks just as good as yours. [*With a laugh.*] Maybe there aren't so many little mats and table runners and things.

PATRICIA. Well, not everyone has artistic taste, I mean, have they? I like my little soft, warm nest, with all my souvenirs around me. The mats and things make it cosy.

PAMELA. Dust traps. My little place is modern, I'm proud to say. Tubular furniture and formica surfaces. Everything neat and bright. No ornaments.

PATRICIA [*with a nervous little sneer*]. Oh, I can just see it —a clinic! I'm not an invalid.

PAMELA. And I *am*, I suppose?

PATRICIA. Well, with those eyes . . .

PAMELA. My eyes may be a little haggard, my dear, but that's because I have a lover who adores me, and that's more than you can say. At least both *my* eyes look in the same direction.

PATRICIA [*squinting nervously*]. Oh! What a thing to say about a physical handicap. Anyway, it's hardly noticeable. How low can you sink? And as for your lover, there's no need to boast about him. A bottle washer!

PAMELA [*laughing quite good-naturedly*]. One does what one can. The great thing is to make a good job of it. I like a job well done. [*She is cooing insolently.*]

PATRICIA. You're unspeakable. I wonder women like you are tolerated in a respectable orchestra.

MADAME HORTENSE [*who has changed the number and is passing the music around*]. Ladies! No arguments on the platform, please! Even when we stop playing, the customers don't stop looking. Smiles, please, charm . . . You can still say what you think with a smile. Your flower, Pamela.

PAMELA. What about my flower?

MADAME HORTENSE. It's drooping. I want all your roses looking fresh!

PATRICIA [*bitchily*]. Like their wearers! [PAMELA *stamps angrily on her toe.*] Ouch!

MADAME HORTENSE. Ladies!

PATRICIA. Little bitch! She trod on my toe!

MADAME HORTENSE [*still smiling, but with a glint in her eye*]. Manners now, whatever happens. You belong to your public. That's the rule. The manager said to me at the audition, when we got the job in preference to Mag's Star and the Symphony Band—and you know they're both reputable orchestras—he said, "I'm taking you because I want women and charm! An orchestra that will catch my customers' imagination."

PATRICIA. Some hopes of catching imagination in a spa for the cure of constipation. Do you think they listen to us? They talk about it all the time. And tote up their bills. Some bills, too!

MADAME HORTENSE. It's not our concern what the customer is thinking, or whether or not he is constipated. Poise and elegance. That's what we were engaged for. And quantities of femininity. Now we're going to play "Impressions of Autumn" by Chandoisy, in the Goldstein arrangement. Lots of feeling and vibrato, if you please. [*She slides a finger in passing under* MONSIEUR LÉON'S *collar*.] Oh, Monsieur Léon, how warm you are! Your collar is quite damp.

PIANIST. I always bring two with me. I'll change during the intermission, after the March from *Tannhäuser*.

SUZANNE D. [*beside herself*]. Stop it, stop it! Or I shall leave the platform.

PIANIST [*pitifully*]. Please, don't let's have a scene. She said I was too warm. I can't very well tell her I'm not.

SUZANNE D. Monster! You're a monster of cruelty!

MADAME HORTENSE [*very much in command*]. Careful of that sharp in the reprise during your solo, Mademoiselle Délicias, won't you, please?

EMMELINE [*finishing a conversation with* LÉONA]. Everything! Everything! I told him everything! The rent not paid, my trouble with my poor mother, my period not coming . . .

LÉONA. So what did he say?

EMMELINE. Nothing. He was asleep.

LÉONA. Well! What an oaf! I'd never have stood that from André.

MADAME HORTENSE *taps discreetly with her bow on her double bass. The music starts up. Very tender and tuneful.*

During the performance at chosen points in the music, the musicians talk as they play.

PATRICIA. I'm a woman. I'm probably more of a woman than you, even though I don't throw myself on my back for anyone that happens along. I'm waiting for someone . . . someone I can . . . I want to be able to look deep down into his eyes.

PAMELA [*puffing out her cheeks as she plays*]. You'll have difficulty doing that with both eyes at once.

PATRICIA [*stifling a sob at this second jab*]. Oh!

PAMELA. He'll have to change sides from time to time.

PATRICIA [*another sob*]. Oh! It's too much!

MADAME HORTENSE *gives her a discreet tap on the head with her bow. She swallows her emotion and plays with a passionate abandon. Music.*

EMMELINE [*continuing*]. So then when we went into the restaurant, an extremely smart place where his friends had invited us, I said to him: "Where shall I sit, Edmond?"

LÉONA. And what did he say?

EMMELINE [*sniffing indignantly*]. He said, sit where you f——

A tap on the head from MADAME HORTENSE's *bow cuts the word off just as by general consent the orchestra has drowned it. The piece comes to an end with much pathos and brilliance of technique. Once it is over,* MADAME HORTENSE *collects the music and changes the number.*

PATRICIA. Why is the waiter hanging about with our refreshments? I'm dying of thirst. We have *some* rights!

PAMELA [*good-naturedly joining in*]. He has customers to serve, so our glass of beer can wait, needless to say.

PATRICIA. Artists don't count, of course.

MADAME HORTENSE [*changing the number*]. During the intermission, ladies. You know that's the usual thing. We have a right to refreshments during intermission.

PATRICIA. Yesterday they served us at midnight. Oh, he's quicker off the mark on Saturdays, he gets a tip. This week I shall give him ten centimes. What a life, among all these yokels. Some people find it quite natural, of course, to the point of taking them to bed. I was brought up differently. An officer's daughter in a clip joint!

MADAME HORTENSE [*vexed*]. The Brasserie du Globe et du

Portugal is a first-class establishment and you were very
lucky to get in, my dear. Don't spit in your own soup.

PATRICIA. And with my gifts! Let me tell you, I've played
at concerts and I've given recitals. Once, at a charity
affair, Massenet, the great Massenet, was in the audience.
At the end of the concert, he kissed my hand. I had been
rendering an arrangement of something by Mignon. I'd
really put the whole of myself into it. The Master had
tears in his eyes. He was so moved, he could find nothing
to say to me. Such an eloquent talker, too. . . . Obviously, you wouldn't understand.

MADAME HORTENSE. We all have our little successes. Monsieur Hortense was once first violin at the Brasserie Zurki
in Saint Petersburg. I am speaking of the time before the
revolution. He used to play to crowned heads. But there
are always ups and downs. It didn't prevent him from
doing his job conscientiously. He would say to me, "Zélie,
music is like greens, it is always good for you."

PATRICIA. Giving all you have to the constipated!

MADAME HORTENSE. Constipation never prevented anyone
from appreciating music. Just the contrary, I should say.
We have some splendid music lovers here. Only yesterday
a big Belgian industrialist came over to congratulate me.
As a matter of fact, he mentioned you.

PATRICIA [suddenly transformed]. Really? How amusing.
What did he say?

MADAME HORTENSE. He asked me if you came from Ghent.
It seems you remind him of someone from there. In
charge of the cloakroom at the Kursaal.

EMMELINE [continuing, to LÉONA]. So I said to him, "Edmond, maybe you don't like it, but don't put other people off!"

LÉONA. Just like that?

EMMELINE. Just like that. Short and to the point. And then
I said, "I'm a woman, and you'll never stop a woman
thinking and feeling like a woman." That, my dear, that
little pay-off line went right home, I could see that.

LÉONA. What did he say?

EMMELINE. Nothing. He just went on brushing his teeth.

LÉONA. So what did you do?

EMMELINE. I put down my scissors—I was cutting my toe-
nails at the time—and went out of the bathroom.

LÉONA. Just like that?

EMMELINE. Just like that. You've got to admit he didn't get away with that! I put on my girdle and stockings. Still not a word, my dear. He was rinsing his teeth. So I put on my dress. I'd made up my mind. You know me. And I just went out and slammed the door. I was in such a rage! The first man, I assure you, the first man to be nice to me I was going to give myself to. Only there was nobody but the night watchman outside—an old Negro—and you know what Moulins is like in the morning! Not so much as a cat in sight. I walked as far as I could, just to frighten him. I went to have a look at the cathedral since everyone says it's so nice, but there was nothing to look at, and at a quarter past two I went back up. I'd had enough. I had those pink shoes on—the ones I gave you because they were too small and hurt my corns. And anyway, I'd shouted out when I left that we'd have to put an end to it once and for all, so I was afraid he might be frightened of the water and call the police.

LÉONA. Is he frightened of water, then?

EMMELINE. Don't be so stupid—there's a river running through Moulins. It's the first thing anybody thinks of in the state I was in—everyone knows that. I did go as far as the edge, too, but it was too dark, so I came back.

LÉONA. Oh, I see! He thought you were dead! So what did he say when he saw you?

EMMELINE. Nothing. He didn't see me. He'd gone out, too.

LÉONA. To fetch the police?

EMMELINE. No. To have a round with his pals at the all-night bar opposite the station.

SUZANNE D. [standing near the piano]. I've put up with everything! Our secret rendezvous, our occasional meetings in that filthy little hotel where the manager talks to me as if I were a tart—me! who has always dreamed of the day when I could go around with my head high and be seen arm in arm with the man I love! But there is one thing I won't put up with, Léon—the advances of that horrible woman to the man I've chosen and given myself to! Your poor, sick wife—that's another matter; I can understand pity even if I do find it cowardly and despise the degrading precautions you take. . . . But here, under my very nose, this exhibition of lust! Right here, in the orchestra!

PIANIST. Our relations are strictly limited to professional matters, my love.

SUZANNE D. Her finger around your collar just now—was that a professional matter? And what about when she ruffled your hair?

PIANIST. She was drawing my attention to the dandruff on the collar of my jacket. It was strictly her professional right as director of the orchestra.

SUZANNE D. [*trembling*]. Your collar is mine, Léon, your hair is mine, even your dandruff is mine! I'm the only one who should be worrying about that little snowstorm! I'm the one who should be brushing your collar! I've given you everything—my saved-up virginity, my illusions, the good name of an irreproachable family—and then there's my religious sister, who'd die if she heard of this. Everything you are is mine now! I shall claw at her like a she-lion!

PIANIST [*mildly*]. Lionesses bite. It's tigresses that claw—I've told you before, my love.

SUZANNE D. Right! Then I'll bite! [*As* MADAME HORTENSE *passes near her, she suddenly shows her teeth with a lion-like roar as though she is about to take a bite at her*.] RRR-RR-RR!

MADAME HORTENSE [*halting*]. Is something the matter?

SUZANNE D. *bursts into sobs.*

PIANIST [*stammering*]. It's just nerves. Just nerves.

MADAME HORTENSE. Nerves or no nerves, my dear, *not* on the platform! We're the center of attention of the entire establishment. [*To* LÉON.] You! Give her a slap on the back; they'll think she was choking. We don't want a scandal in the orchestra!

PIANIST [*doing so*]. My little lamb, my little bunny rabbit, my little stoat . . .

MADAME HORTENSE. Now, now. The *Fables* of La Fontaine can wait. During off hours, I don't care how you pass the time, the two of you!

SUZANNE D. [*to* LÉON, *irritably*]. Stop slapping me like that. You're hurting. [*To* MADAME HORTENSE, *pulling herself up*.] I'm in love and I'm loved, if you want to know, madame!

MADAME HORTENSE. No, Mademoiselle Délicias. No. I do not want to know. We are in the temple of music here.

SUZANNE D. Oh no, that's too easy—trying to shut me up in the name of Art. Do you think I'm ashamed? I can hold my head up! Yes, I can hold my head up! [*She does so on the platform for a ridiculously long interval.*]

MADAME HORTENSE [*snatching the music* SUZANNE D. *is brandishing*]. All I ask of you is that you don't ruin your music sheet. Don't you realize what it costs, this music? Just look at that. "Cockades and Cock-crows" all crumpled up. And it's an extremely rare piece!

SUZANNE D. [*with a contemptuous laugh*]. Extremely rare— really, your taste for cheap music is deplorable, if I may say so, Madame Hortense. Extremely rare! Duverger!

MADAME HORTENSE. Arranged by Benoisseau, my dear! And he was a man who knew his job. I'm sorry I have to tell you that. I knew him at the Casino de Royan, in the good old days of the Symphony Orchestra. There was a musician for you!

SUZANNE D. I was brought up on the classics. Ah, Beethoven, Saint-Saëns . . . !

MADAME HORTENSE. In a place like this, the customer plays cards or dominoes to forget his health troubles. What he wants is a good background noise. This piece is gay, vibrant, lively. And it makes one think of France—that's always a good thing in a café.

SUZANNE D. Oh, I've sunk too low! All these humiliations will kill me! Such mediocrity—it's suffocating. I shan't sing the great aria from *La Vestale* this time. My voice is broken. I'm in no condition to sing.

MADAME HORTENSE [*severely*]. The air from *La Vestale* is on the program. It's in print. A change of program always makes a bad impression. Monsieur Lebonze has absolutely forbidden it. It confuses his customers. You will sing it.

SUZANNE D. [*sits down suddenly, groaning*]. No! No! This is too much. It's too much for my nerves. Help me, Léon! This woman is persecuting me!

MADAME HORTENSE. You are a small person. Monsieur Léon is a man and an artist. He will be obliged to agree with me. [*She continues on her Olympian way, distributing the music to the members of the orchestra.*]

EMMELINE. I'm saying nothing. It's not my lookout. But if anyone took it into their heads to take a tenth of the liberties with Edmond that she takes with that unfortunate boy, I should see red. Once, at the casino at Palavas, I go out for a moment during the interval. When I come back, he's not on the platform. You know where I find him?

LÉONA. No.

EMMELINE. With the lavatory attendant.

LÉONA. No!

EMMELINE. Oh yes. A blonde creature with a horrible reputation. Can you imagine? A pee-pee girl!

LÉONA. What was he doing?

EMMELINE. He pretended afterward that he was asking her for some change, but he couldn't fool me. You know what I said to him?

LÉONA. No.

EMMELINE. Nothing. I just looked at them, like that, said, "Is there any paper?" and walked straight into the Ladies'.

LÉONA. Just like that. And what did he do?

EMMELINE. He went into the Gents', without a word. But let me tell you, he had turned quite pale. I could see he'd taken the snub.

LÉONA. You did quite right. Some people have to be put in their place.

MADAME HORTENSE [suddenly, from the back]. Men! I've had dozens of them! Tall ones, handsome ones, well-set-up ones. Since Monsieur Hortense died, I've been taking a rest. But I just want you to know that if I needed one . . . !

SUZANNE D. May one know what would happen if you needed one, madame?

MADAME HORTENSE. I would choose a better-built one—there!

SUZANNE D. Léon is beautiful. He has a Grecian nose.

MADAME HORTENSE. Grecian nose or no Grecian nose, I couldn't care less. I believe in a chest measurement.

PIANIST. Ladies!

MADAME HORTENSE. Monsieur Hortense was a wardrobe of a man. He crushed a woman in bed. That's love for you!

SUZANNE D. How crude you are, madame.

PIANIST. Ladies!

SUZANNE D. Keep your stevedores, your waiters, your brutes —I despise them. I vomit them! I'd die rather than let them come near me with their great fists. Léon has an Apollo's figure. Not a trace of a stomach. Show her, Léon! I will not have people say you aren't beautiful.

PIANIST [*horrified*]. Suzanne! Not in the orchestra!

SUZANNE D. [*atremble*]. Why not? I'm proud of our love! I want to brave everybody and their opinions—I want to brave the entire world!

MADAME HORTENSE [*who has suddenly cast a terrified look at the end of the room*]. Suzanne Délicias, the manager is looking at us. You know he won't have gossiping in the orchestra. And our contract is renewable every two weeks. [*She calls out obsequiously.*] Right away, Monsieur Lebonze, right away! We're off! Are you ready, ladies? "Cockades and Cock-crows," smartly now. Very lively. Let's go, now—one, two, three, four. . . .

The orchestra, everyone having scuttled back to position, attacks the glossy, heroic music. SUZANNE DÉLICIAS *is muttering to herself meanwhile as she plays furiously on her cello.*

SUZANNE D. I shall kill myself.

PIANIST [*groaning as he plays*]. Suzanne.

SUZANNE D. With laudanum.

PIANIST [*as before, but with a different tone of voice each time*]. Suzanne.

Music.

SUZANNE D. I shall go and throw myself in the river.

PIANIST [*distracted*]. Suzanne.

SUZANNE D. Or under a train.

PIANIST. Suzanne.

With music still playing, SUZANNE *suddenly bursts into derisive laughter.*

SUZANNE D. Not likely! That's just what she'd like. She'd have you at last! You know what I'm going to do tomorrow? I'm going to buy myself a new dress. The most expensive I can find at Petit Paris. I'll blow two weeks' pay on it and make her mad with my wasp waist—showing up her great, fat, undignified backside!

PIANIST. Suzanne!

SUZANNE D. [*demands suddenly*]. Do you love me, Léon?

PIANIST. I adore you, my love. I shall never love anyone but you.

SUZANNE D. You're not afraid of death?

PIANIST. With you?

SUZANNE D. [*beside herself*]. Yes!

PIANIST [*with conviction*]. No!

SUZANNE D. So we shall die together if we are too unhappy.
We'll have them all fooled.

PIANIST [*lukewarm*]. Quite.

SUZANNE D. [*gloomily, over her cello, while the music becomes more and more spirited*]. It's good to die!

PIANIST [*halfhearted*]. Delicious!

A flourish of chords as the music comes to an end. Applause here and there throughout the room. MADAME HORTENSE, *delighted, acknowledges it discreetly and gestures toward the orchestra with her hand.* MADAME HORTENSE *goes around collecting the music.*

MADAME HORTENSE. You heard the way they applauded.
So "Cockades and Cock-crows" arranged by Benoisseau
is still cheap music, mm? What a reaction, my dears,
what a reaction! Did you see that? That piece really penetrates the vitals! The Frenchman knows that it was written
for him. [*She throws this remark at* SUZANNE.] You have
to have turnip juice in your veins and no love for your
country not to feel what that music has to give!

SUZANNE D. My answer to that is utter contempt!

MADAME HORTENSE. Now I have patriotism in my blood!
During the war at the height of unemployment, I refused
a season at Vichy. And I know some who wouldn't have
had any scruples. Even played for the enemy!

SUZANNE D. Your insinuations leave me cold as marble. It
is true that I played in a Paris brasserie in '40, but it was
a resistance orchestra. Whenever there were German officers in the place, the word went around to play out of
tune. That needed some courage! We could have been
denounced—those people were all musicians!

MADAME HORTENSE [*laughing unpleasantly*]. Knowing you,
I should think playing out of tune came all too easily!

SUZANNE D. [*pulling herself up, pale*]. Oh, this is too much!
If you're going to insult my art, if nothing's to be sacred
here, I'm leaving. . . .

She gets up and leaves the platform. The PIANIST, *deathly pale, runs and catches her as she goes out.*

PATRICIA [*to* PAMELA]. There, you see! She's going too far,
attacking her that way. Maybe she didn't play at Vichy,
but she played over the radio.

PIANIST [*at floor level with* SUZANNE, *whom he is trying to deter*]. This argument is ridiculous, like all arguments. Nobody's questioning your talent, Suzanne!

SUZANNE D. [*with a bitter laugh*]. To hell with my talent! It's always possible I didn't even have that! And I thought I was making such a gift of myself! It's too funny. Don't you find it funny? So I've given nothing to Art, or to my country, or to you.

PIANIST [*wearily*]. No, you haven't. . . . I mean, yes, you have! Now, please, Suzanne, don't let's have a scandal!

SUZANNE D. I'm beyond scandal now. I've been putting up with it for a long time, Léon. I've given myself to you in degrading conditions in furnished hotels! [*Shouting madly.*] Furnished hotels!

PIANIST [*stammering pitifully*]. Quiet, now, Suzanne, quiet. Hotels are always furnished . . . in Europe at least . . . and, anyway, when we were traveling . . .

SUZANNE D. [*with a prolonged nervous laugh*]. Oh yes, when we were traveling. Never got very far though, did we? The other side of the town—on foot! We were the sort of travelers who really didn't need luggage! I've suffered enough. Oh, the way the manager would look at me when we asked for our room, the look he gave me—sharing me with you in advance.

PIANIST. You exaggerate, Suzanne. He's a respectable married man. . . .

SUZANNE D. [*contemptuous*]. That makes two of you—respectable married men—sharing me on my so very short travels! We made love with an eye on the time, Léon, so that your so dear and so pathetic invalid wife shouldn't go mad with your everlasting late home-comings. What about me—wasn't I as pathetic and ill as she was?

PIANIST. It wasn't the same thing, Suzanne!

SUZANNE D. [*with rising excitement*]. Maybe we were traveling without baggage, but we did have watches. One each, on the bedside tables. Some lovers lie and play at listening to each other's hearts, to see if they beat in time. But we spent our time in bed checking whether we had the right time by our watches. Oh, that watch, that watch, I hate it. [*She throws it on the floor and stamps on it.*] I'm throwing it out; I'm stamping on it! Give me yours! [*She tries to snatch his watch.*]

PIANIST [*a pathetic figure, defending his own watch as he picks up the other*]. My love, the whole place can see us!

. . . The glass isn't broken, fortunately. . . . You're exaggerating, Suzanne. Everyone watches out for the time these days. Modern life is lived with an eye on the clock. . . .

SUZANNE D. Oh yes, I've lived modern life all right. I've been a free woman, liberated from prejudice as they say. But they're in chains all the same, these free women. All tied up in watch chains! I've been a free woman weighed down with watch chains. Isn't that amusing?

PIANIST. I told you at the start that I couldn't risk killing my poor sick wife. And you told me our love would be so great!

SUZANNE D. [still ridiculous, but with a sort of sincere misery]. Well, it wasn't—it wasn't big enough! It was murdered, murdered with the hands of a watch. It got drowned in the lavatory bowl along with the children I could have had. Ten times I suggested we should kill ourselves, Léon. Dying together would have been clean! To drown the lot, once and for all: father, mother, and children, instead of just the children. That would have been simple!

PIANIST [stammering]. It only seemed simple, my love. . . . I had no right to leave her either. . . .

SUZANNE D. [shouting]. But me, you had the right to leave me at the end of my daily three quarters of an hour. I was a ridiculous old maid and I'd waited all that time just to be a woman three quarters of an hour a day! To the minute. Timed on two watches, if you please!

PIANIST [correcting her idiotically]. An hour! An hour and a half! I'd told my wife I had to be on here a good hour later—you know that!

SUZANNE D. [also idiotic, but somehow touching as well]. Yes, but there was all that walking! And I only had the right to be your wife on the other side of the town. Someone might have seen us otherwise. We had to be good and just walk side by side—as though we didn't know each other!

PIANIST [trying to be romantic]. What did it matter, so long as we loved each other! Does the time count?

SUZANNE D. [serious]. Yes, I've finally decided that it counts terribly. And that that's just what life is made of. [Stating.] I've wasted my time. Funny expression, isn't it? Wasted my time. No good praying to Saint Anthony to give it back to me. [She suddenly bursts out.] What time do you make it, Léon? Do we both make it the same? My watch says a quarter to eleven.

PIANIST [*mechanically consulting his*]. Mine says quarter to twelve. We should be playing, Suzanne. Get up on the platform. We'll talk about it during the intermission—my love. We'll have a long quarter of an hour to ourselves.

SUZANNE D. [*haughtily*]. Thanks. I've already finished here.

MADAME HORTENSE [*who has come down off the platform, in a low voice*]. Now, have we finished with this scene? The manager's looking at us. Do you want to have us all thrown out? That's what you're trying to do, isn't it, you little sourpuss?

SUZANNE D. [*dignified*]. No, madame. So far as I am concerned, I'm out already. I refuse once and for all to play out of tune. Good-by, madame. I leave him to you. But you were right—he's a runt. [*She turns haughtily.*] I hope you have a good watch at least? [*She bursts into a long, nervous laugh and exits.*]

MADAME HORTENSE [*calls after her*]. You'll get five hundred francs' fine, my girl. And I warn you, you'll be replaced on Saturday!

PIANIST [*who has gone back onto the platform, head lowered*]. She's suffering, Madame Hortense. You are abusing your power. [*He groans as he sits down at his pathetic piano.*] You should be ashamed.

MADAME HORTENSE. It's you who should be ashamed, Monsieur Léon, with your poor, sick wife. That hysterical creature will end up telling her everything to relieve her own feelings.

PIANIST [*desperate*]. It's too much—too much!

MADAME HORTENSE. I know men, Monsieur Léon. I've managed other men besides you. A man has need of contentment, it's only human. No one will reproach you for that, in your situation. But entrust yourself to a proper woman, who knows what life is and who will have something to give. I was lying just now. I don't find you skinny at all. A little slender perhaps, but for someone motherly, like me, that's just one of your charms. . . . [*She passes a finger around his collar again.*] Oh! How warm he is, how warm he is, the wicked man. And he doesn't like being petted. He does so need someone to look after him.

PIANIST [*weeping, his head in her arms*]. These scenes destroy my nerves. I'm an artist. I'm not made for real life.

MADAME HORTENSE. We'll help you, we'll help you, my dear.
I understand you so well. Why the need for scenes over
every little thing? A little discreet pleasure—shouldn't that
be enough to make for happiness? You're swimming.
Change your collar, my poppet.

PIANIST [*broken but heroic*]. After the March from *Tannhäuser*. No point in doing it before. [*Snivels.*] You
mustn't think I don't still love my wife. Twelve years—
you can't forget that so easily. I could have put her in a
home. She's incurable. Who would have blamed me? I've
kept her at home, in spite of her insane jealousy. I've
taken a housekeeper, a woman I can rely on. But all that
costs money. Sometimes I feel so alone.

MADAME HORTENSE. You should have someone to help you
instead of torturing you even more. That's all there is to
it. Someone sensitive, like yourself.

PIANIST [*groaning*]. I'm a harp. It takes nothing to break
me.

MADAME HORTENSE. You are an artist. And artists don't
need emotions outside their art. A little pleasure, yes.
That's all. The rest goes into music. Haven't you noticed
that that mad creature was the only one who caused us
any trouble in the orchestra?

PIANIST. She's a harp too!

MADAME HORTENSE. Yes, but a broken-down harp. Leaving
the orchestra like that, just for a whim! Just when we
ought to be striking up "Cuban Delights." . . . Léona,
be a good girl and go and see what she's doing, the little
lunatic. She's probably sniveling away in the toilets!
[LÉONA *gets up and goes.*] Sentiment is all very fine, but
we have a job to do. We're in danger of losing our engagement as well. The manager's on the prowl. I don't
know what's the matter with him this evening, he's so
suspicious. [*She begins to busy herself with the parts.*]

PATRICIA [*pursuing a sudden friendly conversation with
PAMELA*]. All the same, she was absolutely horrible to
her. First of all, people should stop talking about the
war. I resisted, like anyone else. I listened to London
radio every day. I did what I could. But I had my poor
old mother. I had to see she had some comforts.

PAMELA. Does your old girl still live with you?

PATRICIA [*with a sour little laugh*]. Sure. Poor Toots. That's
what I call her. She's my baby now. I've decided to devote

my life entirely to her. To her and my art. There's
nothing else I can do with such a small place.

PAMELA. You know, I just couldn't do it. When I go to
see mine at Batignolles—she's not badly off, she's a
concierge—it's all right for a while: "Hullo, Maman
. . . How are you, Maman? . . . I'm all right, Maman."
Makes me feel I was a kid again. There'll be Irish stew
waiting for me—it's her favorite vice, Irish stew. But by
the third mouthful, without fail, we start bawling each
other out. The plates start jumping around the table and
off I go again home.

PATRICIA [smiling slightly]. You mustn't think we don't
have our little skirmishes, too, poor Toots and me. As she
gets older, she gets more and more like a little girl.
Whims and fancies at every turn. Oh, but I'm very severe
with her! When she goes to steal a sweet, the rascal,
smack! A good rap on the knuckles for her. "Ooh! Ooh!"
she snivels, but after that, she's good. It's obviously boredom that accounts for all these little yearnings. And then
again I've tried to train her to "ask," but it's no good;
the wicked old thing always dirties herself.

PAMELA. It's just a bad phase. It'll probably adjust itself in
time.

PATRICIA. She's getting on for eighty, so I don't hold out
much hope any more. But there again I've decided to be
absolutely inflexible. I change her three times a day, and
if she forgets herself meanwhile, so much the worse for
her. I often think she does it out of spite, you know.
Sometimes, when I'm all rigged out ready to leave for
work, she'll call out "caca" and start whimpering. My
goodness—that's just too bad! I leave her until midnight
to lie in her own mess. That teaches her.

PAMELA. You have to be firm with them. My girl, when I
had her with me——

PATRICIA [cutting in]. And you know what she's been trying
ever since last winter? She's started sucking her thumb!

PAMELA. My mother used to smear mustard on mine, but
I don't know what you'd do with old people.

PATRICIA. Mustard? She'd be only too happy! She adores
mustard. She adores anything that's bad for her. Oh, if I
were to let her eat what she wants! Any time I find her
at it, she gets a jolly good rap. And no pudding. That's
where it hurts most. Oh, the puddings and the sweets

she'd have if I let her—all my pills would disappear,
even! But I'm very firm about that. No sweets or sugary
things in the house. If a visitor brings any, I hide them,
and she can have one a week, on Sundays, if she's been
good. You should hear her blubbering at the cupboard
when I take them away from her. "Sweetie! Sweetie!"
Just like a baby.

PAMELA. It's for their own good. They'd only get tooth-
ache.

PATRICIA [with the same sour little smile]. Poor Toots! She
hasn't got any teeth any more. But it's the principle of
the thing, you see. Once you start giving way to
them . . .

PAMELA. It can't be much fun having that sort of thing
every day.

PATRICIA [gravely]. There's a great satisfaction in knowing
one is doing one's duty. Maman is everything to me,
apart from my art. And I make the sacrifice cheerfully.
Believe me, and I think I can say this without boasting,
I am a model daughter. It's just that she must be straight
with me.

PAMELA. I sent my daughter away to the country. What
with my work and being separated from my husband, I
just couldn't. And then, you know, I'm a real woman,
I need men. And men can never get used to the child.
And even if one did come along by chance who got used
to her, you know how it is, sooner or later he'd change.
Anyway, all I have goes for her clothes. I want her to be
a real coquette, my Mouquette, a real little woman, I
want her to be. On her fifth birthday I gave her a really
sophisticated dress. Silk, you know, with the hooped
petticoat and the ribbons . . . twelve thousand francs it
cost me. You can see I'm not stingy over her. And I sent
her some money for a perm and some nail varnish and
lipstick. She looked so sweet! You should have seen her
with her little nails all painted and her lips made up and
everything. What a love! Me all over, she looked, my
dear. That's what I adore about her. She's the absolute
image of me. It was too bad I couldn't stay. I had a tiff
with Fernand. He wouldn't get out of the car and kept
sounding the horn continuously out in the street. And
there she was calling out, "Maman, Maman, you haven't
even given me a proper kiss." [She sighs.] It would be

nice to see more of them! But what can you do? Life's
like that. Anyway, she had her party frock. She'll remember that, later on.

PATRICIA. When you're an artist, you have heart. My friends
keep telling me I should put her in a home, where she'd
have all the attention she needs, poor Toots. True, she'd
be better off than at home, where she's nearly always
alone on account of my work. But I really couldn't. . . .
I'd rather correct her firmly when she's naughty and know
I've done my duty. She's my mother. My friends say,
"You're a saint, Patricia," but I always say, "You never
recover your losses!" The only thing I ask of her is that
she's grateful. Otherwise, a good smack and no pudding.

PAMELA. But, you know, if you do recover them, you don't
do so well! I could have stayed with her father and kept
her. He found me with Georges, but he thought it was
the first time. These things happen in any family and it
gets forgotten, especially if there's a child. But Georges
said he was leaving for Nice, and at the beginning I
thought I couldn't do without the man. I was crazy about
him. So I left the child. Mind you, two months later we
parted, but how was I to know? That's life!

PATRICIA. Maybe your husband would have taken you back?

PAMELA. I thought about that, mostly because of the child.
The divorce wasn't through and with that man I had
only to appear and everything would have been settled in
bed. So I packed my things and went back. But I met
someone in the train—I was in funds at the time and
had treated myself to first class—we were alone in the
compartment. You know how it is! Ah! Night trains, my
dear, they should be forbidden. [*She sighs.*] And to think
I'd bought her the dearest little regional costume from
Nice, with the matching hat and skirt—well, anyway, I
had to send it to her. . . . She must have been thrilled
with it, my little Mouquette. Apparently her friends at
school were sick with envy. The kid told me in a letter
that the other girls had said, "You're in luck, having a
mother like that." Imagine—I'd bought her the prettiest
model, with the apron in real silk. There's nothing I
wouldn't do for my kid!

LÉONA [*returning*]. I've looked everywhere, she's not in the
toilets. There's one that's engaged, but I didn't dare bang
on the door. I was afraid it might be a client.

MADAME HORTENSE. Bitch! Never mind! Let's tackle "Cuban Delights" just the same. Monsieur Lebonze has just looked at his watch. He must be thinking we're taking our time. Emmeline, be so kind as to leave your instrument and take the cello part. He may not notice the gap so much that way.

EMMELINE. What does he know about music?

MADAME HORTENSE. Nothing, but he can count. And there are only six of us now. We'll tell him she had food poisoning. It happened last week to a customer who ate the wrong sort of mushroom.

EMMELINE [whom LÉONA is helping to the other seat while MADAME HORTENSE is distributing the parts]. She's suffering, that girl. I can understand it only too well—love's a killer. Once I told Edmond, right to his face, "Edmond," I said, "sentiment forgives nothing. If I find you with another woman, I shall shut my eyes and pull the trigger. A woman who has suffered what I've suffered—there are laws in this country—I'll get off."

PIANIST. So what did he say?

EMMELINE. Nothing. But he was yawning at the time. So he stopped and picked up the paper.

LÉONA. Just like that.

EMMELINE. Just like that. I could see it had gone home.

MADAME HORTENSE. Now, off we go. I want this very warm —very sensual.

She has tapped discreetly on her music stand with her bow. She gives them one bar before starting and the orchestra then launches into "Cuban Delights," a syncopated piece heavy with sensuality. They have put on appropriate headgear and are throwing themselves heart and soul into their playing. LÉONA has left her flute for an exotic instrument. The piece has a refrain which everyone sings quietly as they play. It is a tradition. It suddenly makes itself heard during the muted passage at the second reprise.

ORCHESTRA [singing]. Delights, delights, Cuban delights! In Cuba, in Cuba! Delights, delights in Cuba!

Music.

PAMELA [hollowly, to PATRICIA]. This tune makes me feel quite peculiar. It's silly it should be so evocative!

PATRICIA [sourly, as she plays]. Cheap music.

PAMELA. Yes, but it reminds you of love. You wouldn't understand, my dear. But when you have men in your blood, the way I have . . . Take Georges, for example. Oh! How I missed that man. He beat me and he was stupid, so stupid . . . a real moron. But in bed . . . After all, what is there to say to each other during the day, anyway? Have you really never made love, not even once?

PATRICIA. There are questions one woman should never even ask another. I told you I've given everything to my art, and to poor Toots!

Music.

ORCHESTRA. Delights, delights . . . Cuban delights! . . . [*Et cetera.*]

MADAME HORTENSE [*in a hollow whisper to the* PIANIST]. For one thing the girl is a skinny creature anyway. You need flesh for love-making. For small men like you, Monsieur Léon, the woman has to take care of you, wrap you around; men like you have to be kept warm, they must be able to bury themselves in the woman, hide themselves in her!

PIANIST [*groaning suddenly*]. Oh, Mother, Mother! *Maman* was the only one who loved me!

MADAME HORTENSE. I'll be your *maman*, my chicken! You shall bury yourself in my bosom. Skinny women only think of themselves. They have nothing to give.

PIANIST. Oh, *Maman*!

ORCHESTRA. Delights, delights, Cuban delights! . . . [*Et cetera.*]

PATRICIA [*mournfully*]. Don't think I don't suffer! Sometimes when I'm undressing I look at myself in the glass. I'm beautiful! Really beautiful! My figure is nice and round and my legs are smooth, but I just can't!

PAMELA. It's not so difficult!

Music.

ORCHESTRA. Delights, delights . . .

EMMELINE [*to* LÉONA]. But, you know, Edmond's a real boor. I've never, but never, known such a pig. Never a kind word. Nothing. Dumb and clumsy as a carp!

LÉONA. A bull!

EMMELINE. But he's part of me. When that part's taken

away, I'm not complete any more and there's nothing for
it but to wait until he wants to come back—to finish me
off, if you understand what I mean?

LÉONA. It's quite clear. It's no longer his, it's yours.

EMMELINE. That's why he'll get those six bullets in his
head if he ever gets the idea of taking himself off with
anyone! Bang, bang, bang, bang, bang, bang!

LÉONA. Just like that.

EMMELINE. That's love.

Music.

ORCHESTRA. Delights, delights, Cuban delights! . . . [*Et
cetera.*]

The piece comes to an end. Increasing applause. The
PIANIST, *still wearing his Mexican hat, suddenly turns on
the piano like a hunted animal and shouts:*

PIANIST. I do not give a damn! My wife weeping away all
the time in that armchair . . . and the other one as well
with her tears and her emotions! Damn them both! [*He
shouts wildly.*] Damn them! It's torture crying with both
of them, suffering twice over! Once in the hotel room
without any clothes and again at home fully dressed. I'm
getting thin, losing weight, pining away; I've got acid
stomach with it all, but deep down inside me I've got to
admit that I don't give a damn! Sometimes I slip away
all by myself and go down to the river where they've got
that bathing place and I look at them, all those women
in bikinis offering themselves to the sun. I look sort of
preoccupied and you'd probably think I was just going for
a walk, or looking for someone, but it's not true. I'm not
looking for anyone. *I'm* the sun. I'm taking them—I'm
taking the lot of them, one after the other! Slowly,
thoroughly! And what's more I ring the changes. Bru-
nettes, blondes, redheads, coloreds, thin, fat, the lot! Just
as the mood takes me! Young ones, that haven't got
around to it yet, and matrons with rather riper pleasures
to offer. And there they all are—spread out, bottoms up
—you'd never think they were the same you can see so
respectably sipping afternoon tea in the patisserie. There
they are, offering everything to you with the best will in
the world, their beauties and their secrets, offering you
every inch of themselves, so as not to miss a single ray of
sunshine. The magazines have told them it has to be

nicely done all over! [*Shouting with unpleasant laughter.*]
Done! Done! Done! On the spit! On the spit! With me
as chef! I'm Nero! Tiberius! Farouk! All of them, all of
them mine! One after the other—sometimes several at a
time! Some of them I'm nice to, stroking them gently
and putting some feeling into it. But there are others I
take the whip to, and some I have killed off afterward!
[*He is quite out of breath and exhausted, but he adds,
lyrically.*] With tarts you knew you could have it, but you
had to approach them and anyway it's expensive, and
there was always the danger of disease, but these "nice"
women's rumps, these really luscious ones—who'd have
thought we'd have the lot of them one day—all of them,
for nothing! [*Yelling like a mad thing.*] Three cheers for
the bathing stations! [*Adding sharply, cutting it short.*]
An enormous Lido and everybody stark naked! Everybody! By law! On pain of death!

MADAME HORTENSE [*terrified*]. Monsieur Léon, my poor
lamb. You mustn't excite yourself so on duty. Come now,
pull yourself together. There's the manager staring at us!

*There is suddenly the noise of a pistol shot in the distance.
The musicians look up uneasily. There is a flurry, which is
quickly stifled.* MONSIEUR LEBONZE, *the manager, enters
majestically, napkin in hand. A* WAITER *runs across the
stage.*

MONSIEUR LEBONZE. Who in God's name sent me such an
orchestra! Is this what you think you're paid for, you
litter of pigs? To go and commit suicide in the firm's
toilets? And when we're busy, too. Just to put the customer off, I suppose! I'm sick of your scenes. I shall
engage another orchestra tomorrow! Now, get going!
Play! Play! Bunch of boneheads . . . Faster! Faster than
that! And make it loud—and lively! We don't want the
customers suspecting anything!

MADAME HORTENSE. Is she dead?

MONSIEUR LEBONZE. How do I know? They're just forcing
the door. The doctor's coming. Let's have some music
now! God in heaven! Music, immediately! We've told
the customers at the other end that the percolator's ex-
ploded.

He goes off again in the direction of the toilets. MADAME
HORTENSE *rushes madly around changing the parts. The*

musicians get hopelessly involved, colliding with each other
and knocking over music stands.

MADAME HORTENSE. Hurry, girls, hurry! We'll have to skip
the aria from *La Vestale.* Number seven. We'll have to
change the number. Let's take the "Little Marquis
Gavotte." The fool! I said she'd bring us bad luck. What
rhyme or reason does it make to kill yourself, except to
annoy others? Hats on, everyone! Make it lively! [*The
orchestra, distraught, hurl themselves to their seats. They
have all put on ridiculous little Louis XV hats made of
cardboard.*] Ready! One and two and three and . . .
Grazioso!

*They attack the genre piece, which is light and gay, playing
it with spirit and making little simpering grimaces under
the stern eye of the manager, who has by this time returned.
The* WAITER *comes running back, followed by the* DOCTOR.
The orchestra continues playing with many airs and graces.

The curtain falls.

EPISODE IN THE LIFE OF AN AUTHOR

(*Épisode de la Vie d'un Auteur*)

A play in one act

Translated by
MIRIAM JOHN

"C'est une chose étrange qu'on imprime les gens malgré eux."
—*Molière, Preface to*
Les Précieuses Ridicules

CHARACTERS

The Author
Ardèle
Madame Bessarabo
The Photographer
The Maid
Two Plumbers
The Mother
The Friend
A Woman
La Surette, *a tramp*
The Housing Inspector
Gontran

EPISODE IN THE LIFE
OF AN AUTHOR

The décor is as nonrealistic as possible, but the AUTHOR's *study should be distinguishable center, with three doors, a lobby stage left, the bottom of the staircase, and the front door. It is morning. The* AUTHOR *and* ARDÈLE *are discovered on stage in the study, both in dressing gowns. Standing face to face and both extremely agitated, they are shouting and banging on the desk. All the characters in this sketch are realistic, the women charming, but—and this production detail is indispensable—everyone is wearing a false nose.*

AUTHOR [*banging on the desk*]. Exactly!

ARDÈLE [*also banging on the desk*]. Exactly!

AUTHOR [*as above*]. Exactly!

ARDÈLE [*as above*]. Exactly!

AUTHOR [*suddenly icy*]. Good. The play's over. We've no more to say to each other.

ARDÈLE [*no less loftily*]. I hope not.

AUTHOR. Just one thing. That letter was not from your sister.

ARDÈLE. So you're rummaging in my drawers now. It's humiliating.

AUTHOR. Your sister's fond of you, of course, but hardly to the point of calling you "my own love."

ARDÈLE. So I'm not enough. You have to smear my sister.

AUTHOR. I'm not smearing your sister. I'm simply making an observation. Your sister isn't overloaded with culture, but after all she can spell. She wouldn't have systematically left out *all* the feminine endings on her past participles.

ARDÈLE. The things you pick on!

AUTHOR. That letter was from a man.

ARDÈLE. You're despicable. Might I be allowed to put one question?

AUTHOR. Put away.

ARDÈLE. Supposing it was all your fault?

213

AUTHOR [*laughing nastily*]. Ah-ha ha!

ARDÈLE. What are you doing?

AUTHOR. I'm laughing nastily.

ARDÈLE. How horrible! I deceive you and you laugh. You're
not even capable of suffering. I've given you my youth
and you rummage in my drawers.

AUTHOR. The letter was on the floor. In the closet.

ARDÈLE. Rummaging in closets. In two hours I shall have
gone. I'm going back to my mother.

AUTHOR. She died in 1922.

ARDÈLE. Try—go on, *try* to make me more miserable by reminding me that my poor mother is dead and that I've
nothing left in the world. All the same, she did leave a
house. One twenty-two rue des Retaillons in Saint-Malo.
My illiterate sister's living there. I'm going to her.

AUTHOR. Splendid.

ARDÈLE. You're delighted, of course. At last you'll be able
to be unfaithful to me. For twelve years you've been
waiting for this moment, and you've arranged it so that
I'm the one that looks guilty.

AUTHOR [*yelling suddenly*]. For God's sake! Who sent you
that letter?

ARDÈLE [*with marblelike contempt*]. What *can* be the matter? I suppose my sister can't write.

*At that moment someone rings. They listen. In the lobby,
the* MAID, *young and pleasant, but dissolved in tears, opens
the door.*

MADAME BESSARABO. I've come to see the Master. I have an
appointment. Madame Bessarabo. This gentleman is the
photographer.

AUTHOR. She's a Rumanian journalist. I sent her packing a
week ago. We'll continue with this conversation later.
And I'm not even shaved!

ARDÈLE [*sneering as she goes out*]. That makes twelve years
you haven't been shaved.

AUTHOR [*passing his hand over his face*]. You exaggerate.
It would have shown. Am I at least clean?

ARDÈLE [*slamming the door so hard that a picture falls down
and the* AUTHOR *picks it up*]. NO!

The MAID, *still in tears, introduces* MADAME BESSARABO *and
the* PHOTOGRAPHER, *who is weighed down with equipment.*

MADAME B. Master! I am overwhelmed by the tremendous favor. This gentleman is the photographer.

AUTHOR. Do sit down, madame. Excuse my receiving you in these clothes. I was working.

MADAME B. Oh, Master! How very disturbing. I have interrupted a scene perhaps?

AUTHOR. Precisely. [*Recovering himself.*] I mean, er—no. It's of no importance. It wasn't my scene.

MADAME B. [*embarrassed*]. Oh! Please forgive me, I have been indiscreet. I shall go, Master; I shall go immediately. [*She installs herself.*] Do you mind if I smoke? I smoke like a—how do you say it?—like a chimney sweep.

AUTHOR. Like a chimney. Sweeps don't smoke—at least not on duty. In fact it's their job to stop the chimney smoking.

MADAME B. What a fascinating detail! Everything French is quite extraordinary. Now, in Rumania we are all slaves. Master, I've come to talk to you about your last play. You know, of course, that *La Marguerite* had an enormous success in Bucharest. Three performances—for us that is much.

AUTHOR. Really?

MADAME B. We have such a small theatre public. But very enthusiastic too! We are traditionally devoted to anything French. The play made a great impression. The press was unanimous—we almost reached the fourth performance. The general opinion was that it was a little *dur* as you say—a little hard. We Rumanians are such great idealists. We believe enormously in sentiment. In fact, this explains why I am here. We want to know in my country what you really think about love. Our two cultures are so closely linked you cannot refuse us this. [*Someone rings.*] Well, Master, what do you say? I swear to you I shall be absolutely faithful.

AUTHOR [*suspicious*]. Why do you say that?

MADAME B. Because there are journalists who betray. I shall never betray.

AUTHOR. Er . . . well, madame, truth to tell I feel somewhat embarrassed. . . . What shall I say about love and *La Marguerite*? I think you have caught the subtle hint in the title. "Marguerite"—I love you, I love you not, I love you, I love you not.

The MAID, *still weeping, has been to open the door. She lets in* TWO PLUMBERS.

PLUMBER. How do, gorgeous! We're here for the leak.

The MAID *knocks on the door of the study.*

AUTHOR. Excuse me. Come in . . . what is it?

MAID. It's the plumbers, sir, for the leak.

AUTHOR. Well, let them look for it. You can see I'm busy.

PLUMBER [*shouting from the doorway*]. Where is it?

MAID. They're asking where it is.

AUTHOR. Why should we have sent for them if we knew where it was? Let them start in the attic and check the whole house.

PLUMBER. Okay, mister. We'll start with the attic. Which way, gorgeous?

MAID [*sobbing*]. This way.

PLUMBER [*going upstairs with her and his mate*]. What's up, gorgeous? Love's wonderful really, you know.

AUTHOR [*who has shut the door again*]. Please excuse me. Curious phenomenon. Water trickling about all over the place and nobody knows where from.

MADAME B. How strange. You know, almost the same thing happened in the house of my great-uncle, the Archimandrite, in Rumania. I wake up one morning and there is water all over the drawing room.

AUTHOR. Same here!

MADAME B. In the drawing room where there are no pipes.

AUTHOR. Same here!

MADAME B. And the ceiling absolutely intact. As it was the house of a holy man, we thought for a moment it must be a miracle.

AUTHOR. Same here! Or rather, no, I wouldn't go that far. Now, "Marguerite"—I love you, I love you not, I love you, I love you not.

The forestage left lights up and a WOMAN *dials a number on the telephone. Almost immediately, the telephone rings in the study.*

AUTHOR. Please excuse me. Hello!

WOMAN. Is that you, Léon?

AUTHOR. I'm sorry, madame, whom did you wish to speak to?

WOMAN. Oh, Léon, it's you. Why are you disguising your voice?

AUTHOR. No, madame, it's not me. Which number did you want?

WOMAN. Jasmin one two, one two.

AUTHOR. I am Jasmin one two, one two, madame, but I regret to say that I am not Léon.

WOMAN. But listen, monsieur, Jasmin one two, one two is the number of my first husband!

AUTHOR. I'm sorry, madame. There's been a mistake. [*He hangs up and the light goes out forestage left.*] Some woman had the wrong number. It's very strange—they must make a habit of giving people my number.

MADAME B. Do you know, exactly the same thing has happened to me in Rumania. You are aware, of course, that unlike yours in France, our numbers are very long . . . mine was seven, eighty-three, one, one two six-two one four.

MAID [*bounding in*]. Monsieur, monsieur!

AUTHOR. What is it? I'm busy!

MAID [*tragically*]. They're asking if they can cut off the water.

AUTHOR. Certainly. But if they cut off the water, how will they find the leak? [*Noticing that she is weeping.*] What is the matter with you?

MAID. Oh! Monsieur, it's terrible what's going on.

AUTHOR. You mean, the leak?

MAID. Oh no. Not the leak.

AUTHOR. Madame, perhaps?

MAID. Oh no. Not Madame. [*She goes out, crying even more bitterly.*]

AUTHOR [*turning hesitantly back to* MADAME BESSARABO]. Strange.

MADAME B. She's charming. Quite like one of Molière's.

AUTHOR [*smirking*]. You exaggerate, really! That's too high a compliment.

MADAME B. I say what I think, Master. I have such an admiration for all your work—and for Molière's too, of course.

AUTHOR. Thank you. But we were saying—about the water in your drawing room . . .

MADAME B. No—about my telephone number. But let us talk about *La Marguerite* instead.

The WOMAN *has redialed the number forestage.*

AUTHOR. Well, I was saying that the title contains a subtle allusion. "Marguerite"—I love you, I love you not . . .

The telephone rings.

WOMAN. Hello! Léon?

AUTHOR. Madame, you have the wrong number again. Are you dialing Jasmin one two, one two?

WOMAN. Of course, monsieur. I told you it is my first husband's number. Can you explain to me what you are doing on the line?

AUTHOR. What do you mean, what am I doing on the line? I'm waiting for someone to ring me on the line, madame; it happens to be mine! [*He hangs up.*] This is insane. I love you, I love you not, I love you, I love you not.

There is a knock. It is ARDÈLE, *with nothing on but a bathrobe.*

ARDÈLE. So that's how it is. You're starting that?

AUTHOR. Starting what? Do excuse me, madame.

ARDÈLE. Your oafish practical jokes. Cutting off the water just as I'm taking my shower. You know I'm leaving you, and as if that isn't enough, you want to put the blame on me. After what you've done!

AUTHOR. What *have* I done?

ARDÈLE. Don't play innocent—you know as well as I do!

She goes out, banging the door. A picture falls down. The AUTHOR *picks it up.*

AUTHOR. I'm so sorry. Now, we were talking about love and *La Marguerite.*

MADAME B. Quite. The rest is incidental. My great-uncle's leak, the telephone—I can tell you all about these things later when you come to Rumania. But, Master, you were so *dur,* so hard, in *La Marguerite.* Tell me you were lying; confess that you believe in love just the same.

AUTHOR [*embarking*]. Well now, madame, to tell the truth, love like the marguerite, has leaves, or rather petals. . . .

A man has dialed a number forestage right. The AUTHOR *picks up the receiver and yells into it.*

AUTHOR. No, madame, I am not Léon!

FRIEND. What on earth's come over you, old thing? I know you're not Léon. This is Gustave. How are things, dear boy?

AUTHOR. Oh. It's you. Fine, thanks, fine. [*To* MADAME B.]

One moment, please, I'm so sorry. How are things with you?

FRIEND. That's just it, they're not at all good, dear boy. You remember I had a simply fabulous idea for a scenario. I told you about it, I think?

AUTHOR. Yes, yes. I remember. [*To* MADAME B.] Please excuse me—a colleague of mine.

FRIEND. "The Woman with the Boas" I was calling it. You know, it's the story of a madly beautiful woman who meets a man in a train and falls in love with him.

AUTHOR. Yes, yes, I remember. Very original . . .

FRIEND. Paul Zed bought it from me. He was going to film it in the spring for Bourbanski. They'd got Liliane Trésor lined up. She'd accepted, and now she's refused.

AUTHOR [*politely*]. Oh, Lord, what a bore. Why was that? [*To* MADAME B.] I'm so sorry.

FRIEND. She doesn't want to die at the end.

AUTHOR. That's reasonable. Listen, old man, I'm so sorry, but I have someone with me.

FRIEND. How do you mean, it's reasonable? Look at it from my point of view. If I want to kill her off, who's going to stop me? After all, *I'm* the author. Anyway, it doesn't make sense. First of all, who's ever heard of an actress refusing to die? They usually fall over themselves for a good death agony. What's more, dear boy, if you remember the story, you'll see that she can't not die. Damn it, here's a woman who's deceived her husband with two men; she then falls in love on a train with a third man who turns out to be an ex-convict who was a counterspy in the war and takes drugs. That was the whole point. Producers can say what they like about happy endings— life is like that, dear boy, life is like that. I ask you, is life supposed to be a picnic?

AUTHOR. No, it isn't a picnic, but listen, old man, I've got someone here in my study—a journalist come specially from Rumania to see me about a leak in the waterpipe.

FRIEND. About what?

AUTHOR. Oh—no—I mean about love, but there was a leak as well. I'll explain later. Call me again, do you mind?

FRIEND. Oh, all right, I'll call you in ten minutes.

He hangs up. The forestage goes dark. Someone rings. The MAID *opens the door. This time it is an elderly woman, flowerily dressed.*

MOTHER. Is my son at home?

MAID. Yes, madame.

AUTHOR. Do forgive me, what was I saying?

MADAME B. That love had petals.

AUTHOR [who has lost the drift]. Petals.

MADAME B. Yes, Master, you remember—the subtle allusion.

AUTHOR. Oh, yes! The marguerite. So love, like the marguerite, has petals. . . .

MADAME B. [taking notes feverishly]. How moving. I have the feeling no one has ever said that before.

MAID [knocking at the study door]. It's your mother, monsieur.

AUTHOR. Tell her I'm busy and ask her if she'd kindly call again.

MOTHER [calling]. It's very urgent, darling. I must have a word with you at once.

AUTHOR. Would you excuse me? All right, I'm coming. [He goes out into the hall.] What is it?

MOTHER. Aren't you going to kiss me? When you were little, you always used to kiss me.

AUTHOR. Yes, yes, I'm going to kiss you. What is it, now? I'm busy.

MOTHER. The pet. You know, for me, you'll always be a little boy. Now, it's about the apartment. I've been told about one that's up for exchange. I have to let them have my answer this morning.

AUTHOR. Just wait for me a second. I've someone with me from Rumania. She's going back any minute now.

MOTHER. Is Ardèle at home?

AUTHOR. Yes, but do please leave her where she is. Things aren't going so well this morning. No scenes between you, please.

MOTHER. How dare you say such a thing to your mother! Was I ever the one to start anything? Don't you think it's painful enough already to see one's only son married to someone who hates one?

AUTHOR. Yes, I know it's rather painful. So don't stand about. Do sit down. Read the paper. I'll be back.

MOTHER [holding him back]. But you really must give me an answer about this flat. You know I've lost my lawsuit. That means I don't know how much in lawyers' fees and I may be thrown out on the street at any minute. If only you had a different wife—then I could come and live with you.

AUTHOR [*making her sit down and calmly but firmly placing a paper in her hands*]. Read the paper! [*He goes back into the study.*] So. Love has petals. Excuse me, I must be brief, I've so much to do. You've asked me a straight question, and I'll give you a straight answer. I believe in love.

MADAME B. [*with a cry of relief*]. Ah! At last! I shall send a cable at once, Master. It will be a great relief to the whole of Rumania!

At this moment the door opens behind the AUTHOR *and the* TWO PLUMBERS *come in. They feel along the walls in silence, with an air of great mystery, weaving around everyone and putting the* PHOTOGRAPHER *in terror for his equipment. They then go out by another door without a word.*

AUTHOR [*curtly*]. Man is alone, madame—left to himself, with his ridiculous freedom, and no one to call out to him in the desert!

At this moment the FRIEND *has dialed the number and the telephone rings.*

AUTHOR. Excuse me, please. Hello.

FRIEND. Hello. Can I talk to you now, dear boy? Do you know what's happened to me? A phone call from Liliane Trésor. She agrees to die, provided it's consumption. The idea came to her when she had a bit of a cold. But now it's Paul Zed who won't play because he says it would be depressing. He says for Canada and the Channel Islands it would be better if she turned religious and went into a convent. He says that would make it sell better.

AUTHOR. Listen. I haven't finished with my visitor. Could you call me back a bit later?

FRIEND. Right. Fine. I'll call you back. [*He hangs up.*]

While they are speaking, someone rings. It is LA SURETTE, *a tramp, still quite young.*

LA SURETTE. Is he in?

MAID [*who has opened the door to him, still sniffing*]. You again? But he gave you something only a week ago.

LA SURETTE. They're going to cut off the gas.

MAID [*at the door of the study*]. It's Monsieur La Surette, monsieur. He says they're going to cut off his gas.

AUTHOR [*getting up, furious, and coming into the hall*]. No!
Do you hear me, man—no! I know we served together in
the army. I know you saved me from being court-
martialed the time I mislaid my bayonet, but damn it
all! I gave you seven thousand last week!

LA SURETTE. That was for the potatoes.

AUTHOR. And you've eaten seven thousand francs' worth of
potatoes in a week?

LA SURETTE. They're cutting off the gas. I can't cook them.

AUTHOR [*weakening*]. How much behind are you with the
gas?

LA SURETTE. Nine months. They say if I pay half they won't
cut me off. Better take the opportunity, hadn't I?

AUTHOR. How much?

LA SURETTE [*waving a hand*]. Oh! I don't know—here,
here's the bill. You see I wasn't lying. Plus expenses, of
course. They always add that. And then, I wanted to tell
you—I think I've found a place. Only I can't go there
with these boots. Maybe you've got an old pair.

AUTHOR. God in heaven! Wait there! I'll see in a minute.

He turns to go back into the study when the MOTHER *comes
out from behind the paper and seizes him.*

MOTHER. Darling, do you know what I've just come across
in the paper? Another flat. Eight rooms. At the Trocadéro.
Furniture for sale too. Only they don't say the price.
What does it mean when they don't say the price?

AUTHOR [*going out*]. It means a million francs. Let's talk
about it later.

MOTHER. A million francs for furniture? When I married,
do you know how much an Empire commode was worth?

AUTHOR. I don't want to know. It's too late. [*He goes back
into the study.*] I'm all yours, madame. Now, the marguerite . . .

At this moment the WOMAN *has dialed the number. He
takes off the receiver.*

WOMAN. Hello, Léon?

AUTHOR [*howling*]. No!

He hangs up. There is a ring at the bell. LA SURETTE *opens
the door. It is a serious-looking man in black. He greets the*
MOTHER *and* LA SURETTE *and sits down to wait, having
noticed that he is not the first. Meanwhile, the* AUTHOR *is
addressing* MME. B.

AUTHOR. What was I saying?

MADAME B. Man is alone, Master, man is desperately alone.

The door at the back opens and ARDÈLE *comes in, dressed this time and wearing an outrageous hat.*

ARDÈLE [*standing on the threshold, tragic*]. And what about the cats?

AUTHOR. You can see I'm busy.

ARDÈLE. Who's going to look after the cats now that I'm leaving?

AUTHOR. There's Léonie.

ARDÈLE. The maid! You'd leave the cats to the maid. You really mean that? Am I to believe my ears?

AUTHOR. Yes.

ARDÈLE. You monster! Clothaire's ill!

AUTHOR. What's the matter with him?

ARDÈLE. He's miaowing.

AUTHOR. All cats miaow. It's normal.

ARDÈLE. Insensitive brute. He's miaowing hoarsely. He suspects something.

AUTHOR. Talk to him then. Make him see reason. You see I'm busy. Open a tin of sardines.

ARDÈLE. Brute. Insensitive brute. That animal has more heart than you have. He'll refuse your old sardines. He's sad because I'm going.

The man in black, tired of waiting, has come to knock on the study door.

MAN IN BLACK. Excuse me, monsieur. I see there are several people waiting to see you and I have to have a word with you, urgently.

AUTHOR. What about, monsieur?

INSPECTOR. I am the housing inspector. A complaint has been lodged against you for insufficient occupation of the premises and you are under threat of a requisition order for your surplus accommodation.

AUTHOR. Requisition order? But I occupy the entire house, monsieur. Who do you want to put in?

INSPECTOR. A police officer, monsieur. Father of eight. Brigadier Lapomme. Top priority.

AUTHOR. I object, monsieur. The premises are legally occupied.

INSPECTOR. That's what I've come to find out. [*He glances at* MADAME BESSARABO.] Is Madame one of the family?

AUTHOR. Madame is a Rumanian journalist.

INSPECTOR [*taking notes*]. Premises occupied by foreign *émigrés*. Have you a regular permit, madame?

MADAME. Monsieur, I am the Princess Bessarabo and I am staying at the Hotel Ritz.

INSPECTOR [*still taking notes*]. I see. Illegal occupation of further premises in Paris.

AUTHOR. Please don't confuse matters, monsieur! Madame has absolutely nothing to do with this house. Would you be so good as to wait next door for a moment, madame? [*To the* PHOTOGRAPHER.] You, too, please. And take your scrap iron with you.

INSPECTOR. Also one of the family?

AUTHOR. No, you can see perfectly well he's a photographer.

INSPECTOR. Doesn't stop him being one of the family. I've got an uncle who's a painter.

While the AUTHOR *is easing the other two into the adjoining room,* ARDÈLE *has come up to the* INSPECTOR *gleefully.*

ARDÈLE. You can send that policeman right along with his eight children. Let him make another one in the next nine months too if he wants to. He'll have plenty of room here because *I* am going, let me tell you, monsieur.

INSPECTOR [*taking more notes*]. You're vacating part of the property? I'll make a note of that.

ARDÈLE. Please do.

AUTHOR [*separating them*]. Ardèle! Inspector! Please. Let's keep calm.

The MOTHER *comes in, brandishing the paper.*

MOTHER. A flat! Another flat! Darling, this time you'll be able to give your old mother a real treat. Twelve rooms in the Avenue Lamartine, just next door to dear Mademoiselle Pinocle. And for a song—only two million. And shall I tell you something? If I win my lawsuit, I shall keep my little flat at Asnières.

INSPECTOR [*noting*]. Twelve rooms, Avenue Lamartine, and you say you also have a small flat at Asnières? How many rooms?

MOTHER [*mutinous*]. Four, but I've been crafty and only declared two!

AUTHOR [*bawling*]. Mother, I order you to be quiet! And you—stop scribbling down everything people say to you. It's not normal. Damn it all, we're talking about *this* house, aren't we? You'll see that everything's in order here. I have my study on the ground floor, with my secretary's office, a drawing room and dining room, and this is the lobby.

LA SURETTE [*still in the lobby*]. Listen, the gas can wait, but about the boots—I've got to go there this afternoon.

AUTHOR. In a minute.

INSPECTOR [*taking a look at the staircase*]. What about the second floor? What have you got there?

AUTHOR. Three rooms. All occupied.

INSPECTOR. Is there a third floor?

AUTHOR. Only a trompe-l'oeil façade. There's no third floor really. It's just a sort of optical illusion.

At this moment the PLUMBERS *gallop down the stairs triumphantly.*

PLUMBER. We've got it, mister. We've got it!

AUTHOR. What?

PLUMBER. The leak! It starts at the two big empty rooms on the third floor, runs right across the table tennis room, the winter garden, and the two libraries, and finishes up in that big room where you've got your collection of toy soldiers!

INSPECTOR [*rubbing his hands and mounting the staircase brandishing his notebook*]. Splendid! I'm going to have a look at all this.

AUTHOR [*somewhat discouraged*]. We've had it, now.

LA SURETTE. Look, do make an effort. When I lent you my bayonet so as to save you that court-martial, I didn't keep you waiting this long.

AUTHOR [*beside himself, suddenly rips off his shoes and throws them at* LA SURETTE]. Here you are, then! Take mine! But get out!

LA SURETTE [*putting them on immediately*]. Very well. But giving isn't everything. It's the way you do it. One may be poor, but one has one's dignity. [*He hands him the old boots.*] Do you want these? At least you can afford to have them mended. What have you decided about the gas?

AUTHOR [*who no longer knows what he is saying*]. Go and get mine, it's in the kitchen.

MOTHER [*plucking at him*]. Well, darling, what do you think about the flat? The twelve rooms at Avenue Lamartine or the eight at the Trocadéro? In a pinch I could make do with that, you know. I'm old now and I don't entertain much any more.

ARDÈLE [hooking him from the other side]. So it's agreed, you're going to let me go, but it isn't going to be as easy as you're hoping. I demand, you hear me, I demand now to know the name of this woman.

AUTHOR. What woman?

ARDÈLE. Your mistress.

AUTHOR. What *do* you mean, my mistress?

ARDÈLE. Exactly what I said. Do you think I can be fooled by that letter? Let me tell you I can't. I knew all the time that letter was concealing something.

AUTHOR. Ah, you knew all the time! How clever of you. So what was it concealing, may I ask?

ARDÈLE. You may not! I'm asking you. You've discovered that I'm deceiving you. Why should you choose today to discover I'm deceiving you unless you're deceiving me?

AUTHOR [taking her by the arm]. Listen to me, Ardèle, I'm quite calm. I'm absolutely calm, and no matter what happens I shall stay calm.

ARDÈLE. You're molesting me! Deceiving me and molesting me! Look at him, your darling boy, look at the dear, sweet cherub.

MOTHER. Before he knew you, my son was sweetness itself. He has never failed his mother.

LA SURETTE [putting his head through the door]. What have you decided about the gas? You're not going to leave me with two hundred and fifty kilos of raw potatoes on my hands, are you?

AUTHOR [disengaging himself from the two women and storming]. Keep calm, everybody. We must keep exceedingly calm.

At this moment the WOMAN *dials his number.*

WOMAN. Hello! Is that you, Léon?

AUTHOR [smoothly]. Yes, this is Léon speaking. I'd like to be Léon. Why shouldn't I be Léon?

WOMAN. Well then, why are you disguising your voice?

AUTHOR [gloomily]. Just to make you laugh.

WOMAN. Don't be cruel, Léon. I know you love another woman. But I'm ringing you because something terrible has happened to me. I can't stay here. I must find a flat.

AUTHOR [very calm]. Oh, good. In that case I'll put you on

to someone. One moment. Mother. There's a woman here telephoning about a flat.

MOTHER [*rushing to the phone*]. A flat? A flat? Isn't he a darling? You see what a good son he is. Hello! Hello! Madame? Hello! Hello! You say you're ringing about a flat?

AUTHOR. That's one. Now—two: you. [*To* LA SURETTE.] To the kitchen. Eat everything you can find in the icebox. Empty all the bottles in sight.

LA SURETTE. What about the maid?

AUTHOR. Comfort her. Now, number three: you. [*To* AR-DÈLE.] Listen to me carefully. Look me straight in the eye.

ARDÈLE. Oh no! Don't start that. It's not fair. You know whenever you look me in the face I tell everything.

MOTHER [*at the telephone*]. So you really want to talk about a flat?

WOMAN. Yes, madame, I do, indeed.

MOTHER. How many rooms?

WOMAN. Oh, three or four, madame. . . .

MOTHER. But that would be perfect, madame. . . .

WOMAN. Really, would it really be suitable, do you think, madame? I cannot tell you how glad I am. . . .

MOTHER. But it is I who am glad, madame. . . . I don't wish to be indiscreet, of course, but about the furniture and fittings. . . .

WOMAN. It's a little embarrassing, but . . . to tell the truth . . . I'd been hoping we needn't discuss furniture and fittings. . . .

MOTHER. Ah! So had I, Madame!

WOMAN. So, shall we say without furniture and fittings, then, madame? Do you agree?

MOTHER. Certainly, madame, without furniture and fittings. . . . It is so much easier to come to an agreement with people of one's own kind! When may I come along to see you, madame?

WOMAN. At once, madame, if that is possible. You can imagine I simply can't wait. . . .

MOTHER. But it is I who cannot wait, madame. Please, what is your address?

WOMAN. One eighteen Boulevard Ravachol. Madame Fripon-Minet.

MOTHER. I shall wing my way, madame! I'll be with you

immediately. [*She hangs up.*] Darling! Thank you! It's
marvelous. Let me kiss you. Four rooms on the Boulevard
Ravachol! A lovely quarter. And no furniture and fittings.
Really one has only to deal with the right people. They are
much less grasping than one thinks. Good-by now, good-
by. Don't come with me, my turtledoves.

*She flies to the door, younger by fifty years. As she opens
it, there is* GONTRAN *on the threshold. He is a giant of a
man.*

GONTRAN. Is Jacques at home?

MOTHER. Yes, Gontran, yes. Come in, my little one. I adore
you! [*She disappears.*]

AUTHOR [*left in the study with* ARDÈLE]. Now, listen to me
carefully. I realize one may suffer a momentary lapse.

ARDÈLE. So you admit it?

AUTHOR. God almighty! Admit what?

ARDÈLE. Let me go, then. Your dishonesty sickens me. My
mind's made up. I'm going.

GONTRAN [*coming in*]. So there you are, both of you!

AUTHOR [*somewhat ill-temperedly*]. Yes, here we are. As
you can see. What is it?

GONTRAN. I must say I didn't expect that sort of welcome
from you on a day like this.

ARDÈLE. What's the matter, Gontran? You're so pale, little
one.

GONTRAN [*sitting down suddenly*]. It's all over. Have you
got a gun?

AUTHOR. Hell no! I could do with one, though. Why a gun?

GONTRAN. Oh, never mind. I'd have preferred one, that's all.
I'll get by.

ARDÈLE. But what on earth is the matter?

GONTRAN. You know I've left Lucienne?

AUTHOR [*embarrassed, as though it were himself*]. Oh, yes,
I never told you; he's left Lucienne.

ARDÈLE. You mean he's left Lucienne? And you never told
me? I suppose you thought it would put ideas into my
head. Go on, admit that you were thinking of leaving me,
too!

AUTHOR. Let's keep calm. He left Lucienne more than three
months ago.

GONTRAN. I'm in love with Léa.

ARDÈLE. That stick!

GONTRAN. Please make your wife be quiet!

ARDÈLE. That shriveled prune? She hasn't even got any hair!

GONTRAN. I order you to make your wife be quiet, do you hear me?

AUTHOR. He's right. Be quiet. You have absolutely no right . . .

ARDÈLE. To say that she's a prune?

GONTRAN. Léa, a prune? She's blonde—well, anyway, now.

AUTHOR. Now you shut up, too! Let's all shut up. Don't let's ever say another word. Sign language only.

GONTRAN [in tears]. In any case, who said anything about Léa? I'm not talking about Léa.

ARDÈLE. That's better. At least I'm glad I don't know this . . . this . . . tart.

GONTRAN. I'm talking about Lucienne! That's what's so awful.

ARDÈLE. What has she done? Killed herself? I bet she's killed herself. Ring her up at once.

AUTHOR. Do be calm. What's the good if she's killed herself.

GONTRAN. She doesn't answer the phone. She doesn't answer my letters. [He falls weeping into the AUTHOR's arms.] She's deceiving me, old man; she's been deceiving me ever since I left her!

He begins to sob like a child in the arms of the AUTHOR, *who supports his gigantic body as best he can.* ARDÈLE *meanwhile paces up and down the room laughing hysterically and breaking all the vases she can lay hands on.*

GONTRAN. To do that to me! To do that to me! To do that to me!

AUTHOR [yelling like a mad thing]. Do let's be calm. Let's be absolutely calm. Let's try to be more and more calm.

While all this is going on, the FRIEND *dials, forestage. The telephone rings. The* AUTHOR *drags himself to the telephone, loaded down by the dead weight of* GONTRAN, *who has fainted away.*

AUTHOR. Hello!

FRIEND [he, at least, is calm]. Is that you, dear boy? Your line was busy. I've had a marvelous idea for the end of my film story.

AUTHOR [not knowing what he is saying]. Later, darling, later. The main thing is to keep calm. Please keep quite calm.

FRIEND. What do you mean, later darling? What on earth's come over you? Hello! Hello! Hello! Swine. [*He hangs up.*]

ARDÈLE [*bearing down on the* AUTHOR]. Caught in the act! Who were you talking to? I demand to know who you were talking to, you great coward. To your girl friend—weren't you? Deny it. You've just given yourself away. Take that! And that!

She slaps his face. He lets go of GONTRAN's *inert body and it crumples on the floor.*

AUTHOR [*bending over him*]. He's fainted. We must call a doctor. Maybe he's taken poison. I'll go and look for some tincture of iodine.

He goes off to the kitchen. ARDÈLE *calmly steps over the body and makes for the telephone.*

ARDÈLE. Hello! Mademoiselle! This is Jasman one two, one two. I've just had a call and I must find out immediately the number of my caller. Oh, you say it's difficult. Call the supervisor then, please. It's for security reasons. Your job and the whole future of the country depends upon it. You say I'll be in for it if I'm not speaking the truth? Do as I say, please, and check the facts afterward. Hello! Hello! Hello! Thank you, mademoiselle, you're a good Frenchwoman. I'll mention you to the Minister. You'll certainly be promoted.

She dials a number. The WOMAN *takes off the receiver, forestage.*

WOMAN. Hello!

ARDÈLE. Hello. This is Jasmin one two, one two.

WOMAN. So you're Léon's new wife?

ARDÈLE. Oh, so he calls himself Léon these days? Coward!

WOMAN. I must confess I would like a word with you, madame! Was it you that sent me this lunatic who wanted to snatch my flat from me?

ARDÈLE. Your flat? What in heaven's name do I care about your flat? You're trying to snatch my husband.

WOMAN. Let me remind you, madame, that it was you who snatched him from me! Léon adores me.

ARDÈLE. You! With that face? I can see it from here!

WOMAN. And yours, do you think I can't see that, too? I assure you I shall come and get him if you don't give him back to me.

ARDÈLE. Who, me?

WOMAN. Yes, you.

ARDÈLE. Yes, me.

They continue with this incomprehensible exchange of "What, me?" "Yes, you," etc., while the AUTHOR *comes back from the kitchen, dragging* LA SURETTE *roughly by the collar.*

AUTHOR. Parasite! Scrounger! Ill-bred boor! I'll teach you to monkey with the maid.

LA SURETTE. I lent you my rifle, didn't I, in time for that parade? Just because you've become a success in life, it doesn't mean you can grab everything for yourself. Anyway, you told me to comfort her.

AUTHOR. Not that way!

LA SURETTE. After all, she's only your maid!

AUTHOR. Scum! Leave her alone! [*Turning to the Maid.*] And you—stop crying like that. You've been irritating me all the morning!

MAID. But Monsieur doesn't know. It's terrible.

AUTHOR. What is it that's so terrible still? Tell me. Like Oedipus, I want to know everything.

MAID. I'm pregnant.

AUTHOR [*sitting down, quietly*]. Whatever the case, we must keep calm.

MADAME B. [*bursting in*]. Master, Master, I can't wait any longer. The Rumanian intelligentsia is burning to know what you think of love. . . .

AUTHOR [*getting up and going to her*]. Get out of here, you! Get the hell back to Rumania instantly!

MADAME B. He's gone mad. It's terrific! [*She calls out to the* PHOTOGRAPHER.] We'll have to photograph him like that. It'll make sensational headlines.

AUTHOR. Madame, I don't know how these things are done in Rumania, but I warn you that if you have me photographed in these clothes I shall kill the photographer.

MADAME B. That doesn't matter, we'll find another! Come along now, come along!

INSPECTOR [*looming*]. Ah, there you are, monsieur. I've made my inspection. A fine thing! A very fine thing! Twelve rooms to spare. You'll get your policeman all right. In fact, you'll probably get two!

ARDÈLE [*who has hung up a moment ago and has been listening, advances quietly*]. What do I hear? What were you saying while I was on the telephone? Well, *I've* got a revolver.

She goes out, slamming the door. The picture falls down. The AUTHOR *picks it up.*

AUTHOR. Let's keep calm. Let's keep calm to the end. Very well, monsieur. Gentlemen don't lose their heads.

INSPECTOR. Ah, so you want to be funny, my fine fellow? Sarcasm into the bargain. Right, you can have three policemen. A brigadier and two recruits. All of them fathers. And when their children are grown up, they'll make some more and they'll all live here until their children's children marry and make you some more!

AUTHOR. I'm quite calm. Yoga. Remember Yoga.

INSPECTOR. Remember what you like! You're certainly not going to forget me. I'll send you along some old-age pensioners—none under a hundred.

AUTHOR [*having attained a certain degree of concentration, chants*]. I am quite calm. Quite calm. I am becoming more and more calm.

MADAME B. Admirable! Admirable! He really looks like a madman! What genius. What enormous genius. Another picture please, my friend.

At this moment the PLUMBERS *come in, shouting.*

PLUMBERS. Look out, everyone! Look out! Look out!

AUTHOR. What's this?

PLUMBERS. The leak. The real one. We were wrong about the other one. We've only just found the real trouble, but something's gone wrong. There is water trickling all over the place. We can't control it any more. It's everyone for himself now!

At this very moment cascades of water begin to fall from the ceiling while MADAME BESSARABO, *the* MAID, *and the* MOTHER, *who has just returned, rush around in a panic, bellowing with fright.*

MOTHER. A flat, indeed. A fine flat, I must say. No one in this family will ever get a flat again!

The FRIEND *takes up his receiver. The* AUTHOR, *who has knocked the telephone over in passing, picks it up and says mechanically:*

AUTHOR. Hello!

FRIEND. Hello, dear boy, am I disturbing you?

AUTHOR [*trying to bring* GONTRAN *to by slapping his face*]. Not at all.

FRIEND. Ah! So you finally condescend to listen to me! I must say I've hit on a splendid idea for the end, old thing—a fire. Just like that. Everything ends in a fire.

The AUTHOR *is standing calmly beneath the waterfall while the others are running in all directions trying to catch the pictures as they fall. Only the* INSPECTOR *has opened his umbrella and begins quietly making his report under the deluge.*

AUTHOR. That's an excellent idea!

FRIEND. At the same time, you can hear gunfire. Do you follow me? Gunfire and fire—can you imagine the effect?

AUTHOR [*somewhat agitated, since he has just seen* ARDÈLE *come in with a pistol in her hand*]. Indeed!

ARDÈLE *begins to shoot. He dodges the bullets and the water, at the same time trying to protect* GONTRAN'*s body.*

AUTHOR. Indeed! I can well imagine it! [*Dodging a bullet.*] That'll be hilarious!

FRIEND [*pained*]. I don't think you can be paying attention, dear boy. One mustn't be selfish in this life, you know. There you are sitting quietly in your study, without a thought for the agony I've been going through trying to find an ending.

During this time the WOMAN *has been nervously dialing the number, forestage. As the last shot is fired,* ARDÈLE *screams.*

ARDÈLE. Darling! Tell me you're not hurt at least!

AUTHOR. No, my love. Everything's all right.

ARDÈLE. Oh, I was so frightened.

She throws herself into his arms and falls limply in a faint.

AUTHOR [*shouting hysterically into the telephone*]. Everything's all right, do you hear me, everything's all right!

FRIEND [*furious*]. Do you want me to tell you something? You're impossible. You're just saying anything to keep me quiet. You're not even listening. Be honest, for once; tell me straight you don't think this ending's a good one.

AUTHOR [*holding up* ARDÈLE *and endeavoring to hoist up* GONTRAN]. Listen, dear boy, I'll be frank with you. I agree with Paul Zed. I know I wrote *La Marguerite*, but all the same I prefer a story to end happily.

FRIEND [*suddenly venomous*]. You're nothing but a cabaret

turn. Just a piddling little unambitious cabaret turn. A lot of water'll flow under the bridge before I call you again!

He hangs up furiously at this, while the waterfall brings down the ceiling. The WOMAN, *who has dialed the number for the tenth time, gives a cry of triumph.*

WOMAN. Hello! Léon?

She will go on shouting this until the curtain falls, while the AUTHOR *comes forward dragging with him* ARDÈLE *and* GONTRAN. *There is general panic in the background, and the décor falls to pieces as the* AUTHOR *addresses the public.*

AUTHOR. Ladies and gentlemen—one does what one can. . . . And there are so many serious writers in the theatre today, I am sure you will forgive the author's failings if he has only made you laugh.

CATCH AS CATCH CAN

(*La Foire d'Empoigne*)

A play in one act

Translated by
LUCIENNE HILL

CHARACTERS

NAPOLEON } *played by the same*
LOUIS XVIII } *actor*

FOUCHÉ
THE MARSHAL
THE DUC DE BLACAS
D'ASSONVILLE

THE FRENCH SENTRY }
THE ENGLISH SENTRY } *visibly played*
THE FRENCH SERGEANT } *by the same actors*
THE ENGLISH SERGEANT }

THE ENGLISH OFFICER
THE CHIEF USHER *of the King's Bedchamber*
ROUSTAN
THE PALACE SERVANT

CATCH AS CATCH CAN

*The Tuileries Palace—a backcloth. A courtyard with a door.
The* FRENCH SENTRY *is on stage. All the characters have the
slightly coarsened features, the exaggerated stomachs, of
English caricatures of the period.*

The rumble of carriage wheels is heard. The SENTRY *stands
rigidly to attention, presents arms, and cries:*

SENTRY. Long live the King!

Enter the FRENCH SERGEANT.

SERGEANT. Too late! The carriage of his Majesty King Louis
the Eighteenth is speeding toward the La Villette gate, on
its way to Flanders.

SENTRY. Long live the Emperor, then. We're used to this in
France, you know, Sergeant.

SERGEANT. Too soon. The carriage of his Majesty the Em-
peror Napoleon the First is only just entering the rue St.
Honoré, amid the same delirious mob who acclaimed King
Louis the Eighteenth six months ago.

SENTRY. Long live the Republic, then. I don't care either
way.

SERGEANT [*severely*]. You'll do four days for that. You look
like a pigheaded brute to me. I've got my eye on you and
don't you forget it.   [*He goes out.*

Enter FOUCHÉ *and* D'ASSONVILLE.

D'ASSONVILLE. How long do you give him, Monsieur le Duc
d'Otrante?

FOUCHÉ. One hundred days. To the hour.

D'ASSONVILLE [*ironically*]. You seem to be in the confidence
of history.

FOUCHÉ [*winking*]. A little. [*He adds jovially.*] I make it.

D'ASSONVILLE. Is it amusing?

FOUCHÉ. It would be if there were anything unforeseen
about it. But given that one knows the balance of the
powers concerned, the heavy lurch of destiny onto one or
other pan of the scales is no surprise to anyone but a fool.

D'ASSONVILLE [*nettled*]. I'm one then. For I must confess
that the Emperor returning like this——

FOUCHÉ. Did you imagine him ending his days like a retired
battalion commander, with his thousand men, on the
island of Elba—an actor such as he? You don't know the
theatre. He knows he's doomed, but he's come back to
make his exit. He made a mess of it the first time.

D'ASSONVILLE. Oh, but surely his farewells at Fontainebleau
. . . I was there. I wept.

FOUCHÉ [*with a faint smile*]. And well you might, a young
man like you. It was a good scene, if a shade predictable
for my taste. I like my drama a little more subtle. But he
fell somewhat short of the telling exit line, the turn at
the door, facing the audience. The hasty flight, through
a hostile Provence, with his tail between his legs, dis-
guised as a Russian officer. A man as concerned with his
role could hardly let it rest there. He has come back to
give us another curtain, bloody if possible, or at all events
more nobly undersigned by destiny. More in the style of
classic tragedy, which he acquired a taste for during the
lessons in diction he took with Talma. In fact, you may
be sure that's *all* he's come back for.

D'ASSONVILLE. You think he isn't hopeful—really?

FOUCHÉ. One can say a great many things about him, but
one can't say he is stupid. He knows exactly what his
chances are, but a woeful fate will have it that for his exit
he needs bit players. His shows have always been noted
for their spectacle. France had just obtained unhoped-
for conditions from the Allies, thanks to a happy little
piece of double talk which presented us, supporters and
opponents alike, as victims of the tyrant. The borders of
'92—that was a pretty package in the new King's bottom
drawer. In three months from now, with the Allies back
once more as victors, and with France having welcomed
him yet again like a servant girl fawning on a ruffian—
it will be good-by to our pleasant little fiction. This time,
let me tell you, the conditions will be gory. We will be
occupied, torn apart, bled dry, violated—I speak of the
ladies.

D'ASSONVILLE. Do you think he hasn't thought of that?

FOUCHÉ. Oh yes, he probably has. But he doesn't care.
France was never his lookout. He works for the firm of
Bonaparte.

D'ASSONVILLE [*unhappily*]. You're very hard.

FOUCHÉ [*smiling*]. You're soft, my young lieutenant. That's what explains your presence here today. You haven't had time to get to know him yet.

D'ASSONVILLE [*aggressively*]. And what about yours?

FOUCHÉ. My what?

D'ASSONVILLE. Your presence here. How do you explain that?

FOUCHÉ [*quietly*]. That's a lesson you aren't old enough for yet. I won't spoil your natural goodness too soon. I like generosity of spirit in the young—as do all men of state, in fact. Without you and your like, there would be no one to follow where we led. . . . All our beautiful decisions operating in the void! Very galling that would be.

D'ASSONVILLE [*contemptuously*]. To follow you in *all* directions?

FOUCHÉ. No. In one direction at a time. And when we alter course, we find another set of young men equally enamored of the absolute. A different absolute. There are several. But let us go into the palace and take all those white lilies out of the vases. The scent of the royal fleurs-de-lis might bother him. I like you very much. And I was very fond of your mother, too—who never, incidentally, returned my sentiments. . . .

D'ASSONVILLE. Allow me to say I'm overjoyed to hear it.

FOUCHÉ [*with a smile*]. It's such an old story. I was still a seminarist. But that's right, insult me! I adore it when the young insult me. It reassures me of my political sense. Serve the returned Emperor, my young cherub. In two months, in two and a half, I'll drop you the hint. In good time.

D'ASSONVILLE. I hope I shall save you the trouble, Monsieur le Duc. Europe is going to descend on us with ten men to our one. In two months, in two and a half, there are a great many chances that I shall be dead. Cleanly.

FOUCHÉ. What an odd word for such an ugly thing. You mustn't die, young man. You must last. That's much more fun. Especially in a country like ours. After every political disaster in France, there is something in men's behavior that's a delight to watch.

They go into the palace. The SENTRY *stiffens and presents arms. Enter* NAPOLEON, *followed by* ROUSTAN *and a glistening* MARSHAL.

SENTRY. Long live . . . [A *slight hesitation.*] . . . the Emperor!

NAPOLEON. That's a good fellow. A cry from the heart if ever I heard one. Spontaneity, that's what I like to see. You are my first Parisian sentry. Who put you on duty here?

SENTRY. The Captain of his Majesty's Bodyguard, your Majesty. The Duc de Duras.

NAPOLEON. Don't know him. Anyway, you were quick off the mark. Good. What's your name?

SENTRY. Dupont.

NAPOLEON. I knew a Dupont at Eylau. Splendid fellow. I pinched his ear on the battlefield. You can see I have a good memory. I always recognize old friends.

SENTRY. It must have been my father's ear, your Majesty. Or one of my uncles'. I wasn't called up until 1813.

NAPOLEON [*vexed*]. It's the same thing. I'm promoting you to corporal. Marshal, make a note of the man's name. [*To the* SENTRY.] You can go.

SENTRY. Who'll take over my guard duty?

NAPOLEON. Nobody. I am returning as a father among his children. I need no guards now.

The SENTRY *presents arms and goes out. The* MARSHAL *looks musingly at his notebook.*

MARSHAL. We forgot to ask him his Christian name. I've already noted a hundred and thirteen Duponts since we left Grenoble. Not to mention the Durands. It's going to make promotion a little muddled—and also, I'm afraid, a little slow. With a certain glut of corporals . . .

NAPOLEON *has motioned to* ROUSTAN, *who unfolds his little leather campstool.*

NAPOLEON. France is patient, Marshal.

MARSHAL. Are you not going in, Sire?

NAPOLEON. Not just yet. I'll camp here for a while. Until they've done the housework. It seems that Louis the Eighteenth occupied my room. As he must have left somewhat hurriedly, I'm none too keen to find myself nose to nose with his old fleur-de-lis-embroidered slippers. What lack of tact for such a well-bred man! Sleeping in my bed, on the very first night!

MARSHAL. That bed had been his brother's bed before that, your Majesty.

NAPOLEON. Nothing of the kind! I loathed the Louis the Sixteenth style. I'd had it replaced. It was an Empire bed. With sphinxes. They must have been pretty surprised to see that fat old fellow climb in in my place.

MARSHAL. It takes more than that to surprise a sphinx, Sire. They've seen worse in their time.

NAPOLEON [with a sharp look]. Not very pleasantly disposed today, are we? Are you beginning to regret not having arrested me, as you'd sworn to do to Louis the Eighteenth?

MARSHAL. I never regret anything, Sire. I go forward. Whither the wind blows, I might add.

NAPOLEON. I presented myself to your men. I cried, "Shoot your Emperor," as I opened my coat—a superfluous gesture, I admit. You should have ordered, "Fire!"

MARSHAL. My men would not have fired. They knew you had made the same gesture at Lyons. They had no desire to be outdone by their comrades. Besides, by then, it had become impossible. I had seen you again.

NAPOLEON [rises and cries with sudden passion]. I might be a woman the way you talk! I do not care to owe my hold on France to the mere charm of my smile! I can't put myself on show and pinch the ears of all and sundry to make men want me, like a whore. [Shouting.] And what about the Regent Empress? And my son the King of Rome? And the Senate? My creations, all of them! Nobody gave a thought to all that, did they?—while I was out of sight!

MARSHAL. They weren't you.

NAPOLEON [looking with hatred at the Tuileries and murmuring]. All he had to do was appear, six months ago, old and fat, and forgotten for nineteen years, with not a single victory to his name, and without even troubling to stir up the merest show of popular acclaim. The ancient breed! You're right, Marshal. It's his palace. And I am coming back to it, like a common housebreaker, for the second time. Come, let's go in.

He goes in swiftly, followed by ROUSTAN *and the* MARSHAL. *The wall flies up to reveal* LOUIS XVIII's *bedroom, where* FOUCHÉ *is waiting. A* SERVANT *is sweeping a pile of rubbish into a corner.* NAPOLEON *paces up and down impatiently.* FOUCHÉ *waits.*

NAPOLEON. What is that man sweeping up?

FOUCHÉ [carelessly]. Old confidential papers of the King's,

Sire. At the last moment, in all the rush, they couldn't find a tinderbox.

NAPOLEON. Have you read them?

FOUCHÉ. Of course.

NAPOLEON [*with a smile*]. Silly question. In my day, whenever I came home unexpectedly, I invariably found you on all fours over my wastepaper basket.

FOUCHÉ [*smiling too*]. Once only, Sire. It taught me a lesson. You kicked me bodily out of the room.

NAPOLEON. Are you trying to make me believe you never did it again?

FOUCHÉ. No, Sire. I would never try to make you believe such a thing, you'd lose all confidence in me. It was my job to search wastepaper baskets in my capacity as Minister of Police. Since that painful little mishap, I took precautions, that's all.

NAPOLEON [*glancing at the man sweeping the pile of rubbish out the door*]. You're sure there's nothing interesting in that stuff?

FOUCHÉ. Everything of interest is in my pocket. For your Majesty's service.

The SERVANT *goes out.*

NAPOLEON. Show me.

FOUCHÉ *starts to take some papers from his pocket, then changes his mind.*

FOUCHÉ. Oh no. Not that one. Sorry.

NAPOLEON [*seizing his wrist roughly*]. Yes! That one, Monsieur le Duc d'Otrante! That's the pocket for your own service. The one for mine will interest me much less.

FOUCHÉ [*whimpering as* NAPOLEON *twists his wrist*]. Your Majesty! We're too old for such rough games! I have no physical strength at all! You're taking advantage of it!

NAPOLEON. Of course. I've always had to take advantage of everything in my life. I wasn't born on the throne!

FOUCHÉ [*releasing his papers with a snarl*]. Louis the Eighteenth would never have done that! They can say what they like, legitimacy has its points!

NAPOLEON [*jovially*]. It has. But we're all ruffians here, Duke. Are you pining for that King of yours already? Yet you had his predecessor guillotined, didn't you?—if I remember right.

FOUCHÉ [*rubbing his wrist*]. I might point out that with a

man of my feeble strength, you'll never know whether I wasn't pretending to look in the wrong pocket just to fool you.

NAPOLEON [*who has calmly sat down to read the documents*]. Don't you worry. I'll know all right. You know me. I'll search them both. [*Exclaiming.*] Why, this is very interesting! Fouché, come and look.

FOUCHÉ [*going over to him, sulkily*]. I've read it already. Which pocket?

NAPOLEON. The good one, I should think.

FOUCHÉ [*pitifully, as he reads over his shoulder*]. Yes. The good one.

NAPOLEON [*reading*]. A list of suspects, dated three weeks ago! The Duchesse de Saint-Leu, Madame Hamelin, Carnot, Regnault de Saint-Jean-d'Angély, Lavalette, Montalivet, twelve senators. It's a complete dossier of all those who were preparing for my return. Louis the Eighteenth knew three weeks ago! And he did nothing! The simpleton. If I'd been he, all this gay company would have ended in a ditch, the resistance nipped in the bud, and I should never have come back! [*Exclaiming.*] Oh, if I'd been in his shoes!

FOUCHÉ [*calmly*]. You are, Sire.

NAPOLEON [*musing*]. I wonder who could have procured him this list?

FOUCHÉ. I daresay we shall never know. [*He asks a little hastily.*] Have you read the second document?

NAPOLEON *is still studying the list. Suddenly he cries out:*

NAPOLEON. Why, Fouché!

FOUCHÉ. Sire?

NAPOLEON. You aren't on this.

FOUCHÉ [*a little disconcerted*]. Perhaps your Majesty hasn't read it properly. [NAPOLEON *silently hands him the list*.] How stupid. I've mislaid my glasses.

NAPOLEON. It's written very large.

FOUCHÉ *peers closely at the list.*

FOUCHÉ. There's one name that's been written over.

NAPOLEON. Lamarque, and over it they've put Lemarchand. No *F*. If you look closely, they've used the same *L*.

FOUCHÉ [*piteously*]. No *F*! That's an oversight I can't account for at all.

NAPOLEON [*eying him sardonically*]. What do you say to

that, Sir Minister of the Police? This kind of deduction must be familiar to you.

FOUCHÉ. I would say it's rather vexing. I was considered a negligible quantity. Your Majesty should have the charity not to press the point.

NAPOLEON [*coldly*]. Don't count on it. I'm having you arrested. [*He pulls the bell rope.*]

FOUCHÉ [*calmly*]. Not the bell, your Majesty. We have only just arrived. It will be Louis the Eighteenth's staff who'll answer.

An USHER comes in.

NAPOLEON. Who are you?

USHER. Chief Usher of the King's Bedchamber, Sire.

NAPOLEON. Fetch me the Captain of the Guard.

USHER [*with great dignity*]. The Duc de Duras is away just now, Sire.

NAPOLEON [*impatiently*]. Call the first soldier you see outside the window and send him up here!

The USHER goes out. NAPOLEON paces up and down in silence.

FOUCHÉ [*gently*]. You are going to make an ill-considered gesture, Sire. You need me and you are very short of capable men.

Enter the SENTRY.

NAPOLEON. Ah, there's Dubois. My old comrade in arms from Wagram.

SENTRY. Dupont, your Majesty. From Eylau. Well, his son, that is.

NAPOLEON [*vexed*]. Dupont, then. Same thing. [*Indicating FOUCHÉ.*] Arrest that man. Take him to the guardroom. Do you still have a sergeant?

SENTRY. Oh yes, your Majesty. Since I'm the only soldier he's got left, he's always after me.

NAPOLEON. Hand the prisoner over to him and tell him he'll answer for him with his head.

The SENTRY marches over to FOUCHÉ with a clank of arms. FOUCHÉ shrugs and goes out, followed by the SENTRY. NAPOLEON goes back to the pile of papers, which he reads through feverishly, uttering an exclamation from time to time. Suddenly he cries out:

NAPOLEON. Good God! Fouché! Come and look!

He looks around and calls again. Then he rings the bell.
Enter D'ASSONVILLE.

NAPOLEON. Who are you?

D'ASSONVILLE [*at attention*]. Lieutenant d'Assonville, Second Light Infantry.

NAPOLEON [*agreeably surprised*]. The Second Light Infantry? Does that still exist?

D'ASSONVILLE [*blushing like a girl*]. There's myself, Sire.

NAPOLEON [*delightedly*]. Oh, how well he said that! "There's myself"! Oh, Paris, Paris! Since I jumped off my ship at Golfe-Juan, I have turned sixty townships inside out, like so many topcoats, I have rallied thirty regiments, roused hordes of peasants stinking of onions and armed with scythes of no tactical usefulness whatever, but you, with your smile, have just given me back Paris. You are my army, my little lieutenant. We are going to do great things together. I shall bespatter you with glory! [*He pinches his ear and asks roguishly.*] Are you fond of your Emperor?

D'ASSONVILLE, *overcome with emotion, but without being ridiculous at all, only very young, says:*

D'ASSONVILLE. Sire, I want to die for you!

NAPOLEON [*without irony*]. Good, good, that's very good.

D'ASSONVILLE. When I was a child, at school, it was you I worked for. Every mathematics problem I was given—I wasn't very good at them, but I used to stay awake all night until I'd solved it—I'd offer it to you, like my life. . . .

NAPOLEON [*the old star actor*]. Charming, charming. The little schoolboy dedicating his life, along with his homework, to his Emperor. A pretty subject for Béranger. We must get him to write a song about it. We'll do great things together, my boy. I shall bespatter you with glory! [*He concludes coldly.*] As I said before.

D'ASSONVILLE [*ready to faint*]. Oh, Sire! To die for you . . .

NAPOLEON [*tapping him on the cheek, his thoughts elsewhere*]. We'll see, we'll see . . .

D'ASSONVILLE. To march for mile after mile again, in the dark and the cold, with my wounded arm, as in Russia! To keep watch while you sleep, and for someone to come to kill you and kill me instead, and for you not even to wake up! To have them forget to tell you my name even—

to be punished by you, when I haven't deserved it, and
never to complain!

NAPOLEON [*absently*]. Good, good. Very good. Your heart's
in the right place. [*Giving his full attention to something
else.*] Right! Now, where were we? I rang for Fouché. This
palace is full of surprises. Who are you?

D'ASSONVILLE [*springing to attention, a little bewildered*].
Lieutenant d'Assonville, Second Light Infantry.

NAPOLEON. Ah, yes. Your regiment will be re-formed with
the least possible delay, Lieutenant. Tell the Marshal to
come back here as soon as I have finished with the Duc
d'Otrante. [*He turns away and says over his shoulder.*]
And tell him I'm promoting you to captain.

D'ASSONVILLE [*modestly*]. Sire, we will have many opportunities for courage. I would rather win promotion after
some valiant action.

NAPOLEON [*turning, a little surprised*]. It's one in itself, to
be here, and the first.

D'ASSONVILLE [*firmly*]. No. That is only a great piece of
good luck. I should like to give my Emperor something
better than a happy set of circumstances.

NAPOLEON *eyes him coldly, in silence, as if unpleasantly surprised. Then he says, in a different tone:*

NAPOLEON. You're strict with yourself—that's good. [*A
short pause.*] Although, in the course of my reign, I've
had occasion to notice that one never accomplished anything much save with scoundrels. They're the only kind
one can talk to. Look at Fouché, I've just had him locked
up for treason and I need him already. [*He looks at
D'ASSONVILLE again, who has turned to ice.*] You will
stay a lieutenant, my boy. [*He adds peevishly.*] And since
you want to play the little tin soldier with me, I warn you
it'll be a very long time before you are a captain.

D'ASSONVILLE. I ask for nothing.

NAPOLEON. I can't stand that at any price! I prefer to buy
what I want when I want it. Consciences are totally useless. Toward the end my marshals were asking five hundred thousand francs—a million—just like actors with
star salaries, in return for participating in one of my cam-
paigns. I adored that. It reassured me. And I let them
have statues made of themselves as well, for the populace,
who need their history with pictures. [*He asks suddenly,*

excited.] Do you think that old villain Louis the Eighteenth offered them more when they went over to his side?

D'ASSONVILLE. Your marshals are patriots and heroes, Sire,
and if they considered in their soul and conscience——

NAPOLEON [*shouting peevishly*]. I tell you I've a horror of
consciences! They always turn out to be a hindrance—to
governing. I like heroes who are afraid of me and charge a
fortune for their services. It reassures me. Disinterested
men are always ruinously expensive. [*He smiles, reassured.*]
No. The fat old goat couldn't have paid them more than
I did. He hadn't a penny. They must have sold themselves
in exchange for the right to keep what I had given them,
that's all. He had them cut-rate. Like my bed. [*He paces
a little, musing.*] What a game of grab, the history of
France! That's why I love it, the whole lot of it. From
that little hypocrite Robespierre to the Connétable de
Bourbon! [*He paces around the room, light-footed and
spry, hands behind his back, his little paunch stuck out
in front.*] My young lieutenant, I am taking my France
in hand again. [*He declaims, still pacing.*]

O Corsican with the flat hair,
How fair was France, your France
At the high noon of harvest time!
A leaping mare was she, untamed, indomitable . . .

What was the name of the idiot who wrote that?

D'ASSONVILLE. Barbier, Sire.

NAPOLEON. Barbier, that's it. Inspiration came to him a
trifle suddenly, that fellow. You must remind me to think
of him tomorrow morning in case he hasn't managed to
escape—when I have a Minister of Police who isn't in
jail.

D'ASSONVILLE [*a little sadly*]. Is your Majesty thinking of
carrying out a purification?

NAPOLEON [*struck by this*]. Purification! There's a word I
should never have thought of. [*Eying D'ASSONVILLE.*]
You aren't without talent, my boy. It's a pity your head is
in the clouds, I would have employed you. Up till now
one always spoke of repression. It was too crude. [*He
rolls the word on his tongue with delight.*] "Purification."
It has a little hygienic feel to it. It's a brain wave. Have
you a notebook? [D'ASSONVILLE *hands him one.*] I'll
make a note of it. [*He repeats, delightedly.*] "Purifica-

tion." [*He has an idea.*] And "purge" perhaps—how about
that? No, it sounds dirty, it suggests colic. [*He repeats
with satisfaction.*] "Purification." And I'll jot down that
idiot's name too, while I'm at it. What was it again?
Barbier. [*He writes it down, then crosses it out.*] No,
damn it, I'm not starting my purification list with a man
of letters. They're inclined to give themselves too much
importance as it is. I'll slip him into a tumbrel of magis-
trates or actors. Let's see. Who shall I have shot first, do
you think? My marshals?

D'ASSONVILLE. They all went over to the other side, Sire.

NAPOLEON. That's true. And they've all come back to me,
to a man. No fools they! Anyway, I need them—we'll be
fighting soon. It wouldn't be a good idea. [*He shouts.*]
Every one of them! Except Marmont! He followed Fatty
to Ghent. [*He writes down something with glee.*] Ah,
here's a good name to start with—the Duc de Raguse.
I'll give him his title. The populace adores that. They
love star names on the scaffold. Who else? Talleyrand?
Right. But that won't impress anyone much. At least
three regimes have talked of shooting him. [*He tries to
think of other names and then says severely.*] Well, you
were there, for God's sake, when the Bourbons came back!
I'm asking you for names of collaborators! Have you got
any ideas or haven't you?

D'ASSONVILLE [*firmly*]. No, Sire, not about that. I have only
one man's blood to offer—my own.

NAPOLEON [*eying him in disgust*]. An idealist into the bargain! You're lucky that I've no one but you within reach.
I loathe talking to myself. [*Exclaiming.*] Augustan clemency, then? You believe in that, do you?

D'ASSONVILLE. I believe we must rebuild France, Sire, by
uniting her. The Emperor cannot behave like a political
party chief.

NAPOLEON. My young friend, we are not in the theatre, or
rather, yes, we are, but not in tragedy. In melodrama. And
I play to a full house! I am an actor of historical dramas.
I worked for all of France. For the France of the servant
girls who don't know what it's all about but who love a
good cry, and for the France of the workingmen who love
to hiss the villain, up in the gallery, after a pint or two.
Not for a refined little bunch of the best people. I have a
duty to my public. Your Louis the Eighteenth was able

to come back with his crown and his big belly in the nine-
teenth year of his nonexistent reign and say, "I shall forget
all that happened before the day of my return." Darling
brother's death included. Quite noble of him, I admit.
But that was an effect (one that misfired, I may add; nobody gave him any thanks for it) and fine for those born
to the purple. [*Dreamily.*] My son—that fair-haired strip-
ling with a faint air of the Hapsburgs about him—now,
he may well play that role, later in his reign, if all goes
well. . . . [*Nostalgically.*] I wish I'd been my son. . . .
Things would have been so much simpler. . . . [*He
collects himself and goes on harshly.*] But I made myself,
by my own efforts, with my sleeves rolled up, and they
expect a different performance from me. You may have
noticed that great actors nearly always sell the same sort
of wares. They win the public's love in a certain sort of
part and afterward they have to keep on playing it. Or it's
good-by to success! I want to be terrifying! As I was after
the execution of young Enghien. You were too young.
[*He exclaims greedily.*] Oh, if you'd listened to that silence
over Paris! You could have heard a fly buzzing. I like
the silence of fear. So do they. France is always bawling
after liberty, but she doesn't know how to use it. She's
only happy when girding up her loins. If that fool of a
Louis the Sixteenth had only realized that. . . . However, that's another story. [*Dreamily.*] I won't bring the
Empress back just yet—nor the King of Rome either. I
won't assemble a court. My brothers have crumbled like
playing-card kings—which they were. I'll leave them on
the floor. The Revolution—that's the card I shall play
now. I am the Revolution come back again. [*He exclaims
gleefully.*] Now there's a brain wave for you, young man!
It's my trump card against fat Louis. Can you see me?
The skinny little general, risen from the ranks, from the
Toulon days. And I'll have them—just where I want them.
[*He adds.*] And then with my leaping mare—as that idiot
says—well in hand again . . . snap! [*He makes a sig-
nificant gesture, then starts to laugh. He stops on seeing
the frozen-faced* D'ASSONVILLE.] I like confidants who
laugh when I laugh. You aren't amused?

D'ASSONVILLE [*sadly*]. No, Sire. We expect blood and glory
from you, not political chicanery.

NAPOLEON [*glaring at him, hostile*]. Oh, you're too stupid! Go and fetch Fouché!

D'ASSONVILLE [*stiffly*]. Where is Monsieur le Duc d'Otrante?

NAPOLEON. In the guardhouse, catching fleas. I had him arrested. Bring him back. I'll put him under arrest here, so I can have him where I want him. With him one can at least talk!

D'ASSONVILLE *salutes and goes out.* NAPOLEON *rings. Enter* ROUSTAN.

NAPOLEON. Roustan, is the Marshal there? Send him in.

NAPOLEON *takes a pinch of snuff, musing.* ROUSTAN *goes out without a word and comes back with the* MARSHAL.

NAPOLEON. Marshal! I am drawing up my purification list. I need your help.

MARSHAL [*surprised*]. Purification?

NAPOLEON [*delightedly*]. Yes. It's a new word I've just thought of. Repression is no longer in my new line of policy. I am just back from my island, you understand, where I stayed virginal—and with good reason!—and I've come to avenge France for those who gave themselves to a government which was in the pay of the occupying powers. There. It's as simple as that.

MARSHAL. That will make quite a crowd. Acceptance of the Charter was more or less universal.

NAPOLEON. The guilty will be those we designate as such. And that will vastly relieve the rest—who'll thereupon feel safe. That's what I call unity. Unity in appeased fright. Let's see now, in the army . . . I've already put down Raguse. Have you any suggestions?

MARSHAL. I should find it distasteful to give names of colleagues, Sire. And of subordinates even more so.

NAPOLEON [*thinly*]. Right. I see. I shall ask an ordinary colonel. Only men who are waiting for advancement will serve me well. [*Pacing up and down.*] What's more, I shall apply this system to wider fields. I shall ask an unsuccessful painter—preferably from the Academy—for names of painters. An author for names of authors, a needy professor for names in the academic world, a little deputy magistrate for names of judges. In that way, I'll be sure of getting names.

MARSHAL. If envy gives them to you, they will be those of talent, Sire. And you will decapitate the country.

NAPOLEON [*irritably*]. Heads grow again! You're getting on my nerves too, you are! You can go.

The MARSHAL *goes out as* D'ASSONVILLE *ushers in* FOUCHÉ.

MARSHAL. Aren't you under arrest any more?

FOUCHÉ. No. And you? Not yet?

MARSHAL [*at the door*]. Oh, for some fighting, quickly! Give me something I can understand!   [*He goes.*

NAPOLEON *shrugs.*

NAPOLEON [*to* FOUCHÉ]. All he's good for is playing follow-the-leader with a musket, as in Russia. But his sort have their uses too. . . . Come closer, Fouché. [FOUCHÉ *steps forward, unruffled.*] I once told Talleyrand that he was dung in a silk stocking. Talleyrand was a nobleman—a real one, one I hadn't created myself. In your case, it isn't even a silk stocking.

FOUCHÉ [*with dignity*]. I am a son of the people, Sire. And that is precious at the moment. If I have correctly grasped what the lad hinted at as we came up the stairs, regarding your new policy . . . ?

NAPOLEON [*gleefully*]. Does it seem to you a good one?

FOUCHÉ [*smiling*]. It was the line I planned to suggest to your Majesty myself, if we had had time to talk seriously. My Lyons days are back at last!

NAPOLEON. You know what a purification is, do you?

FOUCHÉ [*rather vulgarly*]. I think so, Sire! In the Place des Brotteaux, down in Lyons, I used to line them up in rows of ten, back in '93! And bang-bang-bang-bang-bang!

NAPOLEON [*gleefully*]. Bang-bang-bang! Leave us, Lieutenant. We have important work to do.

D'ASSONVILLE *goes out.* NAPOLEON *offers* FOUCHÉ *some snuff. He watches* D'ASSONVILLE *go with faint irritation.*

NAPOLEON. Why is he always hanging about in here, that boy? Is he a protégé of yours?

FOUCHÉ. He's a loyal soul, Sire.

NAPOLEON. So I've noticed. Without interest.

FOUCHÉ. He worships your Majesty's person. He was the first at the palace to await you. [*He adds, after a slight hesitation.*] And I knew his mother extremely well, years ago.

NAPOLEON [*his eyes lighting up*]. Did you? You old devil, you! [*Offering him another pinch of snuff.*] With the pressure of business, one needs to divert the mind a bit. Fire away. I love spicy stories.

FOUCHÉ [*with a shrug*]. This one is a century old. I was still a seminarist.

NAPOLEON [*severely*]. Just a minute! Nothing against religion! I like a bawdy joke, like all Frenchmen, but I won't have any digs against religion!

FOUCHÉ. Not even in the new line?

NAPOLEON. Least of all! The Revolution, Mother to us all —that they can harp on as much as they like. High principles and speechifying—there's no danger in that. But not a word against religion. It's too useful. That I pay the price for, and protect. Hold the priest and you hold the woman. Hold the woman and ten to one you hold the man.

FOUCHÉ. Then I'll spare you the beginning, which savors somewhat of the sprightly tales of the last century—the happy century, as they called it. They were the lords of the manor in my district. I was father confessor to the mother and the daughter. The daughter now, *she* resisted me.

NAPOLEON. I can well believe it. You are one of the ugliest men I've ever seen, Fouché.

FOUCHÉ. One should never despair, Sire. I must say I was sincerely in love with this girl. It's possibly the only sincere thing there has ever been in my life. I came across her again in Lyons, at the height of the Terror, married, ex-aristocrat, of course, and dispossessed—and in trouble. Incarcerated, both of them, in the worst prison of them all, the one you didn't leave alive. His head was three quarters off his shoulders, so to speak. A classic situation. I save the man.

NAPOLEON [*snickering*]. And you make the woman pay!

FOUCHÉ [*with sham regret*]. By some incomprehensible clerical error, the man's name remained on the condemned list of the Revolutionary Tribunal. An administrative mishap. But the woman, of course, was released. I even had her property restored to her. I was all-powerful in Lyons. Nine months later, she gave birth to a posthumous heir, whom I took steps to protect from afar.

NAPOLEON [*cackling*]. What an atrocious story! To be your son, Fouché! And did you see the mother again?

FOUCHÉ. No. I had become my ugly self again. Add to that

the horror of that accidental execution and her pointless sacrifice—well, I really didn't stand a chance. . . . Loaded with titles and wealth, thanks to your Majesty's generosity, I have, since then, had many mistresses. And —although I was as ugly as ever—some very handsome women, too. With just a little of the small change of power, a man, even an ugly one, can pick and choose. But although that first girl, thinking back on it dispassionately, must have been a rather insignificant little person, you have, thanks to this strange skein of circumstances, a Minister of Police who is actually a virgin to this day, Sire. I have never really made love.

NAPOLEON [*looking at him icily*]. That's a sad story. I don't care for them.

A pause.

FOUCHÉ [*chagrined*]. It was no doubt a mistake to reveal myself somewhat, as I have to your Majesty by telling you, for the first time, something true about myself.

NAPOLEON [*coldly*]. No doubt.

FOUCHÉ [*with a trace of a smile on his thin lips*]. However, I must add, to repair my blunder a little—if repair it I can—that this lady was of Creole origin and an intimate friend of Mademoiselle Josephine Tascher de la Pagerie, even before the latter's marriage to the Vicomte de Beauharnais. I got to know, through her, a great many things which you and I, Sire, are alone in knowing.

He and NAPOLEON *look at each other, two serpents face to face.*

NAPOLEON. We know too much, both of us, about each other, Monsieur le Duc d'Otrante. Only I have the longer arm. And the better memory.

FOUCHÉ [*holding his gaze*]. Quite right, Sire, you have. But my archives, in case my own should fail, are in a safe place.

NAPOLEON [*dismissing the subject for a later settlement*]. Right. Now, let's continue our conversation where we left it before the happy news of this birth. Hadn't you in mind to ask me to be godfather to this child?

FOUCHÉ [*with a smile*]. No, Sire. He is provided for. Madame d'Assonville was also an intimate friend of Talleyrand's, who very kindly consented to hold her son over the font.

NAPOLEON [*sourly*]. I see the web is well woven.

FOUCHÉ [*easily*]. Fairly well, Sire. That is why we can resume, in all liberty of mind, our previous exchange of ideas.

NAPOLEON [*resolved to overlook it all for the moment*]. You're right. Let's get back to business. The purification over, I raise an army of recruits and launch a new set of taxes. War is thrust upon me by a bloodthirsty Europe, Fouché! I must defend myself. France needs men, and she needs money!

FOUCHÉ. As usual.

NAPOLEON [*going nearer to him*]. That is where we're going to start our serious talking. I hope you haven't been there before me? It seems the Treasury is intact, is it?

FOUCHÉ. I did go before you, Sire, of course. That is always the first port of call. It is intact, Sire. Hardly believable, but it is. And do you know what the Duc de Feltre, Head of the King's Household, did before he left, your Majesty? He took out of the till the exact sum needed for King Louis' journey to Ghent—not a penny more—and he left a receipt, addressed to France. . . .

NAPOLEON [*shaking with laughter*]. The fool! Where's the pleasure in fighting men like that! Can you see yourself in their service, Fouché? Why, you'd be bored to extinction —I know you!

FOUCHÉ [*musing*]. Who knows, Sire? Like all aging scoundrels, whose pockets are well lined—as mine are now— I must confess to your Majesty that there is at the bottom of my heart something oddly akin to a nostalgia for honesty. It may be this long-lost young man reminding me of my youth——

NAPOLEON [*interrupts, ice-cold again*]. No nostalgia with me, please, Fouché! It isn't my style. [*He adds, insidiously.*] Especially as, without suspecting it, you *did* let me score a point against you earlier on. That young man, if I've understood you, doesn't know that you're his father, am I right? It would be very sad—eh, Fouché—if he found out?

FOUCHÉ *bows, his mouth twisting slightly, and says simply:*

FOUCHÉ. Well played. I am all yours, Sire.

NAPOLEON [*sitting down and picking up his papers*]. Right, let's make the most of it, then! It can't last. Let's begin this list for the firing squad. You have some names for me, I hope? [*He rubs his hands.*]

FOUCHÉ [*laughing*]. A whole directory, Sire!

As they set to work, the front cloth representing the Tuileries falls in front of them. The SENTRY *takes up his post again. He starts pacing up and down, while the cannon fire is heard in the distance. Suddenly the cannon stops. A roll of carriage wheels. The* SENTRY *presents arms and shouts, as he did at the beginning of the play:*

SENTRY. Long live the King!

The SERGEANT *rushes on.*

SERGEANT. Good man! Don't keep shouting it the entire time, though. With the Emperor, you could start up every five minutes—it was all part of keeping up the enthusiastic atmosphere. But now that the Bourbons are back—and properly back too, with the Prussians and the Russians here as well—we have centuries behind us, and in front of us too, I don't doubt. So quietly does it. Just present arms, my boy, as it's laid down in the regulations; that will do. [*He inspects him and adds.*] You'll do four days' K.P., though, on account of that third button.
[*He goes out.*

SENTRY [*bitterly*]. And that's what they call a change of government!

The front cloth rises. In the King's room, FOUCHÉ *is still standing where he was, only now it is* LOUIS XVIII *who is sitting in* NAPOLEON'*s place.*

LOUIS. Monsieur le Duc, I do not like your condemned list.

FOUCHÉ. May I respectfully point out to your Majesty that if you had taken account of the first list I very carefully drew up for you—a few weeks before the Hundred Days—Bonaparte would not have reached the Tuileries. I found that list in your Majesty's wastepaper basket.

LOUIS. Yes. At the last moment, in all the rush, nobody could find a tinderbox. You collected up my papers, did you?

FOUCHÉ. I went around your Majesty's room, as a precaution, and I saved everything of interest. The documents have been very carefully preserved and are at your Majesty's disposal.

LOUIS [*simply*]. Good. Be so kind as to put them back in my basket. Where you found them.

FOUCHÉ [*obeying with bad grace*]. As your Majesty wishes. [*He asks with a touch of anxiety.*] Isn't your Majesty going to ask me whether I haven't kept one or two back in case they might be useful to me?

LOUIS [*simply*]. For what? I took it upon myself to use you, Monsieur Fouché—despite solid opposition from my immediate entourage—and to include you in my ministry. Despite also a personal repugnance—if you'll excuse the word—which I think you intelligent enough to appreciate. But the King does not consider he has the right to take account of the repugnance—excuse the word again, won't you?—which as Count of Provence he might feel for his brother's murderers. I believe, in the present state of affairs, that you can be useful to the country, with your good qualities and with your bad. That is enough.

FOUCHÉ. I respectfully thank your Majesty.

LOUIS [*tersely*]. Our dealings will be practical. We will also dispense with thanks. But as I have decided to use you, I shall burden you with something you aren't accustomed to, I'm sure: my confidence. It will be total, Monsieur Fouché. I might even say childlike. I don't mind telling you that I expect to inconvenience you more than a little with what must be quite a new sentiment for you. I asked you to put those papers back in my basket. They are there. They are all there, I'm sure. Now, let us talk of something else.

FOUCHÉ [*ill at ease, a little nonplussed even, searches his pockets*]. I shall put these two in as well, Sire—an oversight. [*He throws them in the basket.*]

LOUIS [*smiling*]. Good. You see, it's just another kind of game. All you have to do is learn the rules. [*He adds, still smiling.*] And the last one, which you have no doubt kept back, can be of no use to you because this time you know that I have returned to the throne of my forefathers for good. Our English friends have taken charge of Bonaparte and they are very serious-minded folk where these things are concerned, I needn't tell you that. So you have no other possible master to serve now but me. That simplifies matters considerably, now doesn't it?

FOUCHÉ *sighs and after a short pause puts the last paper in the basket.* LOUIS *smiles again and says after a pause:*

Louis. I am old, Monsieur Fouché. Nearly infirm. I still
love my food, despite the gout, but it's many a day, alas,
since I gave up the ladies. We won't even mention the
other good things of this life. I was so used to them all
as a child that, by contrast, I suppose, I can do without
them very easily. Life has dealt me some hard knocks and
I thought a great deal about human nature in my beds
in roadside inns during those nineteen years of wandering,
when I slept but little. A King is disinterested, in essence
and by function. If we went in for propaganda, like your
former master, we could make use of that argument. For
me, it's simpler still. I am not even working for my son.
Heaven did not give me one. My good brother—on whom
I shall spare you my opinion since it does not concern
you—will not succeed me for very long. He is as old as
I am. My nephews . . . if God wills it! And I'll ask it of
Him here and now, because it would really be too tiresome if the cake went to the Duke of Orléans after all.
That lot have had their greedy eyes on it for long enough.
So let us say, without getting drunk on pretty speeches,
as those gentlemen of the Convention were a little apt to
do, that I have no reason not to be sincere when I say
that I shall work, in the few years I have left to live, for
France's good and not my own. If I have managed to put
a little order in the shop before I present myself to God,
I shall think myself blessed indeed.

You are as old as I am. You have knocked about the
world, in different ways but just as much as I; you have
taken care to make yourself rich enough for it not to
amuse *you* any more either; and you have, I imagine,
learned to appreciate the emptiness of honors and the
insipidity of blood. . . . I ask you, why should I doubt
that you will work loyally with me? In a life as tumultu-
ously full as yours, you have yet to savor the delights of
altruism and of honesty—that supreme luxury which was
denied you until now through your humble birth and the
battles you have had to fight in order to escape from your
condition. All this will be so new to you that—you must
tell me if I'm being ingenuous—I'm staking everything
on it, that's all. You will have every facility for deceiving me, Monsieur le Duc d'Otrante. I shall never
check the truth of anything save in your eyes. It will
therefore be so easy that I venture to think it won't be

any fun for you at all. I hope so with all my heart and I am betting on it. If I perceive that I have made a mistake I shall have to think again. Now, back to business. I don't like your black list. Henry the Fourth, when he marched into Paris, began by embracing the rebels whose dagger thrusts, half healed, he still bore on his body. It was not purely greatness of soul—it was shrewdness and sound sense. To return to France with hatred on my lips would be quite simply the sign of an unintelligent man. And a third-rate politician.

FOUCHÉ. Even so . . . There is the case of the Marshal, your Majesty. You entrusted him with the main body of your troops. He promised to bring Bonaparte back in an iron cage.

LOUIS [with a smile]. He comes from the South. . . . And one must reckon with sentiment. He had an almost feminine affection for the man.

FOUCHÉ. Public opinion will never understand.

LOUIS [seriously]. Yes, now that may be a valid point. My personal feelings must come second, Monsieur Fouché. You say he is in hiding in Auvergne?

FOUCHÉ. I have his address.

LOUIS. He was given those passports on my orders, wasn't he? One for Switzerland and the other for Holland? Under two different names! Good God, he had the choice!

FOUCHÉ. He has them, but he's hanging around.

LOUIS. How inconsiderate people are! I can understand that he's loath to leave France. I was myself. But his fireside slippers will get the fellow condemned to death! He would be so comfortable in Switzerland, instead of appearing at the Supreme Court! He could occupy himself tinkering with clocks—he who hadn't the wit to know the hour had struck on the clock tower at Grenoble.

FOUCHÉ. If your Majesty does not give the order for his arrest, people will not call it clemency but weakness.

LOUIS. I am not weak. I don't intend to be, I haven't the right. But I have a horror of spilt blood. Especially as I find it pointless, and, worse, inept. Let him know unofficially that I give him one more week to clear out. Let him take his slippers with him, damn it!

FOUCHÉ. I shall obey the King's orders.

LOUIS. Anyway, come to think of it, if you've done your job properly, nobody knows that we know where he is!

FOUCHÉ. That's true, Sire. But if it should come out, let us beware of losing face!

LOUIS [*with a kindly smile*]. You know, I'm not so vain about my face as Bonaparte. Thank God I'm not performing a part. At least, not for a salary. I have a very, very old face—which I didn't make up myself—I have fewer reasons than he for fearing to lose it. That is why kings can do their jobs more peacefully than usurpers. They can even treat themselves to the luxury of swallowing an affront or two without flinching—when they must—as I did myself this morning. A thing which those gentlemen cannot afford to do. [*He turns to* FOUCHÉ.] You must have a tinderbox handy, if I know anything about you. There's the fireplace. Now burn those papers, do. Then we can forget about them.

The USHER *scratches on the door and enters.*

USHER. Monsieur le Duc de Blacas, to whom your Majesty granted an audience, is here, Sire.

LOUIS. Show him in.

The USHER *goes out and shows in the* DUC DE BLACAS. *The* DUKE *makes his three bows.* LOUIS *graciously indicates* FOUCHÉ.

LOUIS. Monsieur le Duc d'Otrante, whom I'm sure you recognize, Jules, even though he's on all fours. He is burning documents.

The DUC DE BLACAS *ostentatiously turns away toward the window.*

LOUIS [*To* FOUCHÉ, *dismissing him*]. Thank you, Monsieur le Duc, for this fine blaze. It's most cheerful. I shall myself supervise the combustion. [FOUCHÉ *backs out of the room with three bows, casts a baleful glance at* BLACAS, *and goes out.*] Well, my dear old friend, here we are, back again. [*He graciously indicates a chair, without moving.*] You asked me for an audience. I am listening.

BLACAS [*who is a long string bean of a man, emphatic and conceited*]. Sire! We must avenge the blood of Saint Louis!

LOUIS [*raising his arms in mock despair*]. We have so many

things to do! [*Suddenly.*] I know, let's ask Saint Louis to do it! Don't you think that's an idea? He's better placed than we are for the job.

BLACAS [*tremulously*]. Sire, your august brother died on an ignominious scaffold and I find a regicide squatting on his haunches in your chamber lighting a fire!

LOUIS [*unperturbed*]. The fire I ordered myself. As for the squatting, that's because the fireplaces are low. He voted for Louis the Sixteenth's death, it's true, along with some three hundred of his colleagues. And he was in my chamber. I'll say more—you shall be the first to hear the news—as from this morning, he is my minister! Do sit down, Blacas. You're so tall you make me giddy.

BLACAS [*dropping into a chair, ashen-faced*]. Sire, I am annihilated!

LOUIS [*kindly*]. I'm sorry I can't take you literally, my dear fellow. Annihilation would be a dream solution.

BLACAS [*goggle-eyed*]. I don't understand what your Majesty means. Why, Sire, I am the spokesman here for exile and fidelity. We were with you at Mittau and Coblenz, we were with you in London! What does the King intend to do for us?

LOUIS [*still kindly*]. To be ungrateful.

BLACAS. Sire, I refuse to believe that you would have the heart to mock an old servant, whom you were occasionally kind enough to call your friend!

LOUIS [*smiling kindly*]. You still are, Blacas.

BLACAS [*starting again*]. Sire, we came back to France with high hopes, after that long nightmare——

LOUIS [*interrupting*]. So did I. But *I*, my good man, found myself straight away with reality on my hands. Not that I'm complaining, mind. I like reality. It tastes of bread.

BLACAS [*delighted at the opening*]. It is bread I have come to talk about, Sire! Our children's bread.

LOUIS [*laughing*]. Here we are back at Versailles! When anyone comes to see the King, it's to ask him for money!

BLACAS. No other money but our own, Sire, and justice! What does the King plan to do with the exiles' property?

LOUIS [*gently*]. Blacas, if I were only an ordinary nobleman, I daresay I should be an old fool like you. I am a product of the old days too. But I cannot be King of the little handful of men who have stayed faithful—to me or to their hatred, I've never cared to work out which exactly.

. . . I am not the King of the few folk over in London. I am King of millions of men, who willy-nilly stayed where they were and who had to adapt themselves, as best they could, to what befell them. Exile was a luxury, after all. It has become a badge of glory. I've no objection. But if nobody at all had remained in France, it would have been pretty awkward, you'll admit.

BLACAS [*nettled*]. All those who stayed behind were traitors more or less.

LOUIS [*shrugging*]. They survived. Which is never very easy. And whatever they may have done, all those who stayed during these last nineteen years, which were no more than an interlude for us, were the only France there was during that time. And it is they whose King I am. It is therefore for them that I shall work.

BLACAS. Am I to understand, Sire, that you are not going to restore their property to the exiles?

LOUIS. Yes. I deplore it and it is probably unjust. But effective action is always unjust. I shall not do so. The only thing one may not trifle with in France, Blacas, is the woolen stocking. If you ask them for the last of their sons for the battle front, the French are always ready to cry, "Let him die!" with their hands in their pockets! But try to touch their money and that's different! Just what do you think is the starting date of the Republic? The whole of France was Royalist in '92. The day the ordinary citizen ventured to buy confiscated property from the nation, that day France boarded the Republican ship. And the well-lined woolen stocking went too! Reasons of state therefore demand that the purchasers of national property should sleep easy in their beds.

BLACAS [*rising with a screech*]. Legitimist Europe will cover her face with shame!

LOUIS [*calmly*]. And well she might. She's not a pretty sight to see. After your visit, I am expecting the ambassadors of my good brothers, the sovereigns of Russia, Austria, and Prussia. They have come to do the accounts. I shall have to argue every inch of the way, I can tell you! Quibble over the levies of troops or money. Sit tight on our reserves of corn, cling with my nails to the stones of our strongholds. Those fellows all want a little piece of France to round out their fat domains. Poland has made them hungry!

BLACAS. In return for the immense services rendered, it is quite legitimate that——

LOUIS [*with sudden anger*]. What are you raving about? Nothing is legitimate! Except letting go of as little as possible by every possible means. That is the only reason I am seeing them at all. Patience, my good Blacas. I am a nobleman, but I am not going to do what Louis the Fifteenth did at Amiens. I shall haggle like a big tough horse trader. [*He rubs his hands.*] One minute of utter lowness in a good cause is a toothsome thing. There aren't so many to be had in the life of a King!

BLACAS [*indignantly*]. Is the King going to haggle with his allies?

LOUIS [*purposely vulgar*]. You just watch me! Do you know what those dear brothers of mine had planned to do on Wednesday next? Blow up the Jena bridge!

BLACAS [*who really is as boneheaded as he looks*]. I know! I'd heard the glad news.

LOUIS [*exploding*]. The glad news? Do you think our military gentlemen with their brilliant plans haven't blown up enough bridges since Valmy? I have five hundred and twelve of them to rebuild!

BLACAS [*outraged*]. But, Sire, the Jena bridge commemorates an atrocious defeat!

LOUIS [*laughing*]. For Prussia! You're getting confused, my dear man. Not for us. Come back from London, my friend. We're in Paris now.

BLACAS. But the armies of the usurper——

LOUIS [*shrugging*]. They were ours. Besides, a bridge is a bridge. It was the Jacobins who invented the notion of putting symbols into everything. But I'll tell you something that will make you laugh. Do you know the message I sent those good brothers of mine? That on Wednesday next I would be on the Jena bridge myself, on my two fat legs. Very put out they are! They're just a bunch of shopkeepers, little jumped-up squires with a hundred and fifty or two hundred years of royalty behind them, and as scared of scandal as provincials. But I'm not! I don't give a damn for scandal. I come from an old house where no one ever gave it a thought. I'll be there, on the Jena bridge, they can be sure of that, next Wednesday at daybreak. I'll make the devil of a din and we'll soon see if they let off their fireworks then!

BLACAS. May I as a friend be permitted to say this, even if as a subject I must bow to the royal will. It is deeply painful to me, Sire, to hear the King of France talking like a "patriot."

LOUIS. Don't make me laugh, Blacas! If I weren't one, who would be? In the first place it's my bridge! *That's* patriotism!

BLACAS. It commemorates a victory of Buonaparte's.

LOUIS. Oh, call him "Bonaparte" like everybody else, since it pleases him. [*He bangs the table with a sudden roar.*] But Bonaparte's victories are mine too, sir! Why, you've been living in cuckooland! I can see it's the Royalists I'm going to have most trouble with. France covered herself with glory during the nineteen years when I was dancing attendance at all the courts of Europe, shabbily expelled from each in turn as one by one my dear brothers signed their peace treaties. I'm certainly not going to cross out all that glory on the pretext that I was detained elsewhere at the time. The wars of the Empire I'm adding to my account. The same with the Revolution. I am digesting it. Sometimes I come across a bone, like Fouché, in my ministry. I bring it up, discreetly. And I swallow it down again. It's entirely my affair if I retch from time to time. It's not for me to be finicky. I am France's stomach. I have to digest everything.

BLACAS [*shaking his powdered old head with indignation*]. They have changed our King.

LOUIS [*smiling*]. Of course they have. His number anyway. It isn't Louis the Sixteenth now, it's Louis the Eighteenth. Many other things have changed, my poor Blacas, things we must have the courage to face. That's all we have left now—courage.

BLACAS [*yelping*]. And what about honor?

LOUIS [*calmly*]. I'm the judge of what I do with mine. And it isn't for France to have any. [*Looking at him.*] I grant that you've all remained the same old feathered dodoes. The world is moving too fast and you don't know what's what any more. But haven't you an ounce of manliness and good sense left? Your fathers had, I can promise you; they were a heartier lot of lads than any of *you!* [*Pensively.*] It's Louis the Fourteenth's fault, all of this. . . . After years of keeping you all hanging around at

Versailles in hopes of the good position or the fat pension, he emasculated his aristocracy. There were men in France before that. A little turbulent, it's true. But with a chopped head or so per year one managed to keep order. And then, one day, there was nobody left at all but tightrope dancers. And now it's the great-grandsons who are paying Grandpapa's bill. There's a wilderness all around them. [*He cries.*] I haven't got a Richelieu! Or rather, yes, I have, but not the right one. Never mind. I'll take Fouché. I'll scrub my hands clean afterward. So Bonaparte created a more efficient administration than ours? Brilliant, his system of prefects—all Europe envies us them. Right! I'll pinch it! So he drew up a good civil code? It's mine! And if you see anything else of his, just tell me. I'm a taker. This is a game of grab. And fat as I am on my tottery fat legs, I want to be in the front row! I am twenty-nine million and we've a hearty appetite!

BLACAS [*in a drained voice*]. Sire, I am speechless.

LOUIS [*laughing*]. Don't talk, then. There's nothing left to say. Or do. No more court. I can't dance any more, I'm certainly not going to make others dance under my nose. No more pensions. My household is minute now. And I'm going to be stingy, too! That's new for a Bourbon. Voluptuously stingy! We shall have to have a long period of peace if we're to set ourselves to rights again. France's blood will be her money from now on. I won't let it out save drop by drop.

BLACAS [*emphatic and rather ridiculous*]. Sire, I am profoundly sad. There are forty kings in heaven, your forefathers, who are turning away their eyes.

LOUIS. They're in heaven; let them pray. I'm on earth. I'm the forty-first. And I'm in charge of the political kitchens now. I'm going to brew up a little something for the common good.

He rings the bell. The USHER *appears.*

LOUIS. Are their Excellencies in my antichamber?

USHER. Yes, Sire.

LOUIS. Have Monsieur le Duc de Feltre show them into the ambassadors' audience chamber. Together. Since they are all going to ask me the same thing, it will be quicker. [*The* USHER *goes out. To* BLACAS.] Good-by to you, my dear fellow. Help me out of this chair, would you? [*He*

takes his arm, kindly, walks a few steps with him to the window, and puts on his odd-looking two-cornered hat.]
And to think we used to dance until dawn, you and I, at the Trianon, like the gay young blades we were! Those days are over. You see, now that I'm old and gouty, I have to work for my living. . . . [*He pats his hand affectionately.*] You're still my old friend, you know, Jules, even if I am squeezing the life out of you. Guess what I'm going to do to those three boot-faced old fools who are waiting for me next door—a Prussian, an Austrian, and a Russian—all three in their big new conqueror's boots? They're peeling their velvet gloves off their claws already, I can just see them. But I know what divides them and they don't know I know. I shall support each of them, in turn, against the other two. And when they're nicely at each other's throats, I shall take my pawns back. I mustn't boast, however, it wasn't my idea. It was that old reptile Talleyrand who perfected the technique at Vienna. [*As he speaks, they have gradually reached the window, like a pair of old friends. Suddenly a shot rings out, coming from the courtyard. A sound of broken glass.* Louis *puts his hand to his hat and says simply.*] Missed! But he's made a hole in my lovely new hat, the brute!

There is a commotion outside; then FOUCHÉ *comes rushing in.*

FOUCHÉ. Sire, I've come to set your mind at rest. It was a young officer. A miserable wretch who's lost his wits. But don't distress yourself, your Majesty. It was me he shot at.

LOUIS [*exclaiming, teasingly*]. That's what I call a devoted minister. You're wounded, I hope?

FOUCHÉ. No, Sire.

LOUIS. Too bad. He made a hole in my hat. Where is this young man?

FOUCHÉ. He's in safe custody.

LOUIS. Send him up. I want to see him.

FOUCHÉ. Sire, it might not be wise. . . .

LOUIS. That is my affair, monsieur. Your job is to take away his gun and send him up, since I have ordered you to do so.

FOUCHÉ *bows and goes out.*

BLACAS [*with a grand, ridiculous gesture*]. I shall stay here, Sire! I shall make you a rampart of my body.

LOUIS [*patting him affectionately on the shoulder*]. You old madman! I know I can always rely on you for that. But you're so thin, my poor Blacas, and I'm so fat, that the worst marksman in the world would still contrive to hit me. So it's a waste of time. . . . Anyway, you can go with an easy mind, they've taken away his gun. [*He pushes* BLACAS *gently out of the room. Left alone, he pokes his finger through the hole in his hat and murmurs.*] Another half inch and my poor Frenchmen were saddled with that great loon Charles!

D'ASSONVILLE *comes in with* FOUCHÉ, *who looks a little worried.* D'ASSONVILLE *stands stiffly at attention.* LOUIS *looks at him ironically.*

LOUIS. You stand at attention impeccably, Lieutenant, but you're a bad shot.

D'ASSONVILLE. Sire, I fired at Monsieur le Duc d'Otrante.

LOUIS. He's in the best of health. You're a bad shot. Regiment?

D'ASSONVILLE [*still at attention*]. Second Light Infantry.

LOUIS [*patiently*]. And before that?

D'ASSONVILLE. Before that? Second Light Infantry. [*With a touch of insolence.*] And during the period of your Majesty's first return visit, the Royal Sardinians.

LOUIS. Colonel, the Marquis de Pontorson. I shall recommend you to him.

D'ASSONVILLE [*aggressively*]. I expect to be shot.

LOUIS [*with a touch of impatience*]. If we say so, my young friend! I'll grant a man the right to shoot, if he has convictions, but not to be insolent. Did you talk to Bonaparte in that tone?

D'ASSONVILLE. I had the most profound respect for the Emperor.

LOUIS [*calm again*]. And none for the King? I know, it's the fashion in France. Now that he's gone, he has all the virtues. First of all, stand at ease. [D'ASSONVILLE *remains rigid.*] At ease, I said! He liked it, I've no doubt, but I loathe talking to a rigid automaton. Courtly bowings I don't mind; they may be ridiculous but they're graceful. Standing at attention I just think is stupid. It embarrasses me. [*He looks at him and asks.*] What is it exactly that disgusts you about the Duc d'Otrante? There's plenty to choose from.

D'ASSONVILLE [*springing to attention again*]. He is a traitor.

LOUIS [*smiling*]. To whom? You're very clever if you know.

D'ASSONVILLE. The Emperor!

LOUIS [*quietly*]. And myself too, I expect, my boy, but I'm not making a fuss about it.

FOUCHÉ [*stepping forward*]. Sire, I feel that any conversation with this young hothead will be painful to your Majesty.

LOUIS. Oh, no, no. To you, perhaps. To me it's most entertaining. [*He eyes* D'ASSONVILLE *again, smiling.*] Do stop standing at attention, my child. For you *are* a child. Look, you see, I'm sitting down. [*He motions to* FOUCHÉ, *who draws up a chair close to* D'ASSONVILLE. LOUIS *sits down.*] I'm afraid that if we both stand up, our conversation will take far too solemn a turn. Besides, my legs ache. How old are you?

D'ASSONVILLE. Twenty-two, Sire.

LOUIS *looks up at him, amused.*

LOUIS. And it fires a gun already?

D'ASSONVILLE. I fought at Waterloo. I was a cadet during the Russian campaign.

LOUIS [*gently*]. I know. I know. They started young with Bonaparte. What is your name?

D'ASSONVILLE. D'Assonville.

LOUIS. Any relation to the Vicomtesse Bugniet d'Assonville?

D'ASSONVILLE [*stiffly*]. She was my mother, Sire.

LOUIS. I knew her. Your father died on the scaffold, I believe?

D'ASSONVILLE. Yes, Sire, in Lyons.

LOUIS [*turning to* FOUCHÉ *slightly*]. In Monsieur Fouché's time?

D'ASSONVILLE. Yes, Sire.

LOUIS. And it was to avenge Bonaparte, not your father, that you shot at him?

D'ASSONVILLE *says nothing.*

FOUCHÉ. Sire, I think this conversation is a little ill-timed. I feel I ought to inform your Majesty that the Duc de Feltre has already admitted the ambassadors of the Allied powers. . . .

LOUIS [*with an irritated gesture*]. They'll have to wait! I need to know my young people, Monsieur Fouché. I am educating myself at the moment. [*Turning back to* D'Assonville.] I see a kind of contradiction which I find hard to explain, in what you are telling me, monsieur. When you served Bonaparte, and the Duc d'Otrante was serving him too, you had occasion to see him countless times without disgust, I imagine?

Fouché [*increasingly anxious*]. This boy is a young fanatic who cannot forgive me for genuinely transferring to your Majesty's service. If I needed any guarantee of my sincerity and loyalty——

Louis [*interrupting*]. You do need it, Monsieur Fouché. But I don't know why I can't manage to convince myself that that pistol shot provides you with one. Leave me alone with this young man.

Fouché. Sire, I am very sorry, but my grave responsibilities as Minister of your Majesty's Police and the concern for your safety, for which I am answerable to the realm, do not allow me to obey your Majesty's orders. This young man has just fired a gun. He may have another weapon concealed about his person. . . .

Louis [*tersely*]. If you have done your job, sir, in full awareness of your grave responsibilities, he has been searched and is now unarmed. Do as I say or I shall have you thrown out.

Fouché [*bows and says sourly*]. Sire, I shall stay outside the door.

Louis. That's right. Don't put your ear too close, on account of the usher.

Fouché *goes out.* Louis *studies* D'Assonville.

Louis [*with sudden nostalgia*]. Why aren't you a Royalist, my boy? I like you. I shouldn't say so, but I like cherubs who fire pistols. If a boy of your age didn't feel the urge to fire a shot in the world we live in, it would be a dismal prospect. I'm a little short of marksmen among the sons of my friends. Nothing but lions, as the fashion demands, but without claws, without teeth.

D'Assonville. Sire, I shall remain faithful to the Emperor until the day I die!

Louis [*with a smile*]. But that's such a long way off!

D'Assonville. I hoped I had done everything to make it imminent.

LOUIS. Neither I nor my Minister of Police—I don't know why yet, but I hope to soon—seem to view the matter in that light. I rather feel that this hole in my hat will remain between the three of us.

D'ASSONVILLE [*stiffly*]. I refuse my reprieve.

LOUIS [*smiling*]. That would seem to me difficult. You will personally have to persuade twelve soldiers and a non-commissioned officer, stage an entire ceremony all by yourself. . . . It isn't so easy, you know, to get oneself shot. [*He smiles again.*] I tell you what. We'll strike a bargain. If you answer my questions frankly, I promise to give you a passport to go and join your hero. All right? You didn't know, in your master's day, that it was Fouché who signed your father's death warrant in Lyons?

D'ASSONVILLE [*woodenly*]. My duties gave me few opportunities for contact with the Duc d'Otrante.

LOUIS. Did you know it or didn't you?

D'ASSONVILLE. I thought that my father's name had been one of many on long lists of death sentences which the Duc d'Otrante did, in fact, sign, at the time when the Convention sent him to crush the uprising in Lyons. I did not connect them personally at all.

LOUIS. But since then you have learned something which has led you to believe that there was a connection between them?

D'ASSONVILLE [*on the verge of tears*]. I haven't the right to answer that. The secret is not entirely mine.

LOUIS. Did Fouché know your father personally?

D'ASSONVILLE. No. My mother. That's why I shot at him. I didn't know it before. [*Suddenly he collapses in the chair sobbing like a child.*]

LOUIS. Oh, Lord! And me with my useless legs. [*He struggles to his feet and leaning on a table with one hand and snatching up his stick with the other, he hobbles over to* D'ASSONVILLE *and lays his hand awkwardly on the boy's head.*] My child. My poor child. I don't know what to say to you. . . . We have lived through atrocious times when nobody knew quite what he was doing. You can't ask human beings to remain themselves in the filth of prison life. All prisons are brimming over with innocence. It is those who cram their fellows into them, in the name of empty ideas, who are the only guilty ones. I knew your mother, in the early days of her marriage. In a somewhat frivolous court, she shone with all the splendor of her modesty and virtue. It is that young woman we will talk about, you and I, if you are willing to attach yourself to me.

D'ASSONVILLE [*sobbing*]. I want to die! I'm too ashamed!

LOUIS [*gently*]. Of course. At your age, one thinks that will solve anything. In the first place, it solves nothing at all, and, secondly . . . I am old, my child, and I learned, one pale wintry day, of my brother's ignominious death, and then my sister's—my sister-in-law the Queen's, my young cousin Enghien's, and a large number of my friends'. I also had occasion to learn of the shame of many others. Afterward I was humiliated for many a long year, deceived, derided. . . . I went on living. And now I am trying to make myself useful, as best I can. [*He strokes his hair timidly.*] I can't stay with you much longer. The ambassadors of my brothers the monarchs of Russia, Austria, and Prussia are next door, waiting to rob me. I shall go in, bargain without glory, do my job. Believe me, there is nearly always something better one can do than die. Stay at the palace tonight.

D'ASSONVILLE *stiffens.* LOUIS *goes on firmly, with a steadying hand on his shoulder.*

LOUIS. I want you to. And when all's said, I am your King and your natural mentor, since your father was one of my noblemen. We will talk again later, after the banquet at which I must ape the honest man in all my finery, between my three thieving brothers, late into the night. Tell me, do you sleep well? Not tonight, I imagine? I never sleep. We'll have all the time in the world. I shall tell you what I think remains to be done for a young man of today. And that is to forget this rapacious pie-throwing contest we have all lived through, to go home and get married if he finds a good girl, to have children and to serve his country in his proper place, or to perfect his trade if he has one. That's an adventure in itself. In the old days that's what they meant by a man's life. Before the French began to play at politics and to take life theatrically. Those who tell you that youth needs an ideal are idiots. It has one already, which is youth itself and the wondrous diversity of life—private life, the only real one. It's only old age that needs to titillate itself.

Believe me, all evil comes from the old. They grow fat on ideas and young men die of them. [*He adds, a little wistfully.*] And tomorrow, after you've listened to me, and if I haven't convinced you, you have my royal word that I shall give you passports to join your Emperor. [*He takes a step or two, then stops.*] I said, "your Emperor." . . . You may not have noticed, but this is the first time I have given General Bonaparte this title. I did it to please you, because you are twenty years of age and you are weeping.

Ashamed, D'Assonville stands up and springs to attention.

LOUIS [*cheerfully*]. That's it. You stand at attention. It's idiotic, but it stops the tears. Now I shall go and see my three highborn rogues and try not to let them rob us too much. [*He adds with a smile.*] I say "us" because we're both French after all, and it's our property, yours and mine, that's at stake. [*He changes his mind and goes to him, conspiratorially.*] The Duc d'Otrante is sure to come back. He's waiting outside the door. I'm handing him over to you. Punch him on the nose once or twice if it makes you feel better. But you're sure you haven't another pistol that his minions couldn't find when they searched you—eh, you young rascal?

D'ASSONVILLE. No. Nothing at all, Sire.

LOUIS. Good. I believe you. You see, I need the old villain for what I plan to do. . . .

He goes hobbling out. FOUCHÉ comes in directly afterward.

FOUCHÉ. My boy, dirty linen should be washed in the family.

D'ASSONVILLE [*stiffly*]. I have no family.

FOUCHÉ. Don't be so sure! I was your mother's lover in the Carmes Prison in Lyons in a cell I procured from the head warden, ostensibly to question her in. The Vicomte d'Assonville had been incarcerated for the last three months, he on the men's side, she on the women's. The Lyons prisons were efficiently run, believe me; I was in charge of them. And you were born nine months after that conversation.

D'ASSONVILLE spits, pale and rigid, without looking at him.

D'ASSONVILLE. I hate you.

FOUCHÉ [*dully*]. Of course. I didn't expect you to fall into my arms. But I wanted you to know whose son you were. To each his own cross. I have borne mine. I became your mother's lover as a result of a piece of blackmail which you are entitled to call foul, and I—let us say—allowed them to kill the man whose name you bear. So there is very little chance of any affection between us. But I owe you something. I have secretly made you heir to immense riches. If I know anything about you, my little hero, it's more than likely that you will refuse the inheritance. So I want to bequeath you something else. A story which will teach you something. That is what ordinary fathers do, on their deathbeds.

Your mother was passably attractive—not very, but passably. I am extremely ugly. And that child, conceived in horror and contempt, was to be as handsome as a love child. I watched you grow up—as best I could. Infrequently, when you were small—your mother kept you well guarded—I caught a glimpse of you, riding donkeys in the park. . . . A little more often when you grew older. I made a point of inspecting the Imperial College or the Military Academy more often than usual and I would linger in your class. This interest in the young vastly intrigued the Emperor, who for a long time suspected me of the blackest designs. Later on—as Minister of Police it was easy for me—I kept an eye on your friendships, and your mistresses. You owe one or two of the fair creatures to me, those you hardly dared to speak to, greenhorn that you were, and who must have struck you as astonishingly easy. Fathers who can't appear at Christmas with neat little packages of sweetmeats or gold watches give their sons what gifts they can.

Your beauty hurt me for many years, like a personal insult. Especially when you reached manhood. But one evening I'd jumped into a cab in order to catch a glimpse of you at an Opéra ball—my inspectors gave me an hour-by-hour account of your doings—and I was hurrying up the steps for fear I would miss you when I saw you come down, in the domino my information services had described. You took off your mask at the foot of the steps, laughing with your friends, before stepping into the cab I had just dismissed. That evening your beauty, which had never been more striking, flooded me suddenly with joy, like an absolution. The reason why I've never understood—why the absolution, nor why the insult either. Later, on thinking back, I came finally to the conclusion that I'd simply been happy, that's all, because you had climbed into that cab and taken the seat I had just left. I was fairly humble, as you see, regarding my joys as a father. From that day on, I who had never even thought it possible, from my earliest childhood—which I won't tell you about, but which was ugly—I knew happiness. I had become you.

I thought I would die of joy when my inspectors informed me, shortly after, that you were in love with a young girl and that she loved you. My best men were immediately detailed to shadow her and protect her from all harm, she who had the immense happiness of being your beloved and who would one day give you love. Few Imperial Highnesses—and I have supplied escorts for a great many—were ever as well guarded as that little lawyer's daughter. Nor so inefficiently either, come to that, for the sharpest of my spies were not able to stop her from catching cold in a garden one evening at a ball and contracting the disease which was to take her from us. Later, I broke one of those men, excellent agent though he was, for not contriving somehow or other to approach her and force her to put on her shawl. I mourned that girl, whom I never knew, as long as you did—longer perhaps, for, old as I was, and never having known a love that was requited, I awaited its fulfillment with more delight than you. I was, however, to owe you another human emotion: jealousy.

When you first began to admire the Emperor, like all young men at that time, the effect of your youth made me young and ingenuous too for a while. I do believe that during that period—which was brief—I served him honestly enough and without mental reservations. But the day I realized that you loved him and that he had become a kind of god to you, I began to hate him and to work for his undoing. I am not Providence, he was beginning to undo himself. He had just walked into the absurd trap of the Spanish war and already he was squinting with one beady eye at the white gravecloth that was Russia. My advice, however, drove him to it. I could foresee the outcome. I did not rest there. The morrow of my discovery of your love for him, envoys of mine made contact

with the Comte de Lille at Mittau, to make plans for the
future. Talleyrand—without confiding in me, and for
reasons which did not include any trace of thwarted
paternal love, I do assure you!—was doing the same
thing. We soon divined our mutual aims, without disclosing our motives—mine would have much surprised
and amused the Prince!—and we acted jointly. I'm not
trying to claim that it was in order to inspire in you a
sentiment which I was debarred from ever hoping for
that Napoleon fell from his throne. I might strike you as
a madman and I don't want that. But it is probable that
in an infinitesimal way, it helped. History is made up of
a multitude of little causes. It was because you were
wounded on the Moskva that I allowed the Malet con-
spiracy to break out, in order to teach the man not to
expose you so stupidly! During the French campaign, it
was because I had no news of you that the Allies had me
to thank for the capture of that liaison officer bearing a
letter to the Regent Empress, in which Bonaparte informed her of his strategic plans, a thing he had never
done before with anyone. Typical of him, the fool! Some
hidden instinct was driving him to his doom—but the
capture was mine. It allowed Blücher to ignore the
Emperor's false march toward the frontier, to give up
pursuing him as the other hoped he would do, and to
make straight for Paris, cutting his lines. I had to make
haste; you were perhaps wounded somewhere, without
proper medical care. . . . Paris was taken—finally!—and
to my great joy I at last had news of you.

After that I steered the course of events, right up until
Fontainebleau, where his marshals, worked upon by me,
forced him to sign his abdication. You know the sequel.
Excepting perhaps the fact that if that great apathetic
fool of a Louis the Eighteenth hadn't thrown away that
execution list which I had secretly had drawn up for him
a month before, Napoleon could never have left Elba and
you would not have had the joy of seeing him again.
There. All that was just to tell you that without your
knowing anything about it, you have been a much-beloved
young man, my little pistol shooter. I've finished. [*He
waits. Then he asks, in the same cold tone of voice,
although perhaps a little dully now.*] May I ask you what
your plans are?

D'ASSONVILLE [*who has not moved*]. I shall accept the King's offer of a passport tomorrow morning and I shall go and join the Emperor.

FOUCHÉ [*impassively*]. I am still Minister of Police and very powerful—although fat Louis is harder to fool, in the long run, than your man of destiny. It would be easy for me to stop you from reaching Rochefort. But I shan't do it. [*He adds dully, as if embarrassed.*] I must have started to enjoy being unhappy. Another thing I have to thank you for. [*He adds cryptically.*] Besides, I am counting greatly on your idol himself to complete my revenge.

The lights change. A front cloth drops. It represents the high forbidding hull of the Bellerophon *on the quayside at Rochefort. An* ENGLISH SENTRY, *who must be played by the same actor as the French one, only clean-shaven whereas the French one was valiantly mustachioed, comes on with his stiff British soldier's step to take up guard duty at the gangway—which is pushed on stage from the opposite side—closely followed by a* SERGEANT, *who barks at him as he springs to attention and shoulders arms.*

SERGEANT. Flabby! Take four days' K.P.   [*Goes out.*

Enter NAPOLEON *from the opposite side, accompanied by* D'ASSONVILLE. *One feels they have been pacing up and down the quayside for hours.* NAPOLEON *says absent-mindedly, like someone throwing a bone to a dog that is pestering him:*

NAPOLEON. Very nice of you to have come, Lieutenant. You really shouldn't have bothered.

D'ASSONVILLE. I have nobody left but you, Sire.

NAPOLEON. Me too.

D'ASSONVILLE [*dazed at the immense compliment*]. Oh, Sire!

NAPOLEON [*looking at him with irritation*]. I meant *I* don't have anybody left but me, either. Do you think Montholon, Marchand, and the other four idiots on board are fit company for a man like me? If at least I had been able to take Fouché! Yes, and by the way where did *he* get to? Did I have time to have him shot?

D'ASSONVILLE. No, Sire.

NAPOLEON [*pursuing his own train of thought*]. I managed to pump a young lieutenant from the ship—his eyes popped out of his head when he saw me!—jabbering

away in the little English I know. I'm pretending to be
fooled, because I need to—my indignation scene will
play better in mid-ocean than on this squalid quayside—
but I already know that they aren't taking me to America.
They are going to land me on an island in the South
Atlantic, a rock, some Godforsaken bit of nowhere!

D'ASSONVILLE [*stricken*]. Sire, I shall never see you again!

NAPOLEON [*coldly*]. That's more than possible. The only
thing which amuses me in all this is the faces the others
will make, my four loyal hounds and their ladies, who've
come aboard thinking to leave for a pleasant sight-seeing
trip to the New World! [*He sees the* SENTRY *and takes*
D'ASSONVILLE's *arm.*] Suppose we try to get something
out of the sentry? One always overlooks the sentries—
they're so much part and parcel of the sentry box—but
these fellows listen to everything. You walk past them,
discussing the fate of the world, they stand there like
blocks of wood, and presto! they've heard every word.
History is full of sentries who were in the know before
ministers of state. [*He goes toward the* SENTRY, *who
presents arms and freezes.*] What is your regiment?

SENTRY. Second Royal Highlanders, sir.

NAPOLEON. And your name?

SENTRY. Smith, sir.

NAPOLEON. I knew a Smith at Waterloo. He was wounded
and I gave one of my officers my flask of rum to give to
him. Was that you?

SENTRY. No, sir. I wasna at Waterloo.

NAPOLEON [*vexed*]. Hm. Pity. [*He turns to* D'ASSONVILLE
and says coldly.] My star is deserting me, Lieutenant!
There was one chance in ten thousand, but in the old
days I should have landed on the right Smith. [*He moves
away, somewhat dashed. He paces about a little, in silence,
then asks suddenly.*] What were we talking about?

D'ASSONVILLE [*quivering with hope*]. I was telling you, Sire,
how much I needed to see you again and how unhappy
I had been.

NAPOLEON [*absently, taking a pinch of snuff*]. Oh, yes. And
whose son were you, in the end?

D'ASSONVILLE. Fouché's.

NAPOLEON. Yes, that's right, Fouché's. He told me—I forget
when exactly. . . . Do you know that I wondered for
years if I wasn't the son of Monsieur de Marbeuf?

Although my lady mother's general appearance, in later
life, robbed the supposition of all likelihood. . . . There
must be hundreds of us in this situation. What's the
point of knowing? A real man is his own father. [*Changing
the subject.*] Their little bombshell about the island,
what do you think?—will they serve me with it before
we lift anchor, in the Rear Admiral's cabin, or in mid-
ocean? The cabin, for my big scene, would be a trifle
cramped. I see the thing up on the bridge, during a
storm.

D'ASSONVILLE [*bewildered*]. I don't know, Sire.

NAPOLEON [*irritably*]. You never know anything. Are your
principles as rigid as ever?

D'ASSONVILLE. Yes, Sire. More than ever.

NAPOLEON [*flippantly*]. Hold onto them. They may come
in handy. One should never throw anything away. What
really would bother me is if they made their announcement before my speech. I'm very attached to it. [*Declaim-
ing.*] I come, like Themistocles, to sit at the hearthstone
of the British people! England has always been my
staunchest enemy, et cetera, et cetera. . . . It is most
important for history that I put my declaration of trust
on record before they deal their blow about the island.
If I can say my piece first, the audience is with me. Do
you follow me?

D'ASSONVILLE [*taking the plunge, blushing like a girl*]. Oh,
Sire! I want to do more than that. I should like to follow
you out there, dedicate my life to you!

NAPOLEON [*alarmed*]. Oh, no, no, my good lad, that's out
of the question! In the first place, they've made me draw
up lists in triplicate of all the people I was taking with
me. I thought it was only French bureaucracy that was so
addicted to red tape. Well, foreigners are every bit as
bad. Besides, I don't mind telling you that on a desert
island, with a dismal bore like you, I'd never stand it. I
shall need all the optimism I can get out there.

D'ASSONVILLE [*falling on his neck and bursting into tears*].
Oh, Sire! Sire! My Emperor!

NAPOLEON [*pushing him away, exasperated*]. No tears! No
tears! They're so wet. [*He wipes his face.*] I've always had
a horror of that. I'm counting on you for a pretty farewell speech, of course. The young officer parting from his
Emperor. I hope we'll have an audience of sorts. But for

the moment, we're alone. Let's spare ourselves that. My boy, I don't know how you blundered into my life nor why I see you everywhere I look these days, but if I were your father—who is he, by the way? You didn't finish your story.

D'ASSONVILLE [*crushed*]. Fouché, Sire.

NAPOLEON. Oh yes, that's right. What a slimy specimen, that one! Yes, if I were your father, I should give you a few solid pieces of advice about life. You need them. First of all, no tears. Secondly, no love. That's a bluestocking's invention. Nobody loves anybody. You don't love me. You think you do because you're a young fool who hasn't lived. You're having your little emotional upset, that's all—like a girl.

D'ASSONVILLE [*deeply hurt*]. Sire, I am a soldier! I haven't stopped fighting since Russia!

NAPOLEON. What does that prove? I've known enough soldiers—nobody ever knew more. Girls every one of them when it came to sentiment. Men are rare. You admired your Emperor. Good. That was your duty. He led you to victory many times. Good. Now he's beaten by English gold and he is going into exile to complete his destiny. Right. All those are men's affairs. One doesn't weep. Now, what preoccupies me at the moment, with one foot on the gangway of this damned tub which is going to whisk me into thin air forever, is to bring off my exit. Not the bit about Themistocles and the desert island; that's a curtain raiser with second-string actors. My real exit, my solo, out there. In a word, I've got to die well.

D'ASSONVILLE [*throwing himself at his feet with a moan*]. I want to die too, Sire!

NAPOLEON [*irritated*]. No, no, no. In the first place, you've plenty of time. And, secondly, with you, nobody would be interested. You know, there have been a lot of deaths lately.

D'ASSONVILLE [*sobbing*]. But I'm giving my whole self to you!

NAPOLEON. Keep it, keep it. I don't need men any more. I've got to the final monologue. Alone on stage. The naval lieutenant I questioned told me that the official they've appointed to guard me out there is a certain Hudson Lowe, a man he knows well, and who's vaguely related to him. It seems he's a decent old devil, a bit on the pernickety side. Can you see me ending my days with a decent old devil, a bit on the pernickety side? Playing whist with him after dinner? Can you? They don't know me! I can see that last-act curtain now, on that rock, the two of us. I shall make a monster out of him, an executioner, the fellow will stink in the nose of posterity! You leave it to me! There I'll be, emaciated, unshaven, unkempt, consumptive, or with cancer of the stomach perhaps. . . . It can happen if you will it strongly enough. Man dies when he wants, as he wants, of what he chooses. I'll teach those English, if they don't know already, just how tiresome a persecuted man can be, when he knows how to get himself talked about!

An ENGLISH OFFICER *comes down the gangway.*

OFFICER. General, the Rear Admiral asks you to be so good as to step aboard. We are about to sail. [*He comes to attention and salutes.*]

NAPOLEON [*growling*]. General . . . I'll make them pay for that—for centuries. Good-bye, Lieutenant. Don't be sad. It's every man for himself and winner take all in this world. [*He looks around at the deserted quayside, disappointed.*] I'm only sorry we didn't have a better house tonight. Ah, well, that's how it is. . . . Cover yourself with glory, if there's any glory left. Shoot fat Louis, for instance, or join the *Carbonari.** Or Jacobinism, say. I'm sure there's still a future in that. They haven't squeezed that lemon dry in France yet. Good luck! Write and tell me what your plans are if the mails permit.

D'ASSONVILLE [*stiffly, with tears in his eyes*]. I can tell you now, Sire. I shall marry and have children.

NAPOLEON [*indifferently, going up the gangway*]. Well, it's as good an idea as any. But take my advice, don't talk too much idealism to your youngsters. It's no luggage for life.

The SENTRY *presents arms as* NAPOLEON, *followed by the* ENGLISH OFFICER, *boards the* Bellerophon. *The ship's band is heard playing* "God Save the King" *to greet* NAPOLEON.

D'ASSONVILLE *stands there stiffly, sad and alone.*

Curtain.

* An Italian secret society, working at this time for the unification of Italy.